Praise for the book
The World We Leave Our Children

Holistic approach accompanied by solutions for resource sustainability to save our planet. A must read!!

"If you are interested in the sustainability of resources and saving our planet, then you must read this book. If you are concerned for yourselves, your children, your grandchildren, and your great-grandchildren, you must read this book.
Like the human body needs balance, so does Mother Earth. What is necessary is mind boggling and an undertaking that requires a multi-faceted approach. Despite ALL the challenges, solutions are explained and given. But in the process of achieving sustainability resolutions, Bill Sosinsky is wise enough to not "throw out the baby with the bathwater" due to the consequences of economic loss for people's current livelihoods.

This book will enlighten everyone about the problems, the consequences if immediate action is not taken, but also about where to find the education, and how to successfully participate in the solutions for planet sustainability.

Thank you Bill Sosinsky for sharing your knowledge and compassion."

~ **Julia Scalise, DN, PhD**
  Holistic Health Consultant and Author of the #1 Best Seller
  "Do One Thing   Feel Better / Live Better"
  www.JuliaScalise.com

This book is a must read. Great advice.

"Great book everyone should read. This book shows the fragility of our food system and how simple it will be for it to fall. I love all the practical advice the author gives to help combat this issue and positive solutions we can all take to make a difference. I promise if you read it, you will see things differently and it will help you act now. If we all make small changes, we can make a big difference in our world. Grab your copy as soon as possible."

~ **Ken H. Kamp**

The World We Leave Our Children

The Complete Guide to the Steps We Need to Take to Save Our Planet

William Sosinsky

THE EUC2 PRESS
New York
2019

The EUC2 Press

Published by the EUC2 Press
80 Beekman St. 5D
New York, NY U.S.A. 10038

Contact: Norma Burnson, Publisher
Email: euc2press@energime.com

First Published in 2019 by the EUC2 Press

U.S. Copyright Office
100 Independence Avenue S.E. Washington, D.C. 20559-6000

Electronic File (Text & eService)
Registration Number / Date: TXu001967250/2015-07-18
ISBN 978-0-692-08607-0

Sosinsky, William A. (William Adam)
The World We Leave Our Children / the complete guide to the steps we need
to save our planet.

1. Sosinsky, William A. (William Sosinsky) 2. Business money 3. Climatology
4. Earth sciences 5. Economics 6. Eco-sustainability 7. Economic development
8. Education 9. Environmental economics 10. Environmental policy
11. Environmental sciences 12. Global affairs 13. International 14. Politics & Social
science 15. Public affairs & policy 16. Science & Mathematics

EUC2 Press is committed to publishing works of quality and integrity.
In that spirit, we are proud to offer this book to our readers; however, the narrative,
experiences and the words are the author's alone.

10, 9, 8, 7, 6, 5, 4, 3, 2

Cover Photograph: Source ~Star Trails, NASA

DEDICATION

The World We Leave Our Children was written to provide people with a clear, concise, and comprehensive overview of the critical issues we currently face with the mismanagement of our environment and global resources. It is intended for the reader to understand the underlying reasons why what we are currently doing to save our planet is dramatically failing and the corrective strategies and steps we can employ to start turning things around immediately. In the following pages is described the methodology and strategy we must use and steps we need to take for reversing our current slide towards mass extinction and the destruction of our environment before time runs out.

This book is dedicated to my extended human family and to our children who carry our spirits and dreams within them forever, giving us all eternal life.

INTRODUCTION

When we enter this world as a spark of life, whether that moment be divine or random, we have no part in determining the time, place, and circumstances into which we are born. If we are lucky, we are brought into a world of concerned and loving parents, absent of want and suffering. For those fortunate enough, life can then be filled with the positive experiences and opportunities that provide the enlightened path by which we then evolve. From the moment we emerge from the womb our brains start to evaluate and question our surroundings as it makes a determination of the things we value, trust, and accept as our truths. At the same time, we reject that which is threatening, unclear, or uncomfortable for our mind to assimilate and embrace. It is through this process that we become the human beings we eventually develop into.

Since I became a young adult and started to form the opinions and values that would guide me through the remainder of my life, I have always been aware of the environment. At a very young age I became sensitive to the dual threats we face as a byproduct of global resource mismanagement and environmental degradation. These two issues now pose the single largest impediment to human evolution and our quality of life that our population has ever had to face. How I arrived at that understanding and developed the passion for finding a solution to that threat was entirely random or perhaps a matter of personal fate. Again, it depends on your belief system as to how you tell the story. It was from that moment I became aware as a human being that the challenge of creating the methodology and defining path by which we countered and addressed these dual threats became the subtext to my life.

To understand how humanity got to this point of environmental suicide requires that we detangle the morass of influences, preconditioned behavior, and false assumptions that have led us to the brink. It is through this understanding that we can then begin to see the path that will eventually allow us to find our way back to a sustainable existence. In that way we can forever eliminate the want, deprivation, and inequities that have been the bane of our species existence.

It is only natural we try to place blame for our current situation on the decision makers, corporations, and politicians that have traded our long-term environmental health and resource security for influence, wealth, and power. Ultimately however, we have no one to blame other than ourselves. It is human beings that have made the decisions, created the socio-economic relationships, and established the core values that have dictated our every action and ultimately led us down the wrong path. This could not have happened without our tacit approval and participation.

Every challenge we now face that poses this unprecedented threat to our lives and way of life can be directly traced back to basic human frailties. From the very first moment humankind began to assimilate into societies it has been our enduring primal self-interest and fear that has hampered and distorted our ultimate potential as a species. Those ingrained socio-genetic weaknesses have dictated our desires, spawned our conflicts, and held us back from the enlightened evolutionary track we had hoped we would one day fulfill. The real question is whether or not we will find the courage and wisdom to change our direction before our time runs out as stewards of this Earth. It is the understanding that human beings and human society tend to be reactive to change rather than proactive which may eventually be the defining hurdle that spells our defeat. With that understanding I am cautiously optimistic. I have to be, otherwise I could not continue.

So, I tell my children we are special among all living creatures. I tell them that human beings have a remarkable super power. We have a brain that allows us to predict the results of our actions and change our course in advance of those consequences. We can employ wisdom, compassion, foresight, courage, and ultimately love, such that the decisions that define our path impact the world in a positive and constructive way. I tell them that we live in the most exciting and important time in human history. That the future of our species and our planet will be determined by this generation and that we are fighting for everything. We fight for our lives, the health of our environment, and the future of our species. I tell them if we are to win this battle, we have no choice but to fight together.

If we are to survive the 21st century and traverse this most critical time in our human evolution, it is essential that we change on the most fundamental levels. We must stop looking to place blame. It is a time for us as a species to relearn, refocus, and re-examine our most basic assumptions as to how we live on this planet. We must learn to co-exist in a world which is now burdened by an exploding population, declining environmental health, and diminishing resources. We must address the political divisiveness directly influenced by corporate and banking interests that look to postpone change for fear of losing their power and stake-hold by directly involving those entities in the solution. This must be an evolutionary, not revolutionary process, or we will run out of time before we can rebuild. Time is not on our side. We can no longer spur on tribal conflicts, encourage isolating self-interests, and promote the primal fears that have plagued mankind's time on this planet. Our success will be defined by our ability to cooperate. We must listen to the better angels of our souls and put behind our differences or it will be our epitaph. I would also respond to any critic that believes this proposition is some utopian dream based on idealism or spurred on by some drug induced state that what I am suggesting is the only pragmatic and logical path we can follow if we are to avoid the unimaginable. It is our best, last chance.

It is no longer an option that we hope that we get this right. Unless and until we clearly understand and address the futile and self-defeating misconceptions that define our current corrective actions, we have no chance to reverse our current course. Unless we change, every effort we make to prevent and curtail our decline will be nothing more than an exercise in futility. In the chapters that follow I will lay out the strategies, methodologies, and reasoning that will describe how we must move forward if we are to save our future. I will tell you stories based on my experiences and observations, and explain the science, research, data, and insight that support these conclusions. Finally, I will introduce you to the collective vision of those working tirelessly to make our futures safe, secure, and prosperous in a world with a healthy vibrant environment and an expanding economy.

For the sake of space and to limit your time commitment I promise to keep this information general and to the point. At the end of reading this book you will have a clear and comprehensive overall understanding as to where we are, what our challenges will be, and how we may best move forward. In the end this will hopefully influence your actions from this day forward so we can change the world together. To encourage you to re-evaluate your actions and join the fight and start working to save our future with common purpose is my only objective. It is why I wrote this book. It is based on that result I will either fail of succeed. That is my only goal.

As I said earlier, how I came to this perspective was not a matter of conscious choice. I did not choose when or where I was born, who my parents were, or the influences that shaped my life. Not in the beginning anyway. It is now my fate. I am compelled to try and solve this challenge for which there seems no clear path or unifying approach and to which I have committed the remainder of the days of my life to help define a solution. It is because I see the steps and I can define that path that I try and reach out to you. I hope you will join me. Our children are depending on our wisdom and our resolve. We must not fail them.

William Sosinsky

CONTENTS

Regional Sustainability...Be Specific. The Path of Change

Development

William Sosinsky

Chapter One

How Do We Save Our Planet?

"There are a million excuses why doing what's difficult isn't pragmatic, but when we are talking about the survival of our living planet, our species, our biodiversity, and the quality of life for future generations none of those excuses are good excuses."

William Sosinsky

The skies are not as clear as they used to be in my youth. Food prices seem to rise much faster these days than they did then. Beaches used to be much cleaner with less garbage floating in the water. Seasonal weather patterns seemed to be more reliable and consistent. We had more space and there were less crowds. I never worried about what was in the foods I ate. We drank our water straight from fountains and faucets and not filtered or out of expensive plastic bottles. No one thought the climate would ever change or that the glaciers would ever melt away. Droughts rarely happened and floods were not that common. Oil spills happened in the kitchen. I never heard of Chernobyl, Fukushima, or Three Mile Island, I just worried about the bomb.

We can all argue about to what degree our resources and environment have been impacted by our recent past, or how much or how likely things will deteriorate in the coming years. It is clear however that things have gotten worse and continue to deteriorate. As a species it is clear we face severe and daunting challenges in the years ahead. Yet when I look at all the well-meaning and concerned efforts of my colleagues throughout our global community one thing becomes painfully apparent. There is little or no global cooperation, nor a coordinated methodology that defines a logical path as to how we reverse our course and deal with these challenges. It is for that reason alone that it is clear to me that our response will be ineffective.

Everywhere there are efforts underway attempting to create renewable energy or aimed at producing more and healthier food. There are those looking to manage our waste streams in an intelligent and productive way, and there are those devising new and better ways to produce, maintain, and protect our water supplies. We see calls for new legislation aimed at protecting our environment, or international agreements to redirect our use of resources and limit by law the harmful waste we create which is altering the chemical balance of our biosphere. Yet all these well intended efforts are addressing the symptoms of global resource mismanagement and environmental destruction, not the source of the problem. That is why we are failing. That is why we are falling short.

For those who give up in the frustration that nothing seems to be getting done or live in the belief we are powerless to change our path I would say do not surrender hope. More than that, I would urge you strongly to not give up the fight. It may be true that we have influenced irreversible changes to our climate and environment that will have a profound impact making life more challenging for us all in the years to come. The truth is we have the power to adjust and to prosper through those changes. Also, and this is crucial to understand, there are degrees to the damage we are doing to our planet. Some of these changes we can live with, and some of which if we fail to act will be unimaginable. We cannot and must not allow those extreme consequences come to pass no matter what the cost.

So how do we save our planet? The first major component in addressing positive change simply enough is changing the way people think and act. More precisely, we as a species need to empower our population with the knowledge and skills that promote the proper use and management of our natural resources. Without an educated population acting together collaboratively, what we are currently doing is essentially the equivalent of having everyone on a boat rowing vigorously in different directions. The best result you can manage is to go in a circle.

The second critical ingredient to empower this change has everything to do with the way we promote global economic growth. Economic expansion strategies and job creation efforts will always be in conflict with environmental stewardship unless and until those efforts are married together. Current economic expansion, economic theory, job creation, and corporate/industrial growth are based on what are now obsolete and outdated concepts. We never considered that our resources were finite or that the needs of our exploding population would overwhelm the capacity of our resources to provide those basic needs. Historically this has never really been an issue on a global scale.

To successfully address our environmental challenges there must be an immediate short-term economic benefit for governments, corporations, and individuals such that they "buy in" to the process. Long term investment and responsible development are admirable goals, but the reality is those concepts have failed to create the critical mass of change necessary. It is also essential we promote accessibility to opportunity and an improved standard of living. This must be accomplished while supporting regional economic growth and competition.

The reason is simple. We can trace every major historic human induced shift in societal structure back to an economic stimulus. This includes population expansion, immigration patterns, exploration, war and conflict. That stimulus can come in the form of an opportunity for an entity to improve their economic status and power, or result from the deprivation and perceived injustices and inequalities associated with economic exploitation. Whatever the excuse for these historic events, you can be sure that the desire for wealth, or the absence of wealth played a key factor in those shifts. People do not go to war without a purpose. Nor do they migrate with their families, over-throw governments, create political parties, build great walls, or strap bombs to their chest and rush into a crowded market simply on a whim. You can be sure that an economic stimulus incited that action or was somehow connected to the impetus for that decision.

Resource management which is at the center of our all challenges concerning the environment and basic survival is a two-edged sword. Simply stated, it is an issue of how much you produce and how much you consume. Both require intelligence and planning in order to reduce the unintended consequences of non–sustainable production and the wasteful consumption of those resources. As a result of a global economy focused on expansion and based on productivity, our response to resource mismanagement has been very much directed to "How do we produce more?"

 Unfortunately, history has shown us that there is a clear relationship between energy and food production as it relates to population growth; that is the more you produce, the more it encourages people to have more children. That is a quantifiable and direct relationship which has been undeniably demonstrated since the beginnings of the industrial revolution as our population has exploded on an unprecedented scale. It is also clear that it is this expanding population and increasing consumption that are the root cause of all the issues we face with the deterioration of our environment and our diminishing resources.

So, I will start my argument as to what course the human race must follow to save our planet with the following observation;

The issue of sustainability is not that of too little energy, food, or water, nor is it our thoughtless management of our waste streams. It is rather our inability to educate, engage, and empower the productive and thoughtful participation of our global population in a fair and inclusive model that promotes economic growth while managing our global resources in a manner that promotes environmental stewardship.

Which brings me to the question; "Of the seven billion plus of us who inhabit this earth, how many human beings are truly contributing to our existence in a productive and sustainable manner?" You could argue that a great many of us are productive when it comes to producing and managing the four key areas of industry that support human survival on this planet (energy and food production, water and waste management). Yet how much of that activity is truly sustainable? Sustainability is the key phase here. I would wager that no term or phrase has been misused and bastardized more in the last few years.

The meaning of sustainable as described by the dictionary is "The ability to endure". So, when we dig deeper into how that phrase is applied to many of our current global efforts, we soon realize that referring to them as sustainable is nothing more than a case of false advertising. This is sometimes referred to as "Green Washing".

As an example, fish farming is often looked upon as being sustainable and is widely advertised as being so. Yet the great majority of fish farms derive their feed from protein/omega 3 rich fish species that are considered less desirable as food sources. These include species such as Menhaden, Mackerel, and Anchovies. In the meanwhile, statistical data developed by NOAH indicates that we are reducing global stocks of these "feeder fish" at a much faster rate than we are impacting our reserves of "table fish" (Cod, Pollack, Tuna, Salmon, etc.). The general consensus is we will have wiped these species out as viable feeder source by the early 2030's.

So, what will the farmed fish eat then? Doesn't sound too sustainable to me! It is this lack of predictive conceptual logic and planning which is prevalent amongst our governmental and industry leaders that separates that which is truly sustainable from that which is not.

Then there is the issue of referring to anything that we can produce naturally as being "green" in addition to its being considered sustainable by that very same association. For instance; a development group decides to create biofuel oil by raising Jatropha (a plant that produces high concentrations of natural oil). Their argument is that it is grown and not drilled (So it is sustainable) and the oil is derived from a plant (So it is green). In order to produce the crop, they cut down 300,000 acres of pristine forest in Central Africa to create their farm. This action causes the extinction of numerous species through the destruction of a priceless bio-diverse eco-system and contributes to climate change locally by eliminating the environmentally moderating impact of the jungle canopy. Let's throw in habitat destruction, top soil loss through erosion, reduced regional rainfall, and the loss of animals and plants as a source for food for local populations. Looking at their effort from that perspective makes it difficult to see where this project is either green or sustainable.

After a while you get to realize that the term "sustainable" is being used like a form of Orwellian Newspeak. The point being, whether the term is being employed to deceive people, or it is just a matter of an innocent misunderstanding by the user, it is imperative that we start to clearly understand what is sustainable and what is not.

Once you get past the basics of how we are destroying our planet and using up its finite resources, you are left with the reality that it is part of a historic process to which mankind has adhered to since our emergence from hunter gather societies. The manner in which we relate to our resources is directly mirrored by the way we view and manage our economies and economic development. It is because of this deeply ingrained belief system which influences all of our decisions and directs all of our responses that mankind is in dire jeopardy of collapsing this critical natural balance we depend on for our survival.

So, this is where we must start to reverse our course if we are to be successful. We must stop assuming that the socio-economic structures we have built are still valid and can no longer blindly follow those teachings if we are to evolve past this century. The solution will require re-examination and changes to those very systems we blindly accept as the only models we can follow as it is obvious, they no longer work. After all, if they still worked, we would not be in the precipitous position we now find ourselves as a species.

Chapter Two

The Consequences of Ignoring an Approaching Tidal Wave

"Delay is the deadliest form of denial." ~ **C. Northcote Parkinson**

On Sunday December 26th 2004 a series of tidal waves were triggered by an earthquake centered off the west coast of Sumatra in the Indian Ocean. The resulting devastation killed an estimated 230,000 people in 14 countries. When the first tremors hit, those who knew better fled for higher ground and put as much distance as they could between themselves and the sea. Whether it was ignorance of what the waters withdrawing to the horizon indicated, or an inability of the victims to accept the enormity of what was soon to follow, the majority of people who died just stayed at the shoreline and watched as the waves approached.

The reason I bring this up is that this illustrates a perfect analogy as it relates to our current global challenges. It is not as if we did not see this coming. It is very clear to those of us who are paying close attention that we will all soon face serious and potentially unimaginable consequences. The net result of critical resources disappearing and the increasing damage we are inflicting on our environment. Yet for the majority of our population ignorance, debate, and denial are the norms. We discuss the threats. We move cautiously, taking small steps. We convince ourselves we have time when in fact we have very little.

For me, my awakening started in 1972 when I read a book called "The Limits to Growth". The subject matter was based on a computer simulation program conducted at M.I.T in the early nineteen seventies exploring exponential economic and population growth as they related to finite resources. The book which was commissioned by the Club of Rome with funding from the Volkswagen Foundation was written by Donella H. Meadows, Dennis L. Meadows, Jørgen Randers, and William W. Behrens III. In the book the authors explored different potential futures for our planet proposing several scenarios based on this complex relationship which has defined mankind's emergence and development. It was after reading this book that the clear relationship between our current global economic development models and our inability to insure long term sustainability and survivability of our species became clear to me.

What I found compelling about "The Limits to Growth" was that the book and M.I.T study, for the very first time, clearly laid out the relationship that our booming population's growing consumption of basic resources had on our long term survivability as it related to global resource management. It described undeniable trends that were both quantifiable and undeniably factual. It then drew several conclusions based on our ability as a species to either adjust to these challenges or the consequences of what would happen if we continued to ignore these threats. The authors imagined several scenarios ranging from a measured thoughtful global readjustment of our resource management to business as usual. All in all it examined in thoughtful detail the challenges and issues we have faced since its publication with chilling accuracy. The book described eloquently the present state of our environment and global resources as a result of our "business as usual" approach.

Although it addressed what we needed to do to avoid the harsher consequences of our inaction in general terms, it never clearly defined in anything other than a sweeping philosophical viewpoint the root challenges we faced nor a pathway and approach that would allow us to respond effectively. It was at that moment that I realized the need for a guiding methodology and response that encompassed and understood the complexity of these challenges. This was the impetus for the concept which later became Energime (The Corporate and not–for–profit entity I founded) was born.

Since the birth of the environmental movement a central argument has raged over the costs of protecting the environment and the need to not permit those efforts to cripple economic growth. This has been the central battle ground in which every effort pertaining to reversing our destructive course is debated in one form or another. Yet the basic answer is so obvious and simple that everyone engaged in these arguments cannot see the simplicity of what is necessary;

We need to make the efficient use of resources supported by an over-riding doctrine of environmental stewardship and resource management more profitable then business as usual.

That is the simple challenge we face. The reality is that from the very beginning proponents of environmental protection have been urging governments and corporations to make changes to their operations as a matter of prudence and social responsibility. Those "Green" leaders have pushed the concepts of resource management and environmental stewardship as a long-term investment in protecting our planet's health and conserving finite resources.

It is just as obvious to anyone who is paying attention that those efforts have failed to produce the shift in behavior that they were intended to influence. The reasons for those failures are simple. Governments, central banks, and corporations operate on essentially short-term time frames (relative to environmental/resource impact) when it comes to managing economies and promoting economic growth. Such approaches negate the value of investment in otherwise logical expenditures that will ensure the long-term viability and vitality of a resource or eco-system in exchange for the benefits of short-terms gains that support immediate economic goals.

The examples of this are almost too many to mention. They include valuing short-term profitability over long-term impact by cutting down priceless bio-diverse forests for timber, firewood, and farming (Amazon, Central Africa, Madagascar) failing to put inexpensive safety valves on oil drilling platforms or properly reinforcing the hulls of oil tankers (BP Gulf of Mexico, Exxon Valdez), situating nuclear power plants in vulnerable locations (Fukushima), or using outdated and faulty designs in their construction (Chernobyl). You can throw in overuse of our fresh water reserves, overuse of our soils, overfishing of the oceans, irresponsible disposal of toxic, municipal, industrial, sewage, and farm waste into our lands and waters to name just a few. The list goes on forever. It is all influenced and justified by short term economics. In this instance, the immediate bottom line rules.

The point I am attempting to make is when doing things the "Sustainable" way is more profitable than "business as usual" you eliminate the argument. Instead of debating the point and endlessly questioning the pragmatics as to the potential pros and cons we should be happily embracing that reality and defining the measures that will redirect our efforts. For this to occur will require a myriad of coordinated efforts many of which exist separately today. That being said, it is the lack of coordination and planning that is the real issue we must ultimately come to terms with.

Chapter Three

Understanding The Battlefield (The Science of Global Devastation)

"Adapt or perish, now as ever, is Nature's inexorable imperative."
~. H.G. Wells

It is impossible to address how we change direction until we are absolutely clear on the threats and challenges. Although most of us have a pretty good idea as to what these dangers are I thought a section discussing these issues necessary before we move on. I will try to not belabor the points and just stick to the basics. Later on in the book we will address specific responses and strategies to dealing with these complex and inter-related issues. If this section and the following chapter on our food chain are too overwhelming, rest assured I believe we have the capacity to respond in a manner which will address, reverse, reduce, and avoid the worst aspects of these projections and trends. What I am saying is there is reason to hope so do not despair.

Throughout this book, I will continuously reference 2050 as a key date in our near future. I believe it is by that date that humankind will have either addressed our environmental resource challenges affectively or else will be condemned to reap the consequences of our inactions. Thirty plus years is but half an expected life time for many of us. When I was younger it seemed an awfully long time, but as I have gotten up in age I look back and it feels as if those years slipped away in a heartbeat. The world of 2050 will be here in just a moment and one way or another, it will be a world we will hardly recognize. So let's look at some of those critical trends in a general sense and try to understand how they are currently affecting our planet's environment. It is these threats and the intelligence, vision, and determination we invoke in response that will determine our future and the evolutionary fate of humankind.

Much of the argument concerning our current challenges with the environment has centered on climate change. Although it is not the only critical issue we face as there are several other areas of equal importance, it remains a central area of debate. Additionally there is a strong and inter-connected relationship between all of the following areas of concern as each influences the other and amplifies their impacts. That being said, climate change does play a central role in much of what we will discuss so we will start there.

Climate Change

I believe that whether you fall on the side of climate change being a human induced and influenced issue or you take the science denying stand that these changes are merely a natural cycle, everyone these days it seems are inclined to believe that the climate is changing. We have just lived through (2015) the warmest year on record after seeing that same mark bested several times in the past decade. In fact 15 of the 16 warmest years on record have occurred in the first 15 years of the 21st century and 9 of the top ten. The other warmest year occurred in 1998.[1] This is not opinion but empirical data gathered by NOAH, NASA, and all the other groups that monitor and oversee such analysis. So let's not argue as to whether the planet is getting warmer and whether or not there has been an increase in CO2 levels and who or what's to blame. Those are the undeniable, proven facts.

So why is of this a concern? Climate change (Please note that I do not use the term global warming) is as great a threat to our current systems of existence on this planet as we can possibly imagine.

Ever since our emergence from the last ice age into the Holocene interglacial period we now live in, humanity has flourished in what has been a very temperate and nurturing climate. This period which has lasted more than 11,000 years has seen our emergence from hunter-gather societies through to the development of the civilizations and cultures we have today. Any change to those climate norms we have grown dependent on in the form of a "climate shift" will have immense and catastrophic impacts on our population and our way of life.

How do we know for sure the climate is getting ready for a massive shift? Climatologists and the analytic methods they use to evaluate our environment have made incredible advances in the past decade or so. With the advent of high speed computers and electron microscopes it is now possible for scientists to look back into our history and with extraordinary accuracy determine timeframes and conditions that have existed in the past. Studies conducted on the Antarctic Ice Sheet and with deep sea sediment cores have revealed a vivid and clear picture as to our past and the periodic shifts in climatic conditions that have existed throughout our history. Like rings in a tree core each level and deposit takes scientists back through another year of our environmental heritage.

From the ice core studies levels of CO_2 concentrations, volcanic ash deposits, and even debris from interstellar collisions such as the Chicxulub asteroid impact give scientists a window into the past. Those findings detail the causes of various climate shifts that have occurred over the ages. A direct correlation between increased CO_2 levels or increased volcanic activity/atmospheric debris, have almost always singled a transition ushering in drastic shifts in global temperatures.

Additionally, deep sea sediment studies have illustrated through fossil records changing sea life and algae living in different areas of our oceans at varying times in our history. Increased CO_2 levels impact ocean PH making it more acidic as well. Since different species are known to inhabit specific environments that possess certain characteristics of temperature and PH tolerance it is easy to reconstruct what those conditions were like at any particular time during the past. It is then easy for scientists to combine and correlate those events with the data that has been extracted from ice, sea, and land based geological records to get an even more accurate picture of conditions during that period.

Current research indicates that we have exceeded the historic limits for both CO_2 concentrations and temperature rises that in the past have triggered climate shifts. What is not known for sure is whether or not that shift will be to a much a warmer period, or whether we might prematurely trigger another ice age.

It seems an almost absurd notion that one possibility is that we could inadvertently put the earth into another deep freeze. The thing is, climate behavior is very often a reactive or correcting action. The transfer of equatorial heat through the ocean conveyor belt known as the Thermohaline circulation is responsible for moderating temperatures in our northern hemisphere. That current which brings warmer waters up from the equator northwards is dependent on a salinity balance and water density differentials in the North Atlantic. With the huge amounts of fresh water entering that portion of the system from the melting Greenland ice sheet it is very possible that the diluting of that process might be enough to disrupt the exchange that supports the Thermohaline current. An early ice age could potentially be triggered.

Whether it gets warmer or colder is anyone's guess. What is certain is that any massive shift in climate will trigger a chain of events that will be unprecedented in human history. The one thing we do know for sure from the ice core and sediment analysis is that when the shift does occurs it will happen quickly. Records indicate that these transitions tend to flip in a time frame of approximately a decade once you reach that critical threshold. You have a period preceding the shift where the weather swings back and forth wildly as if attempting a last ditch effort to rebalance itself before it settles abruptly in one direction or the other. When the climate finally shifts we may experience a change in temperature as much as 8 to 9 degrees Fahrenheit. This is what is suggested by the data.

When or how soon this will occur is still open to speculation. It is safe to say that this is something modern man has yet to experience and we cannot know for sure the timeframe or direction as to how this might play out. Anyone who suggests otherwise is just taking a wild guess. That being said, unstable current weather patterns these last few years may suggest we have already entered that phase. So if I were to take a my own wild guess, I would say it is very likely at our current levels that we will soon enter this period of drastic climatic re-alignment, perhaps before mid-century.

Ocean PH and Temperature Changes

I would state quite simply that the single most dangerous impact humanity can potentially inflict on our planet's health and our long term survivability would be to substantially change the PH and temperatures of our Oceans.

When we look at rising levels of CO_2 as an issue it is almost always in reference to warming atmospheric temperatures. Popular debates are quick to argue about greenhouse gases from the singular perspective of climate change and its impact on our atmosphere. Yet we fail to view fully appreciate the impact it is having on our oceans. As with all life inter-relationships, our environment and biosphere are a holistic and symbiotic system. When you increase atmospheric greenhouse gases, those same gases are finding their way into our oceans and changing its chemical balance. At the same time increasing atmospheric temperatures are being transferred into the water column. These two impacts are potentially more significant as they relate to our planets health and the long term survivability of humankind then any simple change in the climate or interruption in our food chain.

To explain this more clearly; Ocean acidification is one of the dangerous consequences that results from increasing CO2 levels in the biosphere. It is estimated that between 30-40% of airborne CO2 is absorbed into oceans, rivers, and lakes. [2,3] These percentages will only increase with continued global deforestation and desertification. As the gas enters the water carbonic acid is produced as nature's way of maintaining chemical equilibrium. Historically the world's oceans have had a PH that was slightly alkaline with a pH of around 8.25. It is at this level of balance and "normality" that the greatest number of current ocean species and life forms can exist and prosper. By 1994 we saw a change in that PH level to 8.14. [4] This may not seem like much, but it is in fact an extremely ominous sign that we are pushing our Oceans into very dangerous territory. With the increase in acidity many species, particularly those that form outer shells as part of their life cycles and ocean coral are becoming increasing vulnerable to disease and system collapse. This may ultimately lead to their eventual extinction.

In the 15-year period 1995–2010 alone, acidity has increased 6 percent in the upper 100 meters of the Pacific Ocean from Hawaii to Alaska. [5] According to a statement in July 2012 by Jane Lubchenco, head of the U.S. National Oceanic and Atmospheric Administration "surface waters are changing much more rapidly than initial calculations have suggested. It's yet another reason to be very seriously concerned about the amount of carbon dioxide that is in the atmosphere now and the additional amount we continue to put out.[6] A 2013 study claimed acidity was increasing at a rate 10 times faster than in any of the evolutionary crises in the earth's history.[7]

The negative impacts of increasing ocean acidity and rising water temperatures are many. Since 1950 as much as 40% of our global phytoplankton may have disappeared. [8] The fact that so few people even know or talk about this simple fact makes me painfully aware as to how large the chasm is in terms of what people understand about these threats and how critical a situation we are now facing.Phytoplankton along with Zooplankton are the small sea creatures that form the base of the ocean food chain and as such are critical to maintaining all the variety of fish and mammals that depend on them for their nutrition. Another thing to consider is that blue/green algae is the main source of the oxygen we breathe. Those two facts alone should be cause enough for great concern.

Additionally increased acidity and rising sea temperatures are being blamed for coral bleaching which is now affecting coral reef health around the world. Such changes in these fragile environments depress metabolic rates and immune responses in the various species of coral. Combined with algae "die-offs" these vital fish nurseries are in danger of permanently disappearing and directly impacting fish reproduction and populations in those areas. This could happen as early as mid-century. Coral reefs are believed to be the nurseries for as much as 25% of all global fish species and as such this should be a major concern. [9]

Still another negative impact is the reduction of carbonate ions available to marine animals that require exoskeletons to survive. This makes it difficult for these creatures to form the biogenic calcium carbonate (A process known as calcification) which is critical to the formation of their protective outer layer. In addition to coral and some plankton species, sea animals that grow shells or external plates such as crabs, lobster, sea stars, clams, scallops, and so forth are at risk. Under these increasingly inhospitable conditions we are seeing higher mortality rates across the planet as regional fisheries decline and collapse. If we continue to see acidification and temperature rises in the future it is highly likely these species will all soon go extinct. Apex sea mammals such as whales, seals, sea lions, otters etc...depend heavily on the krill, crustaceans, and shell fish that are being directly impacted by these declines. So it is no wonder that reports of these creatures dying off due to starvation or the diseases that result from reduced levels of food are now common place.

Furthermore the impact these changes could have on bottom dwelling deep ocean species may be even more pronounced. At current projections we will soon create oceanic conditions that were last seen on our planet around 55 million years ago during in what is referred to as the Paleocene-Eocene boundary/ thermal maximum. During that period which saw a rise in global temperatures between 5-6 degrees Celsius, the deep oceans underwent a mass extinction event. [10] Right now we are seeing an increase in acidification which is about ten time that which was experienced during that time. In fact, we are currently increasing ocean acidity at a faster rate than at any other time in the last 300 million years. [11] This is an unprecedented geological event.

In essence, by burning carbon based fossil fuels that were derived from encapsulated solar energy capturing sources (algae, animals, and plants that have since been converted by time, heat, and pressure into oil/coal) we are releasing those same elements back into solution (our biosphere). This is altering the delicate chemical balance that has supported the variety and vibrancy of the species we have depended on and in which homo-sapiens has flourished off of these past centuries. If we continue on this path we can anticipate that our oceans and atmosphere will soon revert to those same global conditions that were occurring in our distant past. It would then be conceivable that this could spell the eventual and permanent loss of our Oceans as a resource for food for as long as humankind inhabits this Earth.

Combine the destruction of this incalculably priceless resource with the enormous loss of biodiversity and you can begin to see why this nothing short of tragic. Then add the fact that we derive the majority of our atmospheric oxygen from the very species we are destroying, and it becomes clear that we must act and act quickly to reverse these unacceptable consequences.

Rising Sea Levels

For the most part there is quite a bit of misinformation and wild predictions that have been made claiming how extreme and immediate the threat of rising sea levels is to 21st century civilization. Perhaps a bit of background information will help frame this discussion and bring some clarity.

Sea levels have varied greatly throughout Earth's history. For instance, during an ice age enormous quantities of global water volume is encapsulated in glaciers and ice sheets resulting in much lower sea levels. The ice sheet in North America during the Pleistocene epoch (our most recent Ice Age) was over 2 miles thick in certain areas while sea levels were down as much as 390 feet compared to today's levels. This left areas of our crust that are now buried beneath the ocean surface uncovered and available for settlement. It is only recently that discoveries of ancient cities such as the Sunken City of Yonaguni off the coast of Southern Japan, the Bay of Camby ruins off the coast of India, and the Sunken City of Cabo de San Antonio off the coast of Cuba have supported these findings. It is also now being theorized that the flood the bible refers to in the story of Noah was caused by ocean levels rising to the point where they breached the Pillars of Hercules at the mouth of the Mediterranean seas flooding both the those lowlands and what is now the Black Sea. It has only been in this last decade that we have recognized that there is a whole portion of our human history and ancestry that predates our modern records and lays buried under the sea.

On the other side of that coin we also know that sea levels have at times in our past been much higher than what we experience today. When the climate has been relatively warmer less water tends to be encapsulated in polar ice sheets and glaciers. Though those level differences are not nearly as dramatic as what we see with an Ice Age event, there seems to be the potential for the Oceans to rise perhaps another 25 meters or so from today's level with just a 2 degree Celsius increase in atmospheric temperatures and given enough time. [134]

What we can say for sure is that our sea levels are rising. Global temperatures have been on the rise since the beginning of the industrial revolution and as a consequence we have seen a steady increase in sea levels. Current sea level rise is about 3 mm/year worldwide. According to the US National Oceanic and Atmospheric Administration (NOAA), "this is a significantly larger rate than the sea-level rise averaged over the last several thousand years", and the rate may be increasing. [12]

To understand that extent of the threat we face with rising sea levels we have to understand the components that contribute to any potential change in Ocean volume. Presently Oceans make up 97% of global water volume while 2.7% is encapsulated in glacial ice sheets. [13] The great majority of those glacial reserves are found on Antarctica and Greenland. Ice from the Arctic ice sheet does not figure into any equation as to changing sea levels as it is frozen sea ice and merely transforms from frozen to liquid states on a seasonal basis without having a pronounced impact on sea levels.

So if we were to assume a massive collapse of current ice sheets how would that influx of additional water alter sea levels as compared to where they are today? If we include just the small glaciers and polar ice caps on the margins of Greenland and the Antarctic Peninsula, sea level would increase around 0.5 meters or a little over 1 and a half feet. The complete melting of the Greenland ice sheet would produce a 7.2 meter rise (or approximately 23'7"). The Antarctic Ice Sheet would add a titanic 61.1 meters (or approximately 200 feet) of ocean volume. [14] The collapse of the grounded interior reservoir of the West Antarctic Ice Sheet would raise sea level by 5–6 meters (or approximately 16-19 feet). [15]

To bring some reality to these numbers we need to understand that a complete breakdown of these systems is both extremely remote and would take on the order of thousands of years to fully melt. Geologic records also suggest that sea levels have not risen above 30 feet of where they are today on the order of millions of years, even when our planet went through other extended "warm" periods. So although it is highly unlikely we will all be staring as extras in Waterworld 2, that still does not mean we need not be concerned.

The general consensus of opinions that has been circulating around academia recently are predicting that we can expect a rise in sea levels anywhere between 3 to 7 feet by 2100. The truth is there are so many variables that we cannot anticipate, that any guess is just that, a guess. What happens if we go through a full out climate shift which is a distinct possibility? What if average global temperatures were to rise 9 degrees or drop 9 degrees suddenly? All predictive models would be way off. To be fair to the scientists making these predictions, it is difficult to make linear projections based off of past data when rates are increasing and we are very likely to see non-linear acceleration as conditions start to evolve. Higher CO2 levels, deep sea methane releases, advancing deforestation and desertification are all elements that could have unforeseen and unpredictable influences as to how this scenario plays out.

Just for arguments sake, let's go with a prediction of 5 feet by the end of the century. That may not sound like that much, but a rise of 5 feet would have an enormous impact. Around 23% of our global populations live in or near coastal zones, many of whom are in cities that are near or at sea level. [16] Those cities would be in grave jeopardy and far more vulnerable to catastrophic flooding from weather driven storm surge as barrier islands disappear and storm intensities increase. This single impact will necessitate countless billions of dollars in construction costs to build protective barriers to safeguard the huge vested costs of those population centers. Critical coastal wet lands would disappear wiping out irreplaceable fish nurseries world-wide. Coastal agriculture and adjacent fresh water sources would be permanently lost. Additionally, low lying countries such as Bangladesh and The Maldives would either completely disappear or lose much of their land mass to advancing tides creating massive displacement and migration issues. These are just some of the consequences we will most surely have to face as sea levels rise.

Atmospheric Disturbance

One of the most direct and violent consequences humankind will have to adjust to as a result of a warming biosphere is the increased intensity of seasonal atmospheric disturbances. These are the hurricanes, cyclones, monsoons, tornadoes, nor-easters, and other major weather events that can play havoc with global populations. Over the past few decades scientists have been looking at the potential correlation between higher ocean surface temperatures and tropical cyclone patterns world-wide. "A 2005 study published in the journal Nature examined the duration and maximum wind speeds of each tropical cyclone that formed over the former 30 years and found that their destructive power has increased around 70 percent in both the Atlantic and Pacific Oceans." [17,18] "Another 2005 study, published in the journal

Science, revealed that the percentage of hurricanes classified as Category 4 or 5 (based on satellite data) has increased over the same period." [19] The findings from both studies correlate with the rise in sea surface temperatures in regions where tropical cyclones typically originate." [20]

As the atmosphere and oceans heat up, the available energy that powers these storms approximately doubles for each .5 degrees Celsius rise in ocean temperatures. In analysis conducted by the Geophysical Fluid Dynamics Laboratory of NOAA they stated "A new modeling study projects a large (100%) increase in Atlantic category 4-5 hurricanes over the 21st century." Although they expect that the number of storms may remain constant, the potential veracity of these storms and amount of rainfall associates with these events could rise dramatically.

Combined with rising sea levels these increasing powerful weather events could have a dramatic impact on coastal communities and lower lying regions putting formally secure seaside populations in jeopardy. Additionally, infrastructure built and designed to withstand lower wind speeds and less intense storm surge become vulnerable to these new "super cells". We can expect that populations will start to migrate inland and away from the sea as these events become more regular and intense in the decades ahead making living conditions in these areas more precarious.

Desertification

No single repercussion of our inability to manage our resources and limit the destruction we have ravaged on our environment is as obvious and pervasive as desertification. The Princeton University Dictionary defines desertification as "the process of fertile land transforming into desert typically as a result of deforestation, drought or improper/inappropriate agriculture"[21] More than 100 countries in the world are currently in some stage of losing formally usable drylands to expanding desert. The great majority of these nations are located in Asia, Africa, and South America, however this is a global issue that is impacting every continent with the obvious exception of the Antarctic. It is estimated that we are losing over 20,000 square miles annually to encroaching deserts and that 3.6 billion of the world's 5.2 billion hectares of useful drylands for agriculture has suffered significant erosion and soil degradation. [22]

Although the expansion and contraction of desert environments are cyclical on a historic basis, their recent expansion can be traced squarely to human activities. Over recent centuries several major civilizations have collapsed as a result of their managing their agricultural lands improperly which either heavily contributed or led to their decline. These include the Romans, Greeks and Carthaginians of ancient times who fed much of their populations from drylands that they eventually overused and rendered non-productive hardpan. In all cases these "man-made" deserts occurred in densely populated areas of ancient world surrounding the Mediterranean, in the Mesopotamian Valley, or on the loessial plateau of China. [23,24]

There are several root causes for desertification. Deforestation diminishes local rainfall due to a reduction in evapotranspiration rates. An ancillary impact is that it also exposes soil to direct solar radiation and dangerous increases in temperature. Once forest canopies, dry land shrubs and grasses are removed from the environment ground temperatures can soar 20 degrees or more. This has two negative impacts. It increases evapotranspiration rates robbing the soil of its water content while at the same time it also "cooks" the soil. This kills the insects, bacteria, mold, and fungus that retain much of that moisture greatly reducing and eliminating the organic life forms present in the topsoil. When farmers burn ground cover and forest lands to create nutrients in nutrient poor equatorial rain forest soils it has just that impact by transforming once healthy jungles into red expanding deserts. Countries such as Brazil and Madagascar have gained international attention for just such issues.

Aquifer depletion and the "drying up" of former farm lands has also been a major contributor to this problem. Areas such as northern China are losing formally productive agricultural lands as poor farming practices and disappearing water resources turn vast regions into dust bowls. Mexico, India, the United States, and Pakistan are just a few of the countries that are facing or will soon have to deal with these same problems.

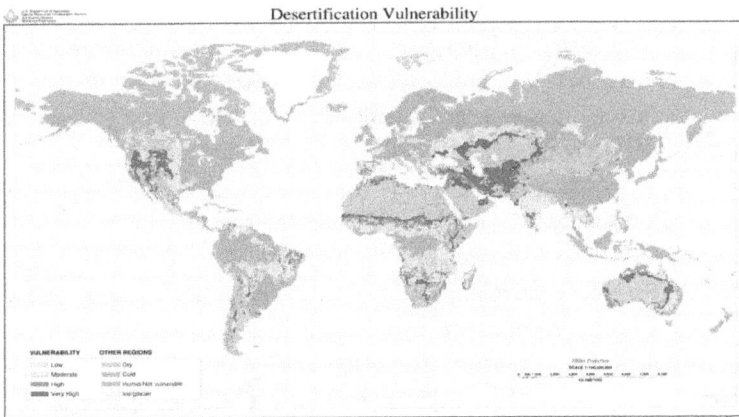

Desertification Vulnerability

[134]

In places like Africa and the U.S. it was believed for years that over-grazing was a main contributor to desertification. Commercial grazing animals and indigenous herds of migrating herbivores such as cattle, wildebeests, and elephants it seemed were stripping the land of vegetation. National polices evolved throughout the world in an effort to stem the decline by keeping vast stretches of drylands off-limits to commercial and naturally occurring grazing. Entire regions were fenced off, or designated as national parks or "protected lands". Some countries went as far as culling animal populations to try and stem the losses in these fragile environments. As time went by however, desertification continued to expand even though the lands were now "protected" from over-grazing.

Recent studies have shown that these policies were a mistake and it was the animal waste from these wandering herds that was providing the basic bacteria, minerals, and nutrients that the soil needed to retain its vibrancy and support plant life. Without those natural fertilizers, plants slowly died and the area would lose its ground cover. It has been a common misconception that these same animals were not only responsible for the desertification but were also producing vast quantities of methane and thus contributing to climate change. As a consequence there has been some public pressure to reduce their numbers. In many countries these policies are still in place. Such have been the miss-steps and mistakes of our land management policies and one of the reasons we are still losing the battle with desertification.

Loss of Biodiversity

Nothing is more important for the health of our planet or as precious for our future as bio-diversity. Mass extinctions have occurred at several times during Earth's geological history, but humankind is now on the brink of initiating our own mass extinction event that could very well include humankind if we are not careful. To understand the importance of bio-diversity it is essential to look at the subject from a number of different perspectives.

The value of bio-diversity to humankind is incalculable and critical to our way of life on many levels. First we depend on a great variety of plants and animals for our sustenance. As we reduce the number of species in any particular genus we eliminate that nutritional source permanently from the food chain thus limiting our availability to food. Additionally, as we destroy species that are lower in the food chain which support the species we rely on for our food, this also reduces or eliminates those sources. The reality is you can't continually move on to the next species when it comes to cultivating, raising, or collecting food. Bio-diversity is finite and eventually (and soon) we will run out of options.

Secondly it is our evaluation and utilization of diverse biological species that have been and are the source of much human discovery and advancement throughout the ages. As examples, we learned the basics of flying dynamics from our observation of birds, jet propulsion design from squids, stealth technologies from chameleons, submarine buoyancy from bony fish bladders. The ideas for consumer products such as Velcro came from plant burrs while the inspiration for glue came from barnacles and mussel excretions. These are just some examples of a recent historic movement by product developers and inventors who use bio-mimicry as the basis for their inventions.

Additionally, the great majority of our pharmaceutical and health related medicines and products are either derived from, based on, or mimic the attributes of smaller organic lifeforms. It is from these discoveries and observations that we may soon develop the life- saving and life improving drugs and treatments that could one day extend life expectancy, cure cancer, heart disease, and a multitude of other ailments. Today there are over 120 distinct chemical compounds that are extracted directly from plants that are in use in medicine around the world. [25] To wantonly destroy species before we have a chance to understand their special traits and powers would be a huge miscalculation as we have just begun to scratch that surface of that potential.

I was always of the opinion that the single greatest tragedy in human history was the destruction of the Royal Library of Alexandria which was the largest and most extensive collection of knowledge in the ancient world. It was estimated that as many as a half million scrolls containing the cumulative knowledge compiled over centuries by some of the world's greatest scholars and inventors were lost in that catastrophe. There were designs and concepts that to this day we have still to discover and understand that were destroyed. In essence a huge portion of our history and brilliance was wiped out in one tragic event. In comparison to what we are presently doing to our global bio-diversity I would consider that loss a minor misfortune.

We need to wake up and recognize the value of what it is we are so foolishly destroying. Every organism on this planet has evolved to devise a perfect harmonic balance with its environment occupying its particular niche through a unique and complex adaptive process that took millennia to evolve. What we can learn from these life forms is incalculable. We are ending the evolutionary tracks of countless plants and animals whose ultimate potential both for themselves and to improve human life is currently beyond our understanding. The fact is we are not gods and humankind does not have the right to be so callous and foolish in our management of this planet. Our planet is unique in this sector of the universe (as far as we know) as a utopia of diverse and complex life forms. It is without question our single greatest asset and irreplaceable treasure. Why is it that so few of us recognize that obvious truth?

WaterAvailability

It terms of the immediacy of the sustainable issues our population faces, water scarcity and accessibility to clean potable water is certainly first on that list. Water is by itself the single most important factor that impacts and supports human survivability, sustenance, habitability, and health. Any substantive change in accessibility or quality has an immediate and pronounced impact on the affected populations.

Water scarcity currently impacts at least 2.8 billion people a year with approximately 1.2 billion people lacking access to clean sanitary sources. [26] By 2025 it is feared that an estimated that 64% of the people on this planet (4.875 Billion) will either be in regions where there is an insufficient supply of fresh water, or where their water resources will be too polluted and contaminated to be used for drinking, cooking, and sanitary purposes. This crisis is already hitting much of the world hard in regions such as the Middle East/North Africa (MENA), as well as portions of Asia, and North and South America. In fact there is not a continent on our planet (excluding the Antarctic) that is not dealing with this issue to some degree.

How this crisis has evolved is the result of a number of converging trends all of which are accelerating dangerously on a non-linear scale. Population growth increases direct water usage and the resources required for expanding agriculture to meet food demands. Climate change alters seasonal rain distribution patterns and volumes. Increasing pollution of fresh water resources reduce potential reserves while deforestation disturbs the water cycle through decreased evapotranspiration. All in all this creates a rapidly shifting dynamic which is affecting vast regions of our planet with what are extremely unpredictable and potentially catastrophic consequences.

Global physical and economic water scarcity

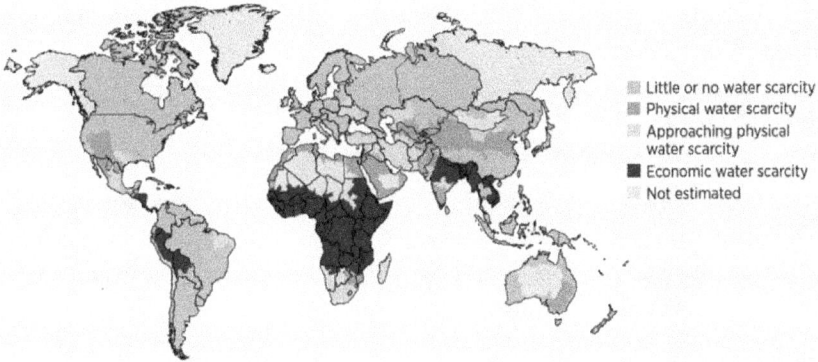

Little or no water scarcity
Physical water scarcity
Approaching physical
water scarcity
Economic water scarcity
Not estimated

Source: World Water Development Report 4. World Water Assessment Programme (WWAP), March 2012.

As an example, when we look at the map above which was done just 4 years prior to the release of this book, the area of South America surrounding Sao Paulo is designated as having little to no water scarcity. Yet, during 2015 there were plans being considered for the immediate evacuation of that city as their water supplies disappeared as a result of an unanticipated historic drought. This unforeseen dry spell impacted a municipality of more than twenty million people reducing their water reserves to dangerous levels. Yet the supportive study this map referenced identified that region as being of little concern for water resources. This is just one indication that the crisis is developing at a much more rapid and expanded pace than previous predictions.

The causes of water scarcity are all inter-related and combine to put populations at great risk. In the developing world where the issues are immediate there may be sufficient volume of fresh water resources, however mismanaged waste disposal and insufficient distribution infrastructure prohibits those resources from reaching those communities in need. Water pollution in the developing world is so rampant that currently one in every two hospital beds on the planet is occupied by a person suffering from some variety of water borne illness. [27]

In the developed or industrialized world climate change and overuse of regional water resources are playing havoc with once dependable supplies. As the atmosphere heats up glaciers are disappearing and snow falls and snowpacks have diminished reducing seasonal run offs. Population growth and increased food demand makes farmers clear more forest for crops thus reducing local evapotranspiration/rainfall levels. The ensuing over-extraction of ground water from aquifers then draws on water reserves faster than the ability of those resources to recharge. This then results in aquifer depletion or loss. All this finally leads to desertification which accelerates this loss of remaining water resources. It is a vicious cycle.

Ocean Pollution

Our oceans are subject to many forms of destructive pollution. These can include pesticides, oil and chemical spills, radioactive materials, sewage, and various forms of solid waste. One of the most significant of these is phosphorus the majority of which come from agricultural runoff and human effluent. This "fertilizer" creates large dead areas throughout the oceans. As the phosphorus flows out of river and sewage systems into estuaries and coastal waters, it initiates a process known as eutrophication.

http://www.ibtimes.co.uk/   www.gceadvancelevel.com

By over-stimulating certain algae species and subsequently causing massive "algae blooms", anoxic events occur which deprives the water of oxygen and creates dead zones where almost all sea life disappears. Each year there are more and more of these areas worldwide, and each year these areas continue to expand. The fear is that if this continues along with increasing CO_2 pollution this could undermine the health of our entire ocean eco-system. This would forever change (as far as humans are concerned) our planet in a way which would be very inhospitable to people and higher organisms such as fish, birds, sea mammals, amphibians, and reptiles. There will be no coming back once we cross that line.

With the recent disaster at the Fukushima Nuclear reactor site in Japan that occurred as a result of the 2011 Tsunami, the world has had to come to terms with the potential impact of radioactive waste on our ocean environment. Although the extent of the damage to the North Pacific is still undetermined to this point, some stories have circulated that are alarming to say the least. Health groups such as Natural News are claiming that the entire Pacific Coast Food supply is seeing advanced levels of radioactive iodine 129 which has a half-life of 16 million year and is starting to show up in the food chain. Fisherman are seeing an absence of ocean dwelling sea mammals in the waters between Japan and North America saying that stretch of ocean which has been historically "alive" with activity is now essentially dead. Divers off the coast of British Columbia are telling stories of hundreds of species disappearing.

In an article published by WND Health on March 5th 2015, written by Steve Elwart the following claims were made:

"There have been many other reports of fish and sea-creature populations dying in the Pacific. Also, there have been many discoveries of cesium–137 in high concentrations in seafood caught in the Pacific and sold in North America. There have also been many reports of unexplained deaths among wildlife:

• *Vast amounts of sea stars are "melting" off the west coast of North America*

• *Killer whales are dying off the coast of British Columbia*

• *There is an epidemic of sea lion deaths due to starvation along the California coastline. The question is: Why are they starving? Has the food chain been disrupted?*

• *Polar bears, seals and walruses along the Alaska coastline are suffering from fur loss and open sores*

• *Along the Pacific coast of Canada and the Alaska coastline, the population of sockeye salmon is at a historic low*

• *Something is causing fish all along the west coast of Canada to bleed from their gills, bellies and eyeballs*

• *Experts have found very high levels of cesium–137 in plankton living in the waters of the Pacific Ocean between Hawaii and the west coast, affecting the food chain in a process called "biomagnification"*

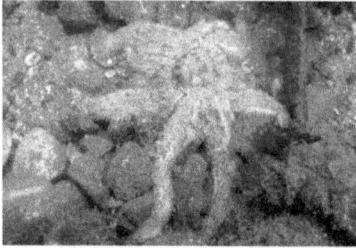

Whether you wish to dismiss all this "information" as hyperbole and fearful over-reaction, or accept the government's explanation that the
rise of background radiation levels is minimal, within safe limits, and not the cause, I believe a certain level of skepticism is in order. History has shown us time and again the willingness of many governments to bargain human health and food chain impacts against protecting existing economic markets and jobs

In addition to the phosphorus and other assorted pollutants we flush into our oceans, they have also become a collector of our consumer and municipal solid waste. Each of our oceans has an area in or around their mid points known as a "Gyre".

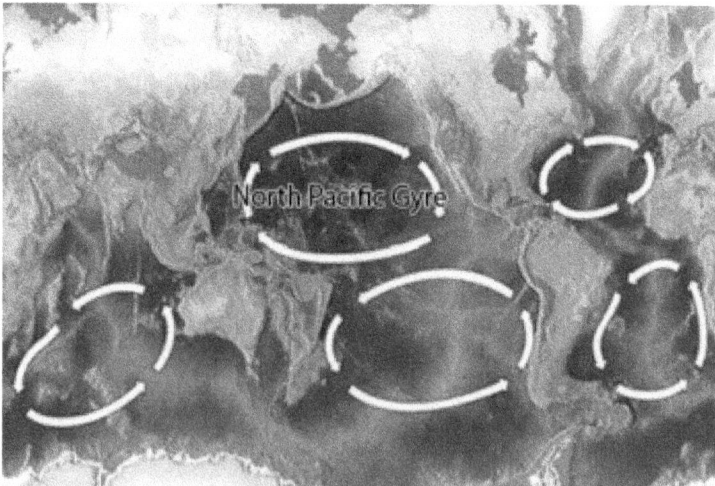

These areas are a central vortex where all floating debris tends to accumulate. This is a particular issue as it pertains to the huge quantities of
"garbage" plastics and chemical sludge that find their way into the Oceans via direct

dumping or being flushed out through river systems. Current estimates as to the size of the Pacific gyre range from the size of Texas, to twice the size of the United States. [28]Accuracy however is a matter of conjecture.

Land Based and Atmospheric Pollution

Many of the issues we face today in regards to climate change, ocean health, and water scarcity are directly related to how we manage our waste streams and the environmental pollution they create. Pollution is defined as the introduction of a contaminant or contaminants into a natural environment that causes an adverse impact. Every industrial, agricultural, and human activity that relates to our daily existence produces a variety of waste products. It's when those waste streams are released into the environment that they can create negative consequences and have an environmental impact. For the sake of this section I will limit the discussion to those waste streams and impacts that directly relate to the larger issues of environmental stewardship from a bio-chemical perspective and not those of sight or sound.

Air Pollution

The invention of the combustion engine/generator will be recorded by history as one of the most significant moments in human development. It both ushered in and enabled our great technological leap forward during the industrial revolution, and all but guaranteed we would one day destroy this favorable climate and healthy eco-system we depend on for our existence. The issues we now face with the pollution of our atmosphere are a direct result of the machines we depend for electricity, heat, transportation, and global commerce and the profitability of the fossil fuel commodities that power those systems.

Air pollution comes in many forms that are both harmful for the environment and potentially dangerous for human beings. We've already discussed CO_2 and the huge impact fossil fuel pollutants have on our biosphere in terms of influencing our climate and chemical changes in our oceans. There are however many others types of pollutants that are the byproduct of human activities we need to be concerned about.

SO_2 (Sulfur Dioxide) enters our atmosphere from the burning of coal and petroleum or the slashing and burning of forests, jungles, and grasslands for agriculture. When it combines with other airborne compounds it creates acid rain which impacts crop/soil health and can "kill" lakes or streams when concentrations become too high. This is a big issue in areas where factory and coal emissions are untreated before they enter the atmosphere such as eastern Asia and many parts of the developing world.

Particulate matter (PM), or the small dust like materials that are a byproduct of incomplete combustion contributes to health related issues such as heart disease and lung cancer. PM can include persistent free radicals and toxic metals. PM 2.5 (2.5 microns) is of particular concern as it is easily absorbed through nasal membranes and the lungs directly into the blood stream. The negative impacts of this form of pollution are becoming an acute problem for populations in Eastern Asia such as India and China, or in cities in undeveloped nations where air borne particulates are reaching historically high levels. This form of pollution is turning formally blue skies consistently grey. The main contributing factor in those regions is the percentage of coal used for electric generation and the absence of regulations limiting car emissions and industrial waste streams.

Particulate matter pollution in Linfen, China Photo:sheilaz413/Flickr

Chlorofluorocarbons (CFCs) damage the ozone layer letting in dangerous levels of ultraviolet radiation a major contributor to various skin cancers. Along with VOCs (Volatile Organic Compounds), Ammonia, and Radioactive particulates mankind impacts our atmosphere in a variety of ways that are not conducive with a heathy and vibrant environment.

So this leaves us with the question of where does all that pollution come from and who is responsible for reducing its impact? This has been the central theme of governmental discussions and negotiations that have been going on for decades.During that time countries have labored to identify those sources and come to agreements on acceptable strategies to limit the levels of pollutants entering our biosphere. The debate has centered on defining a fair and balanced approach to reducing pollutants in terms of each states individual responsibilities. It is because these discussions and initiatives always lead directly back to the energy that fuels regional economic development that there has been such little forward movement on this critical issue.

When we delve down into the main sources of air pollution most people are quick to identify motor vehicles as being the single largest contributor. The reality however is that the two largest contributors are industries that powers their operations through the burning of coal, and global transport, particularly large transoceanic shipping. An April 23, 2009 article in the The Guardian reported research that showed just one single large container ship emitted the equivalent pollutants of 50 Million cars annually. Currently the fifteen largest transport ships in the world may emit as much pollutants as 760 million cars. This is a result of these vessels using low grade bunker fuel in the completely unregulated environment of the open seas. When you realize that these transports account for 90% of global trade you understand why addressing this issue is so difficult.

South Korea's STX shipyard says it has designed a ship to carry 22,000 shipping containers that would be 450 meters long. There are already 3,693 new ship builds on the books for ocean going vessels over 150 meters in length due over the next three years. The amount of air pollution just these new ships will put out when launched is equal to having another 29 billion cars on the roads. [29]

2013 Global Emissions of CO2

Country	CO$_2$ emissions (kt)[30]	Emission per capita (t)[30]
World	35,270,000	-
China	10,330,000	7.4
United States	5,300,000	16.6
India	2,070,000	1.7
Russia	1,800,000	12.6
Japan	1,360,000	10.7

China contributes twice that of the next largest air polluter which is the U.S. mainly because of their huge expanding manufacturing base and the widespread use of unfiltered coal burning power plants. After China and the U.S, India, Russia and Japan are next in line for CO2 emissions and airborne pollutants. Generally speaking, the more developed the country, the higher individual impact per person. The less developed the country, the faster growth rate of CO2 emissions annually as those societies strive to improve standards of living and economic expansion as quickly and cheaply as possible.

Right now we are increasing the levels of CO2 and pollutants in the atmosphere at a rate that is unprecedented in human history and it is predicted that we are going to increase these levels substantially in the near future. With the impact climate change is already having on global weather, atmospheric turbulence, and ocean PH, one can only imagine what might be in store for our children.

Radiation

Fukushima and Chernobyl are well known and historic nuclear disasters. There are literally dozens of other events known and speculated about where large quantities of highly radioactive materials have been dumped or discarded without the public being aware. Governments rarely like to admit to or disclose knowledge of these releases, however over the years many have come to the public's attention as secrets have leaked or evidence of their impacts have become apparent.

Radiation is deadly to all animals and plant life depending on the concentrations, volatility, and exposure time. Lake Karachay, a lake in the Southern Ural Mountains which was used as a dump site for early Soviet Nuclear development is so radioactive that you would die from less than one hour of exposure at the site. [31] When drought hit the area recently and dried up one end of the lake, radioactive dust was blown into a neighboring city exposing over 500,000 people to these highly dangerous materials. The Italian mafia is rumored to have sunk approximately 30-40 ships carrying both highly radioactive and toxic waste in the Mediterranean and off the coast of Africa. [32] Russian nuclear subs are rumored to be scuttled throughout the Arctic Ocean leaking their nuclear fuel into those otherwise pristine waters. [34] These are just some of the stories out there.

The half- life of some radioactive isotopes can last tens of thousands of years or more and make those areas they pollute absolutely unlivable. Through accident, ignorance, or greed and a blatant disregard for the health of our population we are losing more and more of the space and resources we need to live and survive due to radioactive contamination. These losses will be permanent as far as modern humankind is concerned.

Industrial Accidents/Chemical Pollution

Second only to nuclear catastrophes in terms of a pollutant's long range impact on our environment are the damages caused by industrial accidents and the negligent management of toxic chemicals. These can include a wide range of occurrences such as poorly managed industrial growth, oil spills, chemical spills, mine tailings and residues, and the illegal or unregulated disposal of industrial waste.

Every few years we're reminded by a BP disaster in the Gulf of Mexico, or an Exxon Valdez oil spill, or Bhopal India Union Carbide chemical explosion of our vulnerability to these highly destructive events. The problem is, just as with nuclear accidents, most people are only aware of a fraction of the damage that occurs. Additionally only a small portion of the many instances of severe pollution that happen on this very small planet are ever in the news. These events are occurring in so many places in such large and uncontrollable levels that it is difficult for the average person to grasp the enormity of the damage.

When the oil companies were finished drilling for oil in the Niger delta, one of the lushest, bio-diverse, and important eco-systems in West Africa, they neglected to cap the wells. Years later those wells are still leaking oil and the Niger delta is a black, oil soaked, toxic polluted wasteland that no longer functions as a healthy environment. Divers reviewing the aftermath of the BP disaster are finding the sea bottom in the affected area of the Gulf of Mexico devoid of life. There are many cities in Eastern Europe, South America, Asia and Africa that are severely polluted from mining operations and toxic heavy metals such as lead, mercury, and cadmium. Arsenic is also a major issue. Often nothing will grow locally because of the soil contamination. The residual toxic dust which blows away with the wind often end up throughout the food chain and water supplies. The city of Dzerzhinsk in Russia is so polluted that the death rate exceeds the birth rate by 260% and an average life expectancy is in the mid-forties. More than 300,000 tons of chemical waste were dumped there up until 1998[135] There are similar issues throughout the world on every continent wherever you find people and industry.

Whether it's Love Canal or a small mining village in Ghana, the legacy of toxic waste lasts for generations. Cleanup is costly and in many cases impossible. Whereas most developed nations are being far more proactive in monitoring and regulating toxic waste management and disposal, this is still a huge and growing problem in the developing world.

Sewage, Industrial, and Agricultural Waste

What we flush down our toilets and dump or drain into our rivers and lakes has a direct impact on our health and the health of our environment. How we manage various types of sewage and agricultural waste is a major issue. It compromises healthy soils, regional water supplies, and the vitality of aquifers, estuaries, wetlands, and coastal waterways.

Into those vulnerable and pristine resources we introduce a witch's brew of toxins, chemicals, detergents, pharmaceuticals, heavy metals, bacteria, and pathogenic organisms.

Many of these undesirable waste products find their way back into the food chain, our fresh water supplies, or dramatically impact the bio-chemical composition of those eco-systems.
Sewage can be broken down into several categories, each of which is comprised of specific waste streams. Domestic or sanitary sewage is primarily made up of grey water from showers, sinks, and toilets, the majority of which includes human effluent, detergents, food preparation waste, and bio-solids such as toilet paper. In addition certain toxins, chemicals, and pharmaceuticals also make it into that waste stream when they are part of our excrement or dumped directly into those systems. Pathogenic organisms that can cause a variety of illnesses such

as dysentery, hepatitis, and cholera are commonly found in those discharges. Uncontrolled flows of these materials are a blight in the developing world contributing to millions of deaths annually and countless numbers of illnesses.

Agricultural waste releases a combination of unwanted nutrients, chemicals, and pesticides into soils and water systems as a by-product of the fertilizers, sprays, and pharmaceuticals used in raising crops and livestock. Those nutrients contained in the manure and livestock feces may cause eutrophication, a condition we touched on earlier. Uncontrolled they promote the unwanted and rapid growth of algae in both inland and coastal waterways.

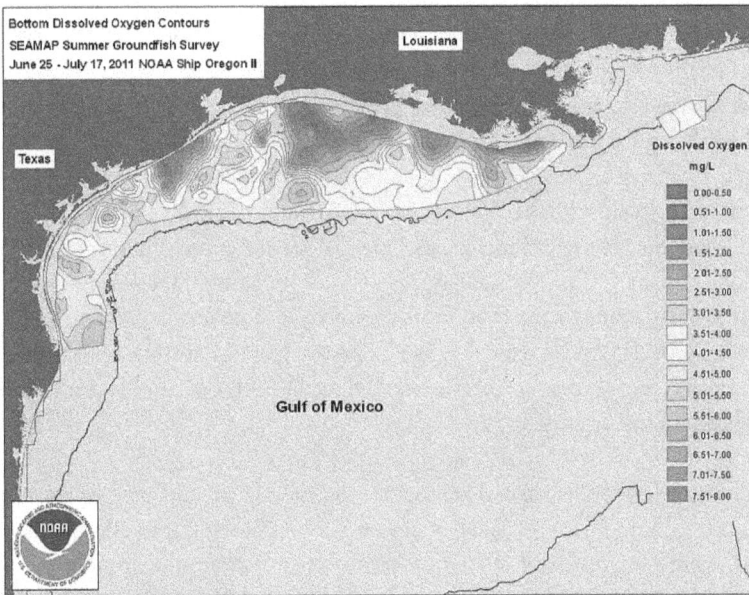

This, in turn, can create "Dead zones" or hypoxic low oxygen areas leaving the waters virtually lifeless, or contribute to another potentially deadly condition known as ecotoxicity.

Another by-product of uncontrolled runoff is the growth of toxic algae. Cyanobacteria have been an increasing issue in our lakes and coastal waterways. In addition to killing sea life, these bacteria are toxic to humans when ingested in drinking water or as a concentrate of the seafood we consume.

Additionally animal wastes are full of antibiotics and other medicinal by-products. These residues impact us directly through the fruits, vegetables, grains, and sea food we eat. They can also leech into the soil and show up in aquifers to then be ingested by people as part of their water supply.

Industrial waste can contain some very harsh chemicals, toxins, heavy metals, and in some cases low-level radioactive waste. This is currently much more of an issue in developing countries where oversight and regulations are either non-existent or very laxed. There is however an existing legacy of past mismanagement that still exists in the brown fields, industrial storage tanks, lagoons, and super fund sites located throughout the developed world. As we discussed earlier, some of the most polluted and toxic environments on the planet are the direct result of this issue. The health of both the environment and the populations in those areas pay a terrible price in terms of life expectancy, poor health, livability, and reduced bio-diversity because of these wastes. Increased cancer rates, genetic birth defects, and a variety of nerve related illnesses are just some of the resulting consequences.

As we move forward into the 21st century we can anticipate that water scarcity issues are going to increase globally. More and more of our population will be forced to use marginal sources for drinking, cooking, sanitation, and growing their food. This is already a huge and expanding issue in the developing world. We can expect to see higher incidences of illnesses, disease outbreaks, and increasing mortality rates as a result of our dependence and exposure to these contaminated waters.

Another impact of contaminated sewage is that these toxic outflows are destroying the healthy soils and inland/coastal waters we depend on for agriculture and seafood. Increasing levels of the toxins, pesticides, pharmaceuticals, and heavy metals that are so destructive and dangerous to our health will be showing up in our food chain in ever growing concentrations. This is the direct result of having to use sewage for irrigational purposes, growing crops on contaminated farmlands, and harvesting fish from polluted waters. It is a by-product of a process known as bio-magnification. Many experts are claiming that our increased exposure to these contaminants is resulting in higher incidences of autism, and the general breakdown of our auto-immunity systems in addition to increased cancer rates.

Municipal Solid Waste

Generally speaking, Municipal Solid Waste or (MSW) is not nearly the threat from a bio-chemical, toxicity, or biosphere altering perspective as some of the other forms

William Sosinsky

of pollutants we have covered. It is however the most pervasive and visible waste stream that most people relate to in the course of their daily lives. MSW is comprised of the general garbage and consumer waste we create continuously without paying it much thought. That being said it is a huge problem that has reached untenable levels around the world.

Whether it is the mass of garbage circulating at the centers of our oceans gyres, or the endless piles of refuse choking our landfills, our consumer waste problem has gotten out of hand. You cannot travel through the developing world, or walk through the streets of almost any large municipality that lacks a robust waste treatment infrastructure without being overwhelmed by the endless quantities of garbage everywhere you turn. It is piled by roadsides, strewn about the streets, and dumped into local streams, rivers, and lakes. In the developed world the landfills are overflowing and running out of space.

MSW is not without its adverse impacts in terms of toxins and contaminants. Consumer electronics, solvents, batteries, household and garden chemicals, motor oils and a variety of other common waste products can poison the water table and foul local bodies of water. When MSW is burned the fumes can be overpowering and create substantial local air pollution from such items as tires and plastics.When plastics get into the ocean they can strangle sea going mammals and birds. Particalized plastics can be eaten by fish and get into the food chain creating a health risk for people who consume those species.

While these are all big issues none of them are going to destroy the planet in and of themselves. What MSW does however is greatly diminish the landscape and destroy the natural beauty of our environment. It turns gardens into wastelands, neighborhoods into slums, and lakes, streams, and rivers into cesspools. MSW is a prevalent and ongoing issue in practically every corner of the world that lowers our standard of living and quality of life in a very direct and visible way. We are turning the Garden of Eden into a garbage dump.

Over Population

It is not my intention to challenge any religious beliefs or be misconstrued as to how I view the extraordinary value and potential of every human being on our planet. There are simply too many of us. To be a bit clearer, there are just too many mindless consumers and careless producers on this planet. If we do not change fundamentally how we manage our resources or learn how to manage our population growth, we will soon permanently alter our environment and our ability to survive as

a species. It is a direct result of the sheer numbers of us who create waste
and overuse our finite resources that we are now destroying the eco-systems and
extinguishing the reserves that every living thing depends on. No single contributor
is more central to our current dilemma and more dangerous to our future, than our
inability to control the size of our population.

For centuries aboriginal tribes throughout the world have lived in small groups
essentially living off of the land in a somewhat non-invasive and symbiotic lifestyle.
It was not until mankind expanded our population and started developing larger
communities, villages, and cities that we threw out of balance the delicate
equilibrium that had existed throughout our history. We used our ingenuity to
efficiently move water resources from place to place, cleared the land for living and
agriculture, and altered landscapes to suit our purposes. Technology advancements
allowed our industries to strip the soil for minerals and dig deeper and more
productive mines. We now search for oil and coal deposits from remote and
previously unreachable sources, cut down a forests worth of timber in a day, and
catch vast amounts of fish that would have been unthinkable only decades before.
With all these great achievements and increases in efficiency we never questioned or
worried what the potential consequences for these actions would be.

We now have over seven billion of us on this planet. In areas such as Eastern and
Southeastern Asia, Central Africa, the Middle East, as well as other highly
developed regions our population have completely overburdened their natural
resources. If it were not for foreign imports and resources flowing in from distant
lands those regions would already be standing on the precipice of imminent resource
collapse. Instead of intelligently managing our resources we have acted like rats or
pigs. We carelessly take what we need, foul and poison the lands and water we
depend on for sustenance, and go on to new areas without a single thought as to
finite nature of these resources.

Nature is always striving to create equilibrium. All natural ecosystems and
environments without abnormal or external outside stress eventually find that
balance. Humankind has completely ignored that essential reality as we have sought
to expand our reach and develop our world to suit our own purposes. Right now the
planet is desperately trying to find that equilibrium. The weather fluctuates as
climate change becomes more pronounced creating erratic and severe fluctuations in
our atmosphere. Plants are dying in areas where they no longer are suited to be later
replaced by newer and more climate appropriate species. Sea life is diminishing
rapidly as over fishing and the chemical and temperature changes in the oceans
sweep away those life forms not strong enough for the more challenging

environment. Humankind was never meant to upset and destroy this tenuous balance that we depend which is exactly suited for us and our long term prosperity. The aboriginals knew this. We are about to learn this the hard way.

Chapter 4

The Threats to Agriculture,

and the Collapse of Our Food Chain

"Saving our planet, lifting people out of poverty, advancing economic growth... these are one and the same fight. We must connect the dots between climate change, water scarcity, energy shortages, global health, food security, and women's empowerment. Solutions to one problem must be solutions for all."

~ Ban Ki-moon

The 21st century will be about food scarcity, not a lack of energy.

It amazes me how every discussion on sustainability and going green always seems to center on energy and not the impending collapse of our food chain. I guess that's somewhat understandable as CO_2 has had such a pronounced impact on the environment while fuel and electric costs have skyrocketed. After all, it is the way we consume energy and the fossil fuels we depend on that are central to the issues we now face. It is also our focus on the challenges we are experiencing right at this moment as a species that tends to draw our attention. Human beings have a penchant for being preoccupied with immediate issues of self-interest while neglecting the future impacts of trends they either do not see or fully understand. It just seems to me that while everyone is focused on the source of our problems, very few people are seemingly concerned or preparing for its gravest consequence. At our current trajectory we will see the largest loss of life and reduction in human population in history by, or around mid-century as a result of mass starvation.

That's a pretty harsh statement that most people would find hard to believe. Markets in most developed countries are stocked to the brim with meats, fish, poultry, vegetables, grains, fruits, and assorted delicacies from every corner of the globe. You can drive up to a fast food window and they hand you a hot prepared meal, or pick up a (Smart) phone and magically someone delivers your meal or groceries right to your door. How could we possibly be running out of food? It is therefore hard to believe that the overwhelming odds for the cause of your demise (if you are young enough) or that of your children will very likely be from starvation or diseases that result from malnutrition.

This is not my opinion but an undeniable fact. We are facing an issue that will severely affect every family, country, and region on the planet, not just the poor and developing nations. Our food chain is currently in the early stages of collapse. It is already a reality for the majority of our global community, with the exception of those living in Europe, the U.S., the developed world, or having lots of money. For those fortunate enough, acquiring food in its seemingly endless varieties and preparations may be an after-thought, however that is not the case for much of our population and those percentages are increasing daily.

There are a number of opinions on how this will all play out. Some experts feel we can adjust and stabilize our current situation if we are proactive, while there are other opinions and models that suggest our planet's population carrying capacity could be reduced by as much as 3/4 (to approximately two billion people) by the middle of this century. These are not the fear-based rants of "over-sensitive, end-of-the-world environmentalists", but computer models analyzing core data that directly affects food production capacity and future production levels. We need to pay close attention and start preparing for shortages.

World Overshoot Scenarios
Anatoly Karlin @ SublimeOblivion.com

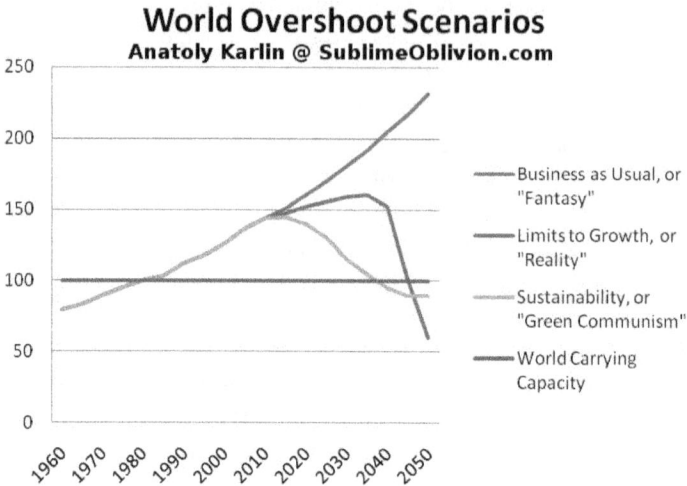

Legend:
- Business as Usual, or "Fantasy"
- Limits to Growth, or "Reality"
- Sustainability, or "Green Communism"
- World Carrying Capacity

To get a better handle on this, we need to look at all the issues involved. Outdated farming and fishing practices are currently being pushed to their limit. Over-harvesting, climate change, soil nutrition loss, and collapsing bee colonies are just part of the problem. When you also consider pollution, aquifer depletion, biodiversity reduction, and habitat destruction we begin to see the threats to a system already overwhelmed by an expanding population. For the first time in history, in an effort to make up for recent short falls, India has had to import rice, [34]Russia has stopped exporting wheat, [35] and China has leased farmland in more than a dozen separate countries to make up for their own production deficits. [36]

Many of us may counter that we are producing more food at this time in history than ever before, and they would be right. In addition, it is a said that we have plenty of food and it is just a distribution problem made more difficult because of fuel costs and the distance most food has to travel to get to consumers these days. Again, if this opinion is based on supply and demand today, then it would be hard to argue that point. However, we need to pay heed to the trend lines which indicate that the food we take for granted will not be so available in the years to come. Starvation may likely be the norm and not the exception. This is difficult to imagine as most of us have never experienced real hunger, but it will surely be the reality that our children will have to endure if we do not take decisive action and soon.

So, let us break down some of the major areas where the food chain is currently vulnerable and examine the threats to our resources that are behind this prediction. I will keep these sections as concise as possible and concentrate on the specific issues (How we provide solutions will follow later in this book).

The Impacts of Climate Change

The key impacts of climate change that make our crops vulnerable are the shifts in hydrologic patterns (the disbursement of atmospheric moisture) and the effects of altered temperature ranges. This can have a negative impact on agriculture, biodiversity, and ecosystems in general. Our agricultural farm belts where we are able to raise crops worldwide exist only in areas where there is a suitable balance between land/water resources and climate. Flooding, droughts, longer warm seasons or unseasonably cold temperatures throw this balance out of whack. When these changes occur, plants in those ecosystems become weak due to stress and either die, fail to blossom, or become prone to insect infestation and plant viruses. We can all feel and see this impact as food prices trend higher as a result of crops failing with greater consistency resulting in supply chains being squeezed.

One of the clear impacts with a climate "shift" will be its immediate impact on our food chain. Global agriculture infrastructure is located in regions suitable for those crops where those specific plants get adequate water and consistent seasonal temperatures. All agriculture depends on adequate rain fall, or access to available water supplies from rivers, lakes, and aquifers which make it possible for them to flourish. Our distribution systems of dams, canals, and irrigation networks are all designed to work within those parameters and with those stationary local resources. Additionally, each of the local species of plant we raise for food has adjusted to a consistent length of a season and a temperature range that deviates only slightly from year to year. A dramatic shift in climate, rain patterns, and water distribution will leave much of our supportive food production infrastructure in the wrong place and most of those crops in inhospitable conditions in which they will not do well. If all this happens abruptly, we will not have the time to reorganize and bring back global food production to pre-shift levels. As such, we will assuredly lose a large portion of our population to the ensuing famine.

www.uky.edu   http://k2radio.com/ wyoming -drought-disaster/

The fact that the weather is changing is undeniable. Since 2009 there have been 100 year droughts in Australia, China, India, East and West Africa, and devastating dry periods in Russia, South America, the southeastern U.S., and throughout California. This is not "normal" as some people would argue. The scientific data now available through recent studies of ice cores and deep-sea ocean sediments, have increased our understanding of climate patterns exponentially to where we have a clear idea of what is "normal". Recent record warm and cold temperatures, floods in areas that rarely if ever flood, powerful storms and unusual seasonal weather systems have filled news headlines increasingly over the last few years.

The Loss of pollinators

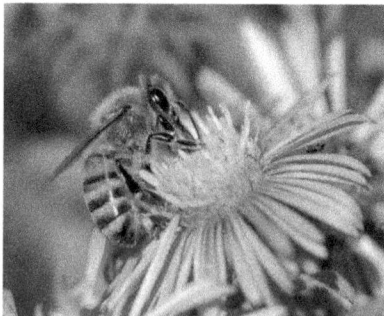

http://inhabitat.com

Bees are responsible for pollinating 90% of fruit and vegetable growth world-wide. CCD or Colony Collapse Disorder is rampant throughout our global agricultural network and soon threatens to eliminate perhaps the single most important species on our planet in regards to supporting human food production. A look at just some of the crop dependent on Bees for their growth cycle include:

Nuts, berries, broccoli, cauliflower, Brussels sprouts, cabbage, beans, turnips, peas, peppers, papayas, apples, melons, tangerines, coconuts, okra, kiwi, onions, coffee, herbs, spices, cucumbers, squash, lemons, limes, oranges, carrots, buckwheat, figs, fennel, mangoes, alfalfa, avocados, apricots, cherries, plums, peaches, nectarines, guavas, pears, eggplants, cocoa, tomatoes, and grapes...

...to name a few.

Try to imagine for a minute what your life and diet would be like without just some of those options. The US Department of Agriculture showed a 29 % drop in beehives in 2009, following a 36 % decline in 2008 after a 32 % fall in 2007. Losses globally were comparable. In 2010, the USDA reported that data on overall honey bee losses for 2010 indicated an estimated 34% loss. [37]After bee populations dropped 23% in the winter of 2013, the Environmental Protection Agency and Department of Agriculture formed a task force to address the issue. [38] Below are recently updated figures from the US Department of Agriculture published in a May 2015 article in the Wall Street Journal.

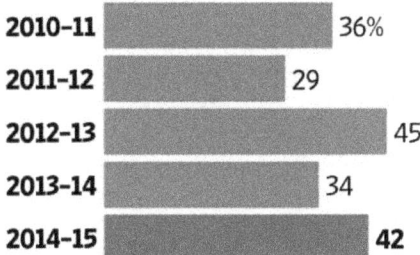

Diminishing Buzz
Annual loss of honeybee colonies
April–April

2010-11	36%
2011-12	29
2012-13	45
2013-14	34
2014-15	42

Source: USDA
THE WALL STREET JOURNAL.

Einstein once said that two years after the bees have disappeared, civilization will collapse. He was a pretty smart guy so perhaps we should start paying attention?

The Loss of Farm Lands

As populations continue to grow our need for living space and additional industrial output to service that increased consumption is putting increased pressure on our land reserves. More and more land that was historically used for farming is being converted to more profitable use such as housing or commercial development. In turn this has forced our remaining farms to try and produce more to make up for that reduced production space as demand rises. Additionally, the movement to start utilizing former food producing lands for biofuel production such as ethanol and organic fuel oil is cutting into our traditional agricultural lands on a massive scale as nations try to augment their fuel needs with cheaper home-grown alternatives.

UN special rapporteur Olivier de Schutter said in an October 2010 Rome meeting for world food security that a combination of environmental degradation, urbanization and large-scale land acquisitions by investors for biofuels is squeezing land suitable for agriculture. "Worldwide, 5m to 10m hectares of agricultural land are being lost annually due to severe degradation and another 19.5m are lost for industrial uses and urbanization," he said in his report.

Soil Nutrient and Topsoil Loss

If reducing our production space for food were not enough of a threat with an exploding global population, plant nutritional content is also becoming an issue as soils around the world are lost or depleted of critical components by overuse and mismanagement. Years of poor farming and careless irrigation practices have contributed greatly to a systematic stripping of key elements from our soils that are needed for healthy crops. This has also created an unnatural reliance on fertilizers making once prime farm lands now completely dependent on massive amounts of industrial additives in order to grow our produce and grains.

Additionally, in order to flourish in these poorer growing conditions, native crops have been replaced by genetically modified varieties that are better able to deal with these conditions. The result is fewer nutritional crops that are comprised more and more out of nutritionally poor cellulose (plant cell walls). It is a real issue as the vitamin and nutritional value of the produce we consume and need as part of a healthy diet is reduced.

Then there is the loss of topsoil. It is clear that we are eroding soils at a rate much faster than they can regenerate. Cropland in the U.S. is being eroded at least ten times faster than the time it takes for lost soil to be replaced according to the National Academy of Sciences. The United Nations has been warning of soil degradation for decades. This is a major concern in the third world where soil loss has contributed to the rapidly increasing number of malnourished people. Topsoil grows back at the rate of an inch or two over hundreds of years and can therefore not be taken for granted. Like all our resources, it is finite.

Furthermore, pesticides and weed killers have also played havoc with our farm lands. In an effort to eliminate the unwanted weeds and crop destroying pests that have always threatened a farmer's crops, we have introduced chemicals into that system that were created to eliminate those twin nuisances. Unfortunately, while they may kill the weeds and insects they were meant to defend against, those same chemicals destroy the bacteria in healthy soil that breaks down the raw elements which provide the nutrition for the plants. This renders the soil incapable of producing crops without the addition of fertilizer.

Finally, poor farming practices have also impacted soils. This is an issue particularly in developing nations where growing populations are forced to try and make marginal drylands agriculturally productive. Overuse makes these lands increasingly unproductive as the sparse organic components native to the soil are removed by the crops. Additionally, irrigation tends to concentrate salts in that same soil rendering them infertile as time goes by.

Limited Phosphorus Reserves

That reliance on fertilizer is ultimately one of our greatest causes for concern. Phosphorus is one of the three main elements that make up fertilizer and there is no substitute for it. Phosphorus is essential for cell wall, root, and flower development in plants. Without this crucial and irreplaceable mineral there would be no "fertilizer" and our current global agricultural model as we know it today would collapse. The loss of phosphorus as a feedstock would lead to more than 2/3 of our population (4-5 billion people) starving to death from the resulting scarcity of food. Phosphorus cannot be synthesized and without it we will soon run out of sufficient food to feed our growing population. It's that simple.

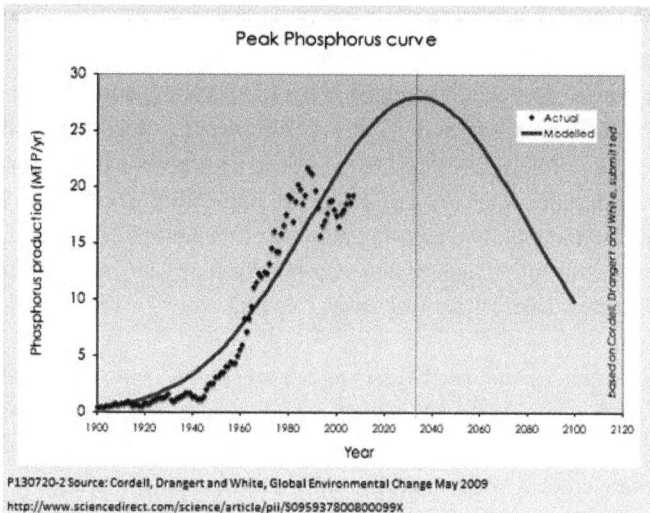

P130720-2 Source: Cordell, Drangert and White, Global Environmental Change May 2009
http://www.sciencedirect.com/science/article/pii/S095937800800099X

Although opinions differ on the subject (similar to the argument on climate change) most experts without a financial stake in the issue believe we have perhaps just 50 to 70 years of easily mineable reserves left. Some believe that number to be much closer to 40 years. Peak production levels are now quickly approaching and once we start our decline the impacts of reduced availability and increased cost will start a cascading collapse of agricultural stocks in poorer countries unable to afford fertilizer. At that point our global population will start to starve in mass. The U.S is believed to have less than 25 years of these crucial reserves left.

Aquifer and Groundwater Depletion

Most areas of the world depend on aquifers, healthy river systems, and inland water sources for their agricultural needs. Agriculture is the single largest user of the world's freshwater resources consuming 70% of those reserves. [39] It takes around 2,000 - 3,000 litres of water to produce enough food to satisfy one person's daily dietary need. [40] When you consider that the average person requires just two to five litres a day for drinking purposes alone, this is an extraordinary number. Water dependence (the need for additional fresh water supplies) is growing annually and a critical challenge for farmers. This is becoming even more of an issue as rain patterns begin to shift with our changing climate making a once dependable resource a thing of the past. Additionally, farmers in many areas of the world are now over-using these diminishing finite resources in an attempt to grow their crops, or in many cases increase their output to keep up with accelerating demand.

Northern China is losing farm land at the rate of 2100 square kilometers per year due to a regional system collapse of their aquifers. The same is true for India as both countries are burdened by explosive demand for more fresh water and agricultural output as a consequence of huge, growing populations. River systems have been so overburdened by the irrigation needs of farmers that bodies of water such as the Aral Sea which was once the fourth largest fresh water lake on the planet have all but disappeared.

In the U.S., the Ogallala aquifer which runs from the Dakotas to Texas (the major water resource for Midwest U.S. farming) has seen water levels drop over 150 feet in some areas threatening farm production. Current water use is at 130-160% of the recharge rate. In addition, the Colorado River which is the main water resource for the U.S. Southwest and Southern California is being de-watered at a rate of 1% per year (USGS Fact Sheet). In California's fertile central valley snow pack depletion in the Sierra Mountains threatens to turn arguably the most important farmland in the world into a desert by mid-century.

Depending on who you ask we could look at a global agricultural model where as much as 75% of our current production will be dependent on water sources that will no longer exist by 2075. This reduction of resources will happen in stages with each phase ushering in a new era of untold suffering and deprivation to the populations directly impacted. Water security and planning for continued water scarcity must be a central goal of governments globally or this crisis will have a devastating impact on human society as we now know it.

Agricultural Biodiversity Reduction

The majority of the fruits, vegetables, and grains that our society consumes today are the result and end product of scientific modification. GMO's (Genetically Modified Organisms) have replaced the huge diversity of ancestral stocks that used to feed our masses.

In an effort to provide a more profitable, dependable, and uniform product, commercially-grown fruits and vegetables have been manipulated by biologists to produce a more consistent look and flavor with higher yields. Very often these varieties are less nutritious sacrificing vitamins and mineral development so that the plant builds cellulose (Cell walls) faster and mature more rapidly. Additionally, a small number of "super grains" have been created that can adapt more easily to varied growing conditions and harsher climates. Although this has been quite successful and of value for many aspects of our agricultural production, it has also made our farm production vulnerable to targeted viruses that can potentially wipe out singular varieties of a species. By purposely reducing the number of strains we cultivate in an effort to homogenize our agricultural products, we have left the door open for a potentially catastrophic collapse of those limited crops.

Now when a virus breaks out in a particular agricultural food source it has the potential for wiping out that entire strain worldwide. This is evident in the wheat blight known as Ug99, a new form of stem rust that has spread out from central Africa that now threatens to destroy the world's entire wheat supply. Loss of this food stock would create a global crisis and result in potentially tens of millions of people dying from starvation as a core food source disappears. Another crop, the Cavendish banana is being wiped out by the tropical race 4 virus. [136] This will eventually eliminate the second strain of mass marketed bananas to fall victim to a worldwide sickness in the last two decades.

Biodiversity is the natural defense that protects our food supply. To limit the variety of crops we raise when it is both reduces their nutritional content and makes those crops more vulnerable to a catastrophic collapse is nothing short of madness.

William Sosinsky

Dependence on Fossil Fuels for Food Production and Transportation

Our current food production system is completely dependent on fossil fuels for commercial production and transportation. If we look at charts (see next page) you can see that there is a direct correlation since the beginning of the 20th century between our ability to produce fossil fuels and the growth of our global population. By all industry estimates, we hit peak fossil fuel production between 2006-2009. Industry experts also estimate that we will only be able to produce less than half of our current levels by 2050. That estimate factors in our ability to tap all available known sources still left on our planet. Should the population curve continue to follow this trend line (as it has for the last hundred plus years), a reduction in population matching that trend line would seem inevitable.

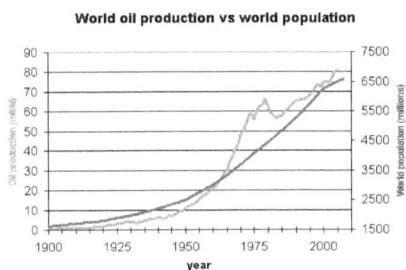

World oil production vs world population

State of the World

http://energyskeptic.com

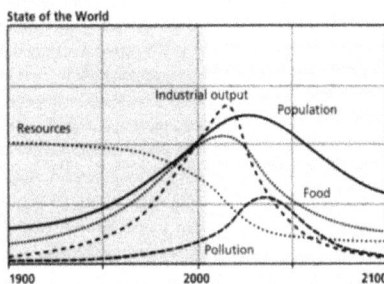

www.macrobusiness.com.au

Over-harvesting Ocean Fisheries

An international group of ecologists and economists in a 2009 U.N report warned that the world will run out of seafood by 2048 if steep declines in marine species continue at current rates. This conclusion is based on a four-year study of catch data and the impact on collapsing fisheries. Steve Palumbi from Stanford University in California who served as one of the other scientists on the project, added: "Unless we fundamentally change the way we manage all the ocean species together, as working ecosystems, then this century is the last century of wild seafood." This position is supported by NOAH.

Right now over 75% of the ocean species we consume for food are in decline and being harvested faster than they can reproduce. Additionally, 90% of our larger fish such as tuna and swordfish have been removed from the food chain all together.[41]

Hundreds of millions of people globally rely on fish from the oceans as their primary source of protein and when those fish are gone there will be nothing to replace those essential nutrients.

William Sosinsky

Chapter Five
The Tipping Point

"A man's conscience, like a warning line on the highway, tells him what he shouldn't do - but it does not keep him from doing it."

~ Frank A. Clark

As far back as I can remember since we began to recognize our potential to destroy our planet's environment, experts have spoken of a tipping point. This is a theoretical time frame where our collective action would no longer offset varying degrees of catastrophic damage to our biosphere. The concept of a tipping point has been a focus of arguments and the impetus for calls to action. As such, opinions have varied widely as to the actual timeframe and consequences of this subjective moment in time. Whether those who still insist we have not reached the tipping point are just plain ignorant or using their opinion as a strategy of creating doubt to delay action, the reality is we passed that proverbial tipping point years ago.

The wheels of change are now unalterably moving forward with a momentum we are powerless to reverse. The manifestation of our impacts on the environment will change our planet in fundamental ways that will have a huge impact on every human being on earth in the years ahead. The icecaps will continue to melt, sea levels will continue to rise, oceans will continue to become more acidic, weather patterns will continue to change and become more severe, atmospheric temperatures will continue to rise, and the general health and vitality of our food chain will continue to deteriorate regardless of what mitigating steps we now take. Anyone who does not realize these truths has failed to acknowledge the scientific trends and cumulative data which points to these undeniable facts. Too many of us are living in a fantasy world too afraid to admit the consequences of our failure to address these issues preemptively. The sad truth is we are about to enter an unprecedented age of resource depletion that has the potential to turn our future into an extended "dark age" the likes of which our species has never experienced.

We are not without options however as to how this will eventually play out and what we can still do to respond to these threats. The reality is there are degrees of austerity and damage that could occur as we push forward into the 21st century. Much is still yet to be determined and will be the result or consequence of the actions we take or our continued lack of a coordinated and decisive response. If we were to collectively put into action a massive restructuring of our planets supportive infrastructure and resource management policies much of the more potentially severe consequences could be avoided. In some cases, they could actually be reversed. In that case we could avoid some of the other tipping points which would then have permanent and irreversible consequences to humankind.

That being said, there is another tipping point that we need to focus on and is much more significant that no one really talks about. What happens when we run out of economic resources to respond to these threats and prepare our population for the changes that are sure to occur? How will we answer these challenges when societies around the world start to collapse under the pressure of diminishing resources so that regional response becomes impossible? If you think that unlikely look what has happened in Somalia. You might also consider the recent events in Egypt, Tunisia, Yemen, and Syria during the Arab spring. The harsh reality is when populations don't have sufficient food and water they stop listening to the authorities.

More than 75% of our global population lives in countries which are in jeopardy of having their ability to support their population's basic necessities for survival completely collapse before mid-century. Additionally, neighboring countries which can somehow manage to get by are also at risk. Those remaining regions will quickly come under pressure from migrating populations desperately seeking the resources they need to survive. This is the frightening reality our modern world now faces.

All is not lost however. We still have the opportunity to avoid the worst of this scenario but time is running short. Every year as food, energy, and commodity prices rise as a percentage of family income globally, our ability to counter these trends diminish. Reduced financial and available capital resources will result in families and countries having less and less money available for discretionary investment and infrastructure development. This will eventually erode and cripple our ability to respond. Subsidies will disappear, philanthropic efforts will diminish, and money for education and health diverted in an attempt to make up for those shortcomings till we are eventually broke and powerless. Read the papers or listen to the news. These challenges are the subtext of practically every global challenge we now face. The days of large humanitarian aid efforts will soon come to an end and we will be powerless to act as we watch regions of our world collapse under these pressures. This will be the consequence if we fail to prepare in advance of that tipping point.

Never before has it been so important and necessary for humanity to act in common purpose if we are to substantially counter this momentum and re-establish balance back to our broken planet. Actions and projects need to be coordinated, prioritized, and quantified for efficiency and impact. All of that will take financial resources we can ill afford to squander. Our failure to accomplish these changes will usher in a series of events that few of us can imagine in terms of the human suffering and environmental destruction that are sure to occur as a result of our inaction. This particular tipping point can and must be avoided at all costs.

Chapter Six

Knowing the Role You Play in the Solution

"Individual commitment to a group effort -that is what makes a team work, a company work, a society work, a civilization work."

~ Vince Lombardi

The reason we have found it so difficult to coordinate and focus on a game changing methodology in response to our current challenges has been a universal lack of understanding as to what steps are critical to achieving that end. Most of our leaders tend to view their "sustainable solution" from a limited perspective. Depending on their background and area of expertise, specific intelligence, or influence, their efforts tend to be myopically directed towards political solutions, technical solutions, social solutions, environmental solutions, or financial solutions, etc. It is only natural that these leaders try and approach and direct a response from their area of specific understanding, influence, and skill set. Yet those approaches have by their very nature been uneven and lacking proper perspective and coordination with the other critical pieces key to solving this puzzle. It is this systematic lack of understanding as to the complexity of these inter-relationships that is undermining our inability to direct our response to global resource depletion and environmental destruction.

The key to mounting an effective response to our global challenges requires a diverse understanding of all the contributing components that together form the societal structures which are now failing in the gross mismanagement of our natural resources. So let's dissect some of the major participants in this imperfect system and try and understand what makes their efforts fall short and what they can do to improve their focus and impact.

William Sosinsky

Government and Politicians

Government is a central player as to how we define and develop the socio-economic models in which we all live. Politicians, particularly in a free society, are in many respects the mirror image of the people they represent. We elect officials in the hope that their vision, experience, and leadership will help fulfill our own best hopes for our societies. We expect that during their tenure they will improve and protect our communities, enhance the quality of our lives, and that they will vigorously promote those values we embrace. Politicians almost always mirror the demands, expectations, and agendas of their constituency whether that allegiance is to a population, political ideal, specific stake holders that support their power base, or in the case of dictatorships, themselves.

Into that political arena enters every variety of opinion and personality type. The way free societies were designed to work assumes that those leaders will get together to discuss and decide on the steps that will ensure we respond effectively to our common interests. Then through a process of debate, compromise, and pragmatic logic leadership will find the best and most appropriate course of action to address these issues. Unfortunately, it does not always work that way. This is particularly apparent as threats and events become more challenging and the answers less clear. It is at this point either visionary leadership emerges, or the entire system starts to break down as infighting, self-interest, and blame dominates the discussion and nothing substantive is accomplished.

Such is the current political impasse we see occurring in a majority of countries throughout the world. Even though the threats are obvious and the need for action painfully clear, there is a lack of knowledge and insight guiding our decision makers. The result is they struggle to enact policy that will start us back on the right course and decisively address these challenges. Worse yet, many are not even interested in understanding the issues or be willing to take the time to try and grasp conceptually what needs to be done. I don't mean to insinuate that most of these leaders are not well intentioned and doing their best to provide that leadership. The harsh reality is however that very few of these politicians understand the overwhelming complexities of economic modeling, environmental science, and sustainable technologies such that they can properly analyze and formulate plans to address these challenges.

As an example, when President Obama moved to allocate hundreds of billions of dollars at the beginning of his first term for "Green and Sustainable" development, much of that money ended up going into projects that were anything but green and

- 55 -

sustainable. In order to reach a majority consensus for those bills to pass Congress compromises had to be made to include "ethanol production" from corn and "clean coal" as part of those allocations. Just to be clear, producing fuel from what would otherwise be food crops when so much of the world is struggling with malnutrition and outright starvation is obscene to say the least. Additionally, as of right now there is no such thing as "clean coal". That's just another example of the Orwellian Newspeak I spoke about earlier.

Then you add to that unwise investment into technologies and businesses that were predestined to fail such as the $500,000,000 dollars wasted on Solyndra (The Solar Module Company in San Jose) and you can begin to see how ineffective these efforts really are. Any business expert who understood the solar module market prior to that investment would have known that the Chinese would drop their own pricing of exported solar modules to undercut Solyndra's market (A standard China market tactic) and put them out of business. Supporting Solyndra was a naïve business decision that resulted in disastrous consequences as the company went bankrupt.

And just so we do not misunderstand each other, many of the projects supported by Obama were successful and strides forward have been made. I do not argue for a second that his intentions were anything but honorable and sincere. I would only argue that he was way out of his league from a business/economics perspective. He did not understand the "battle field" and as a result huge sums were wasted and the overall impact of the invested monies minimized as they related to his goal of creating a sustainable economy. It would be fair to say that as much as 65-70 % of all the money spent on "Green and Sustainable" efforts during that time were either misdirected through concessions or outright wasted due to poor decisions on market development methodology.

Another impediment that some leaders and government officials show is a complete lack of knowledge or concern towards the issues of sustainability. When you realize that most of these officials are more concerned with maintaining their power base and getting re-elected than enacting real change, our political response becomes even more diluted. Additionally corporate, banking, and business interests have exerted an ever increasing influence on government through extensive lobbying, campaign financing, and political action committees and organizations. This has had a very pronounced and negative impact on decisions which support public interest as policy shifts to protecting those influential private stake-holds. The end result are legislation and laws made for the "Stated" public good which are skewed towards short term economic results that support those stake holders rather than long term system improvements and needed infrastructure investment.

It is essential we elect smarter and better informed politicians. Campaign and lobbyist reforms with legal limits on contributions from the uber rich, super packs, large corporate, and banking interests would also be a good idea. I would also argue that government needs to restrict themselves to creating smarter regulations and enacting policy that helps direct positive change rather than sticking their noses into areas where they are ill equipped to compete. That would include backing businesses in markets they do not understand and in which they do not have the power or agility to maneuver effectively in.

Although government investment into new and emerging technologies plays a critical role as an enabling force in pushing forward positive change and innovation, the system as it now stands is terribly flawed and overly influenced by naïve and misdirected effort, and systematic cronyism. When proper legislation that takes into account the complexities of sustainable market development are in place and rewards through tax breaks and incentives individuals and businesses moving in the right direction, much can be accomplished. Additionally, creating surcharges and penalties for behavior and operations that are wasteful and destructive can have a very positive impact for encouraging change.

Another area where government can play an important positive role is education. Governmental action that directly supports and subsidizes the spread and access to specific knowledge and skills training relating to resource management would be invaluable. Disseminating those empowering skills and general knowledge to as wide an audience as quickly as possible both enhances our time critical response as well as supporting efficient economic growth.

Ultimately government functions best when it is supportive in a general sense by acting as a fair and thoughtful commissioner without actually being a player. That being said, going against the entrenched short term interests of the dominant global stakeholders requires courage and a singular vision along with unparalleled wisdom to manage the required compromises intelligently. Right now I would say that the world is desperate for that leadership as it will take such leadership to truly ignite the masses to action.

Big Business (Corporations and Banks)

Governments may be visibly out in front of social change and large infrastructure projects, but it is big business that ultimately holds the strings and dictates the course of global economic development. This will be a recurrent theme throughout this book as a core consideration as to how we manage our economics and current challenges as they relate to resource management and protecting the environment. For most of modern times and certainly now in our current global society, central banks and large corporations have held a disproportionate amount of influence and power in determining the directions we take on core global policies. They write the checks that empower change and without their support you have no chance to substantially change the world or the way it works. They are that central to the process.

In the world of global finance, relationships go way back and wealth and influence are very much viewed in historic perspective. It is fiduciary ties that bind these entities together and those considerations weigh heavily on policy and investment implementation strategies when it is time for them to invest. Once central banks commit to large investments as is the case with oil, coal, and fossil fuel infrastructure they are very reticent to back potential technologies that could potentially render those investments less profitable or in some cases worthless. On the other side of that coin major corporations and stakeholders fearful of those changes can use their financial or political influence to pressure banks to refrain from making commitments to potential competing entities or project concepts. This has many ramifications and demands a sober perspective when defining a strategy to enact substantive change.

If we extend that concept further you can see the logic as to why corporations spend huge sums of money on lobbyists and in their support of political candidates. It is those individuals and groups backed by big business who do their bidding in an effort to expand their influence/opportunities and defend their perceived vulnerabilities. Although this may have the net result of holding up needed reforms, it is however fiscally responsible and strategically sound from a fiduciary perspective. So it is not beyond big business to try and buy an election, "own" a political party, or dictate a political campaign platform that supports their interests. From their point of view it is just good business and they are just being fiscally responsible and proactive.

Additionally, from a historical perspective we are now at a point in economic history that draws a clear parallel to the U.S/Soviet cold war nuclear policy of Mutually Assured Destruction or MAD. These central banks and huge corporate interests are so powerful, exert so much influence, and are so completely integrated into governmental/societal infrastructure that there is virtually no way to go around them without completely destroying or abandoning the system. The irony is however, that by doing so we would also destroy or eliminate any chance we might have had to create substantive change. So the key here is we need the corporations and the banks if we are going to turn things around though that relationship may at times be contentious.

Central banks and large financial/funding entities tend to see their world in terms of risk management, return on investment, cash flow, capitalization, bond-ability, leverage, vulnerability, and strength and weakness. Whereas most of us fully understand those concerns as they might apply to specific projects and investments, for major financial institutions and corporations those same concerns extend to their long term strategic planning and management. This can put them directly at odds with the environmental and resource management concerns of our population when those two perspectives do not align. Existing fiduciary commitments, policies, plans, and financial investments can make them susceptible to denying or being adverse to any scientific data or evidence that negatively impacts those interests. Moreover it creates a co-dependent environment with their major supporters, strategic business partners, and associate investment groups. As a consequence they instinctively back any perceived solution that flows through their common pipeline and commitments, or supports the vision of those they have backed with investments. This can have a devastating impact on new ideas, technologies, start-up companies and concepts from ever seeing the light of day as they can be perceived as being directly competitive to those core relationships and models for change.

The reality is that money or in this case "Big business" does not take orders, they give orders. Big business is an inevitable, irreplaceable, and absolutely necessary partnering entity if we are to respond effectively and reverse our current course. They control the infrastructure, wield the influence, and have the means to turn things around. We do not have sufficient time left to address these challenges by rebuilding the system from scratch before conditions would deteriorate beyond our ability to respond. It is therefore essential that any visionary strategy aimed at saving our planet fully consider their stake-hold, profitability, and long term vision in any plan meant to find compromise and common ground. These are very smart people who know they will eventually have to change. All that is needed is a business plan and implementation strategy that makes long term fiduciary sense for them which protects their interests to encourage them to turn things around. The devil as they say is in the details.

Scientists and Technology Developers

One of the best parts of my job is that I am privileged to interact with some of the world's foremost scientists, inventors, and visionaries. Not a day goes by that I am not stunned and amazed at the depth of creativity, brilliance, insight, and single-minded passion that these exceptional people contribute to our societies. I love every aspect of science and any opportunity I have to get innovative perspectives from the people who do the planning, design, research and development is beyond exciting for me. It has only been through this experience that I have come to realize that intelligence is sometimes quite specific.

Just because you can do advanced trigonometry and land a space module on Mars doesn't mean you know anything about business, logistics, project development, politics, financing, legalities, social behavior, or have the least bit of common sense. That isn't to say that some of these great minds don't on occasion stretch their understanding of complex inter-relationships into efforts that support their vision, but generally speaking there is a huge void in their understanding when they step outside their areas of expertise.

CEO's and CFO's of technology companies are not usually scientists but businessmen who understand science. The reason scientists don't commonly hold those positions is it takes much more than a great idea or invention to create the supportive structures for that inspiration to find its potential expression in the real world. Creating real impactful change in the new technologies/applications market is a whole other skill set requiring a diverse and specifically trained team to orchestrate.

It is also the rarest of occasions when you see a scientist leading a nation or very high up in a government structure. Scientists were the geeks future business tycoons, politicians, and CEO's made fun of in grade school. Very commonly they do not communicate or translate well. After all, they were warning us about climate change and CO_2 emissions as early as the start of the industrial revolution. I guess nobody was listening? Also, generally speaking, they do not frequent the same social avenues as the average consumer. Many of these intellectuals do not buy into the "I want money, power, and fame" care-free lifestyle and values the rest of world is conditioned to pursue and aspire to. These are cerebral types who very often gravitate to relationships and social communities they can relate to. These are some of the reasons as to why they do not translate well and as a result fail to communicate the necessity for change, action, and innovation. In a way, they are viewed as outsiders.

When you combine that inability to communicate along with their not understanding the subtleties of creating change you can see why our best and brightest are not necessarily the ones to lead change. They should however be listened to very carefully. Everyone else needs to do a much better job educating themselves and appreciate what these "geniuses" are so concerned about. Scientists function as the brains of our society and when it comes to preemptive thinking and innovative solution solving, they are our only hope. These brilliant people will develop the technologies, applications, and provide the vision of the future for the rest of us to develop. What is needed is a much more efficient way for our leadership (both Political and Business) to understand and translate what are these best ideas and best responses to our current challenges into actions that impact change.

Environmental and Humanitarian Groups and Organizations

The people who dedicate their time and their lives to protect our environment and to try and bring hope to those who have nothing are the eyes, ears, and heart of this process. They are on the ground and the first to see the results of these drastic changes we are inflicting on our planet and the first to try and initiate efforts and devise strategies to try and correct those imbalances. They are the communications bridge into the at-risk populations who understand on a front-line level who we need to talk to, what does and does not work, and what can and cannot be accomplished. Much in the same way that Scientists are the technical visionaries whose advice and guidance must be heeded, so too are these groups who oversee and link us to the people and conditions where we need to focus our efforts.

The problem is that all the philanthropic and subsidized good will in the world will not solve our current challenges or reverse our course. We need to be honest with ourselves and accept that truth. Every year there is more need and bigger problems, every year there is less money. Very soon we will start to run out of resources. Finding money for those problems and people in need will be one of the first casualties of that process. Every year as food, energy, water, and basic commodity costs rise as a percentage of individual income on a global basis, less and less of a percentage of that income is available to go to help others in need. When the planes carrying bags of flour and rice to hungry populations are no longer flying to those countries to come to the rescue, the world will start to starve in mass.

Don't misunderstand me. I hold true to the ideals of helping those who cannot help themselves, defending those who cannot defend themselves, and speaking up for the oppressed who have no voice or say in their treatment. There is an important place for providing assistance to those in need. It must however be a process of increasing empowerment, not continuing dependency. There are many non–for–profits and foundations that understand this imperative and are actively moving in that direction. This approach which projects assistance into at-risk areas and lifts up at-risk populations by providing education, training, access to tools and technologies must be the future standard as to how we address these challenges.

The road to ruin is paved with good intentions. Our humanitarian/environmental groups only have the very best of intentions. They must however take a much more instructive role in addressing global needs and employ a strategy that reduces outside dependence through fazed empowerment. What was it that Confucius said? "Give a man a fish and you feed him for a day. Teach a man to fish and you feed him for a lifetime." Let's hope there are still fish left to catch.

Educators

Specific education directed towards sustainable management of our resources will need to play a central role if we are going to mount an effective response in combating resource depletion and environmental degradation. If this is a battle we are planning on winning then we'll need well trained troops for that effort. Educators are the drill sergeants that will prepare those recruits for the challenges ahead.

If I have an issue with why we are currently failing in that effort it is that there is little to no coordinating methodology guiding this essential mission. As I will expound upon further on in this book, I believe there is a need for future education efforts to be linked directly to skills training for ongoing regional efforts at rebalancing our resource management. Time is a critical factor in our response and all efforts need to be streamlined and focused if our impact is to be maximized.

Right now, the majority of education available only provides a backdrop for getting a job without directly leading to one. Military and Corporate training on the other hand make huge investments to improve the specific skill sets and knowledge of their employees/work force/troops as it relates to their business development plans or ongoing mission goals. For re-establishing a sustainable balance our societies and governments would do well to follow that lead once those entities have a clear idea as to what needs to be done. This is most efficiently accomplished by designing an expanding education model with a focus on supporting regional project implementation strategies to complete that mission. Not only would this help solve our current challenges as they relate to resource management, it is also the most direct and efficient way to build an economy and increase the standards of living as it leads right into job placement and a salary.

Additionally, the empowering education and skills training required for this effort is still extremely limited to those fortunate few who can pay and have access to such resources. For most of the developed world higher education is a business. Don't get me wrong. There is incredible work being done by some of the most knowledgeable, dedicated, and passionate people on our planet who feel compelled to impart to others what they can to help heal our planet. Not–for–profits and some wonderful and concerned educators are doing all they can to disseminate critical knowledge throughout the world. It's just that the majority of these "sustainable education" efforts were developed as part of a profit producing model that was designed to "sell" education rather than empower maximum change. In most cases the knowledge is not reaching the masses desperate for that information and training.

In this particular instance collaboration rather than competition would be a much more efficient and logical course to take. As long as the spread and access to this critical knowledge is directed by the profitability of the education process, the competition for paying students, and the exclusivity of access to knowledge we are delaying by design an effort that needs to occur with all due haste. Linking sustainable training and education directly to a profitable project development strategy that supports relevant education and training would be a much more efficient way for that process to take off and spread quickly on a global basis.

Organizations and Groups

Organizations and groups have a crucial role in organizing public participation and focus in any successful effort. These "Special interest groups" are the equivalent of today's modern "tribes" having set agendas, values, and concerns that bond their constituency together. For many individuals their association with an organization or group whether that relationship is political, economic, religious, issue, or community related serves as a main influence on their views and their focal point for community involvement. It is within and through these associations that they strive to impact the world in a way that reflects their common interests and values.

It is therefore essential that any organizational effort to bring together our population in coordinated action reach out and educate these diverse groups of people on the need for collaboration. This can be a huge challenge considering the polarizing opinions, ideas, and beliefs that separate us. That being said, the threats we now face are common to all these "tribes" and we must tailor the message such that each of these separate entities understand the threats as it relates to their interests, beliefs, and values. As an example, you may not be an environmentalist, but resource management is also critical for a healthy growing economy.

My point is protecting our environment and the sustainable management of our resources is in everybody's best interest. In a general sense poor, struggling, and starving populations are a threat and can have a direct negative impact on all these diverse interests. As examples: a likely scenario is that struggling, desperate populations replace their leaders or overthrow their governments (Political impact). Societies have no extra money to invest in innovation, growth, or purchase consumer items such that markets collapse (Economic impact). Parishioners can lose faith or no longer have the means to support their places of worship or incite violence blaming other religious groups for their troubles (Religious impact). People start seeing their existence from a "me first" survival perspective and withdraw from larger associations (Community impact).

We need to stop arguing amongst ourselves and find common ground quickly as the clock is ticking. A strategy that links our common concerns to a message that resonates directly with these diverse constituencies and gets them working in common purpose may well be the determinative factor as to our eventual success.

Individuals

Our world and the systems that support our daily existence are going through the most extensive re-organization in human history. As individuals it is necessary for us to embrace that change. Those changes need to be reflected in the way we manage our relationships with food, water, energy, and waste, in our homes, work places, and communities. It must be an expression of how we purchase, who we vote for, how we contribute and relate to our community, and what we expect from our schools, and teach our children. It is imperative we educate ourselves on the best options available to make those improvements and extend that knowledge to our neighbors to encourage their participation. We must demand of our leadership focus and action that makes sense and hold them accountable for their inaction. Our governments, corporations, and communities must recognize the need for responsible and continuous investment in the pre-emptive measures and infrastructure projects necessary to avoid the potential shortages and needless losses that lie ahead. We must act quickly and with singular determination.

It is imperative we remove fear from the equation and start to look at all the positive steps we can accomplish TOGETHER that will improve life on a global basis. If we don't do this, and allow our destructive and blind self-interest determine our inaction, we will eventually destroy or lose all that we hold dear. Each of us must add our voice to this purpose. No one else will do it for you.

William Sosinsky

Chapter Seven

We Have Met the Enemy and It Is Us

"Any person who thinks you can have perpetually increasing industrial growth and production in a world with finite resources is either a complete moron or an economist."

~ *Anonymous*

You cannot help but look around at all the pollution, environmental destruction, industrial disasters, and ineffective leadership and not want to blame someone or some group for the terrible challenges we now face. As painful as the truth might be, we have no one to blame other than ourselves. We have stood idly by and been active participants in empowering all these groups we now wish to condemn. We encouraged their irresponsibility by purchasing their products, elected leaders who supported short sighted public policies, bought larger houses and bigger cars. We demanded more luxuries, more convenience, bigger selections and better availability. We were seduced. We bought into those values and dreams and gave in without a fight. Worst of all we designed and participated in an economic system that does not allow these entities to change insuring that we will ultimately destroy ourselves along with this planet.

Take a moment to consider that last statement.

The entities we blame are compelled to behave the way they do. Most people never stop to consider how economic models define societal evolution and dictate and influence every level of social behavior, development, and interaction. I grew up in a liberal family in lower Manhattan and attended what is probably the most left wing, neo-socialist private school that has ever existed in the United States, The Little Red School House/Elizabeth Irwin High School. I am as passionate an environmentalist as exists on this planet having dedicated my life to the protection of our environment. I am also a strong believer in capitalism, albeit with certain modifications that I will discuss later on in this book. Yet I do not fully blame those powerful corporate and political entities who are at the forefront of environmental destruction for the predicament we now face.

In my youth I was raised to vilify corporations such as Exxon, BP, Monsanto, Dupont, and Dow for the irresponsible, calculated, intimidating, and destructive manner in which they operated valuing profitability more than people, health, or the environment. These days I have developed a more even perspective on these huge corporate entities which is not quite as polarizing. They are not entirely to blame. I now recognize there are socially conscious, caring, concerned, and remorseful people who work within those companies who are sensitive to the impact their operations have on people and the environment. They would change and do business differently given the chance if they could make those changes without hurting their company's bottom line. The issue they face is they are constricted by an economic system that does not allow them to fundamentally change to the degree they need to if they are to be friends of sustainability and not at odds with the "green" movement. Our economic model does not allow or encourage them to act in a way that is in the best interests of humanity. They act in the best interests of their stakeholders and investors. That is their fiduciary responsibility.

Consider for a moment that most of these entities are publicly traded companies. The investment community has set up a structure for evaluating performance and value of a company that requires these corporations to report their performance accomplishments on a quarterly basis. If they make or exceed their projections and hit that forecast number along with continued strong growth anticipated for the future, the price of that stock and the value of that company generally increases. That is the criteria. Not how well the company is responding to public pressure to become more socially responsible. Not how much the company is investing into long term modifications to their operations to limit the damage they are inflicting on the environment or the unsustainable manner in which they manage their production. They are required to hit that number come hell or high water because there are serious consequences if they do not.

What are those consequences? Not performing up to expectations is almost always followed with a drop in the stock price and a reduction in company valuation. This reduces a corporation's ability to borrow and invest in system improvements, market expansion, research and development, new hiring and so forth. It can also force a company to contract in size, fire members of their work force, limit their competitive edge in the market place, and ultimately makes them vulnerable to their competition in terms of market share loss and possible takeover. It is because of these pressures to maintain their corporation's vitality and the struggle to survive on the battle field of global competition for market share that these companies make some of the disturbing and counter intuitive decisions they do. I am not excusing these actions. I am just trying to bring context and understanding as to why they make such poor short-sighted decisions that end up having such adverse impacts on the environment, our resources, and our population. It is this bottom line, have to hit that number mentality that is at the core as to why we overuse our resources and exploit our work force in the effort to increase profitability.

The role of the key corporate leadership is a fiduciary responsibility to build the brand, increase profits, and deliver increasing value to the investors in that company. So, making any investments that they cannot see as directly increasing that value and that may potentially impact short term valuation and performance is something that they do not generally perceive as being in the best interests of that corporation. Understanding human nature, it is easy to understand where these business leaders start looking at any negative trend from climate change to increases in cancer rates from a position of denial as to their company's impact or contribution to that problem. It is a survival instinct that compels them to protect their company from the negative implications of those impacts and to not accept the empirical data that supports those conclusions. After all the most prevalent type of dishonesty humans' practice is self–deception. It is at the root of all lies for any person who considerers themselves a "good" and "responsible" member of a society. Rationalization and denial are our defense mechanisms. We tell ourselves what we need to in order to justify our actions as not to have to deal with guilt and self-recrimination that comes with an overt act of "evil" or bad intent. These leaders do not view themselves as being irresponsible or having negative aspirations and act in what they believe are with the best of intentions. When faced with data which directly threatens their company and creates all sorts of impediments as to how these officers maintain and increase profit share and company value, it is easy to see why they instinctively deny impact and causality.

After all, do we not behave similarly? Be honest. You must have known that using gasoline was adding to the CO_2 in the atmosphere and contributing to climate change? Have you taken your car to an appointment when you could have used public transportation? Ride alone when you can car pool? Ever toss a battery or compact florescent bulb into the trash bin? Ever use a weed killer or pesticide? Maybe purchased a product and disposed of the recyclable waste without recycling? Bought a disposable shaver, a plastic bottle of water, or an individually wrapped food items? Throw out old furniture or appliances that were still serviceable without considering the consequences of what becomes of that waste once it goes into the trash bin and is hauled to the land fill? Ever flush a toilet? Eat food that was not grown or raised locally?

The point is you felt compelled to act, consume, and dispose in a manner that you may have consciously known was not good for the environment but either denied the impact or simply decided to ignore that outcome. You may have rationalized that you had no realistic or convenient alternative choice in that behavior. There was not a viable option or easily available and affordable means for you to act otherwise. That is exactly the way corporate officers generally look at what they do. We convince ourselves that we have little option and that to act otherwise is neither practical nor pragmatic. The end result of that instinctual response is why our planet's environment is in such dire jeopardy.

Chapter Eight

We Are All One Human Family

"Until human beings accept the truth that we are all members of the same extended family, our dysfunctional, divisive, and competitive nature is ultimately destined to destroy us and our environment."

~ William Sosinsky

To understand our circumstances and the real challenges humankind now faces we must start at the beginning. Before I commence to present the facts and figures that describe our potential self-induced destruction or the path and methodology that will provide our eventual salvation, we must understand where the heart of the problem lies. There is a cause and effect relationship that is the seed from which our current challenges began.

If we are honest with ourselves, we know there is a problem. Although there is existing argument and debate as to the depth of our dilemma and the eventual outcome of our current historical course, the undercurrent of concern and trepidation as to the health of our planet and the future of our species is almost universal. My son likes to point out to me that the "Web-bot", a technical term for a program that tracks global sentiment and opinions voiced online as a predictor of future events, is foretelling the most troubling of consequences for our population. You can hear it during casual conversations at informal get-togethers. You see it reported online and in the newspapers. It is the subtext of the content that streams across our television sets or watch when we go to the cinema. We experience it when we shop or go to work, and it is embodied into the fabric of our daily lives and colors the unconscious background of each and every experience we absorb during the course of our day. We can all sense that as a species, as a population living on this fragile Earth, as individuals trying to make a go of it and survive, that things are soon going to change... and we can sense that they will not be changing for the better.

The deluge of stories, influences, and input that predicts and suggests this eventual fate is something that frightens most of us at our most subliminal and survivalist level. Whether that moment is defined by an oil spill, nuclear disaster, drought, unprecedented weather event, or if it is as benign as the rising costs of our groceries and fuel bills, we can feel the threat. It has gotten to the point where we both expect and accept these changes as being unavoidable. We've become desensitized to these threats as a result. The fact that these events impact us without our consent and are too large for us to influence triggers a response that inspires varying degrees of fear, self-preservation, anger, concern, action, curiosity, or denial depending on the individual. It's just human nature. Yet with all the evidence and continuous empirical reinforcement, we as a species have still not realized the enormity and severity of the changes to our existence that will soon threaten all of us.

This brings me to my first key question:

"Must we as individuals witness the complete devastation of our planet before we commit ourselves to actively participating in changing our course?"

To further complicate and distort our perception and understanding of what might occur in our future are the predictions of the so-called experts that we rely on for the information from which we form our opinions. These scientists, educators, and data analysts are more than willing to make predictions of the future, or sight data that supports whatever theory they are committed to that week. These predictions often border on the ridiculous to being outright misinformed. Yet very often they present their findings as fact. I could certainly be viewed in that category depending on your personal opinion. That being said I would argue that there is a stark difference as to my observations and predictions as opposed to these experts. I would argue that it is their limited and specific viewpoints no matter had educated and esteemed, which both colors and influences their perspective. It is that limited perspective that makes their predictions so unbalanced. Climate change, global warming, resource depletion, population growth, rising sea levels, CO_2 levels, acidification of our oceans as well as a hundred other influences and effects are all inter-related to a certain extent. If you fail to account for any of these extremely complex inter-relationships as you try and predict the course of future events, your opinion as to what might or might not occur is going to be uneven. By the very nature and complexity of the issue, it requires a very universal and general understanding of all the components that contribute to the problems in order to account for the influences each part plays in the eventual impact these processes will have on our planet and population. Yet these experts voice their opinions for the most part based on their specific area of expertise. As such they often ignore other areas of influence, data, and observation that are keys factors in affecting the outcome of their "prediction".

As an example, I have seen reports recently of population growth projections published by experts in their field of expertise that predict at our present rate of growth based on current trends that we can expect to see 12 Billion people on our planet by the end of this century. Such a report was issued not so long ago by a fact-finding group working with the United Nations. [42] My immediate reaction was "Really…twelve billion people?" My question to that "fact finding" body would be "What would you suppose they will eat to survive?" Did these experts not realize you need to feed all those mouths in order to support their existence? Were these experts not aware that there have been predictive computer models around since the mid 1970's that have clearly defined the limits of our ability to "feed" our population? Did they not realize that there are comprehensive studies available addressing and predicting agricultural output, farm production, nutrient depletion, ocean biomass decline, finite phosphorous reserves (A key ingredient of fertilizer), topsoil loss, ground water depletion, loss of pollinators, habitat destruction, and increasing consumption rates that will greatly impact their predictions? These "counter" studies have definitively and eloquently demonstrated through real statistical analysis and predictive modeling that our food chain will *likely* be incapable of supporting a population larger than 2.5 billion people by mid-century. These are undisputed facts and projections based on clearly definable trends and quantifiable reserves. So, it is clear they made a huge over-statement based on an incomplete assumption. That is of course unless we counter those trends by undertaking a massive reorganization of our food production and management practices…but I'll get to that latter.

So, the U.N. report was announced as fact and widely reported throughout the media. Worse yet, it is now accepted as the basis for policy decisions by many governments and regions throughout the world who must direct the actions and planning that will determine the future of their countries.

Then you have those experts who try and determine how high oceans levels will rise this century by siting exact, definitive figures when the truth is it's anyone's guess. They'll base their opinions on ice caps and glaciers melting at a linear rate while completely neglecting to factor in the accelerating non-linear environmental changes that are much more likely to occur in these next decades as conditions deteriorate. Or they will ignore historic models of previous ocean levels under similar environmental conditions that are clearly demonstrated through geological records and ice core/ocean sediment studies in their predictive data. What happens if we go into a complete climate shift? My point is that are a lot of folks out there taking wild guesses and making predictions based on a limited perspective and incomplete understanding of the subjects they are "experts" on. It would be much better if they just explained all the possible permeations and outcomes and left it at that. Yet once these learned and esteemed experts are published or reported by a "trusted" and "informed" media source we accept those definitive opinions as fact. As a scientist this disturbs me.

This brings us to my second question:

"If our leaders and so called "experts" do not clearly understand the issues and challenges we face, how can they possibly hope to properly focus and direct the responsive effort required to reverse the negative impact we are having on our planet and the future consequences it will have on our population?"

These misconceptions are directly related to improper and incomplete education. The human race has never had to deal with the concepts of finite global resources or worldwide demand for basic necessities overwhelming supply. As a result, we have never structured our education models nor were those platforms ever designed to prepare our students to respond to such challenges in a real-world sense. Even now we have separated all of the inter-related areas of sustainability into their own divisions of learning without providing the necessary linkage required for students to grasp the complete picture of the issues they will face. We teach renewable energy, advanced agriculture and food production, waste and water management, yet there is no inter-connected methodology as to how you implement these changes that relates to sound fiscal policy planning that supports economic expansion. Without that connection all this effort is nothing more than an ill-founded social experiment with a clearly predictable outcome that will assuredly fall short of its intended solution.

At the core of all these shortfalls is a general disconnect between what we fear as a population and our ability to confront those threats with decisive action. Every effort so far put forth on a global scale such as the Kyoto, Copenhagen, Rio and Paris Summits have been dramatic failures. I have watched each of these world summits only to come away with the impression there is no current workable idea as to how we are going to resolve our differences and start working together. All you get are idealistic, meaningless pledges that will soon be ignored by the countries that issue them as the economics of those promises sink in.

The results are that we as a species are now driving towards a cliff edge with the occupants of that vehicle arguing over who planned the trip, who should step on the brakes, and who will pay for the gas. When we do act it is in measured half steps perpetuated by the uncertainty that our leaders feel as a result of their incomplete and incorrect understanding of the threats and challenges.

Finally, I guess my last and most important questions would be:

"When did we forget that we are all one Human Family?"

When did we stop telling the story to our children of how once upon a time and long ago, every human being in the world lived together on the great plains of central Africa? That it was there that we can all trace our common lineage? That this was where our ancestors lived together and scratched out an existence? That this is the shared past which every human being on the face of the Earth today shares? When did we forget who we were?

Was its self-interest and fear spurred on by our desperate struggle to survive, or the politics of power that which made us forget we were once related? Perhaps it was those influences that divided us into tribes, villages, societies, political parties, ethnic groups, religions, and countries such that we waged war on our brothers and sisters, stole their riches and lands, laid waste their homes, and slaughtered and enslaved their children? When we could no longer trust ourselves to act benevolently, we expected nothing more from them and acted accordingly. We had the excuse of protecting ourselves and our vital interests to fall back on. When did we decide that "those people" were no longer our relations? When did we decide that they had fallen from grace and were now a threat? When did we conclude that they deserved it and had it coming? They were less than... less human, less civilized, less intelligent, less deserving. You know...those people. Those communists, those capitalists, those extremist Moslems and infidel Christians, those uppity niggers and racist crackers, those hypocritical Catholics and self-righteous Protestants, those money-grubbing Jews and godless fascists, those tree hugging liberals and those right-wing religious nuts. Gooks, micks, rag heads, spics, wops, camel jockeys, yankees, ruskies, japs and krauts. You know...them.

The undeniable and scientific truth is there is no "them". There are only us. Today's advanced genomics are capable of tracing every human being's common lineage back to basically a score of mating couples that lived more than 2 million years ago on the central plains of Africa. Any variations in appearance and customs are the result of small changes that manifested themselves over thousands of centuries of our specific histories as we separated and settled throughout the world in an effort to find new resources to survive and prosper. Still, with all that current knowledge and clear understanding of our shared past we consciously or subconsciously feel comfortable with minimizing, disregarding, exploiting, or at worst dehumanizing those with customs we don't understand, and physical features we view as foreign.

And that's the real issue isn't it? In order for us to solve these challenges which are global in scope we need to get all these diverse groups to work together to solve what are now are our two major threats: resource depletion and environmental degradation. It will require cooperation and collaboration on an unprecedented scale if we are to mount an effective response. After all, if one group stops burning fossil fuels sending CO2 into the atmosphere and the others continue polluting, or over-harvesting ocean stocks, or over-consuming global resources, you still have the same problems and suffer similar consequences even though you did your part to be sustainable. These are not issues, that any one country or region can solve by themselves. Yet human beings are cursed with an over-riding preoccupation with self-interest and an underlying fear of the unfamiliar that hamstrings all our efforts to bridge our differences and work together with common purpose. That is unfortunately human nature in its purest and most prominent form.

The reason I bring this up is because it is imperative, we remember this truth and that the great majority of us understand and embrace this reality on an emotional, spiritual, and ultimately practical level. This will be the only way we can surmount our current challenges and prosper as a species past the middle of this century. With it we evolve. Without it we usher in a very austere and dark future. It has come down to that one simple concept. It is from this understanding that the structure and impetus for our solution must flow if we are to counter our current threats. Gandhi, Einstein, Jesus, Confucius, Muhammad, and countless other visionaries throughout our history have dreamed of unifying principles and ideals to elevate us from our ignorance, yet Mankind has failed to embrace this higher purpose. We must get beyond our divisive nature born of years of separation, self-interest, and fear of one other or it will ultimately be the reason we destroy ourselves and our environment. We must remember we are all one human family.

William Sosinsky

Chapter Nine

Human Nature Will Ultimately Be Our Greatest Challenge

"Human nature Mr. Allnut, is what we are put in this world to rise above."
~ *The African Queen*

Perhaps nothing will be a greater impediment to our working together to rejuvenate our environment and gain sustainable control over our global resources than human nature. Mankind through years of conditioning has been modeled to be subconsciously dominated by two basic impulses and behaviors. They stand as the main road-blocks to our ability to evolve to the point where we can work together to maximize our impact in reversing our current course; Self-interest and fear.

Self-interest influences us to seek disproportionate advantage, to view mutual interests and issues from a limiting singular perspective; "How does that situation impact me or us?" Self-interest compels us to negotiate and enter into agreements where we attempt to gain leverage by dominating, controlling, or maximizing relationships to our own advantage. In its darker forms it is expressed as greed, exploitation, inequality, or injustice. Business leaders, politicians, and warriors are rewarded and admired for their abilities to excel in these areas as it is viewed as critical to their "tribes" success and survival. Our global economics and politics are dominated by this consideration and because of that, logic and long-term mutual planning that benefits the masses almost always loses out when matched against self-interest.

Fear immobilizes our ability to act decisively. It holds us back, opposes change, limits us to conservative steps and wants to take a wait and see approach before moving forward. Fear stops us from innovating, changing, taking risk, seeing impending threats, communicating and depending on one other. It is expressed through skepticism, denial, mistrust, condescension, inaction, and often aggression.

When our leader's decisions and actions are heavily influenced by fear they are admired as being pragmatic and cautious. So, when the time comes for bold and collaborative action to address our common threats, it is that fear of change and each other's intentions that puts a stop to any progress.

Additionally, self-interest and fear have an evil step-child that in many ways is the single most threatening human element that makes collaborative action and coordinated change almost impossible: The Human Ego. It is what drives us to be irrational, self-delusional, disproportionate in our responses, and uncooperative. We all want to drive the bus. When I say "we all", I mean all the type A personalities who look upon their own intelligence and their own opinions as being the final word when it comes to wisdom and how we direct action. If common sense, practicality, empathy, generosity, concern, self-preservation, expediency, and positive action were the rules of the day and the path we all seek, we would not face the issues we now face. That is unless of course you inject ego into that equation.

At some point ego transforms our actions into an expression of self-rationalizing, self-induced, self-interest and fear. It turns a leader into a dictator, an ambitious business person into a greedy exploiter of others, a reasonable diplomat into an intransigent advocate, a cause promoting activist into a fame seeking egotist, friends into adversaries, and acquaintances into enemies. You see it in the infighting of governments as politicians grab for power and influence, when championship sports teams and successful musical groups disintegrate and disband as individuals want more recognition and individual acknowledgement. It is evident by the need of the visionary who is only interested in getting credit, the leader who's afraid that changing their opinion will be perceived as weak and indecisive, the partner who deserves a larger share of the profits. Put any group of creative drivers of change in a room together and sooner or later you are bound to have an argument. We just can't seem to leave our egos at the door.

A mentor of mine used to tell me "you are only as strong as your weakest element." If that is the case which I believe it is, we do not have sufficient time to change human nature before the proverbial shit hits the fan. We simply cannot evolve quickly enough as it will likely take many generations of enlightenment before we are able to rise above the limiting behavioral norms of Homo Sapiens. At best under current projections we have till mid-century to complete our preparations if we are to effectively combat our coming global crisis.

Accepting mid-century as a likely timeframe, our best course of action is to try and create societal economic models and methodologies that utilize human tendencies and preconditioning to our best advantage. To address the twin headed monster of self- interest and fear you must make a friend of self-interest by rewarding those ingrained responses and reactions in a way that promotes positive change and action. As long as economic development does not overuse a resource or destroy the health of the environment it meets that basic criteria. If you make people well off and rich through the process of sustainably improving the planet, it becomes effortless to encourage their participation.

The issue of fear is far more complex. The fear of change must be replaced by the fear of inaction and its resulting consequences. Illogical fear must be exposed for its dangerously limiting qualities. A disciplined structure of advanced rules and guidelines established and accepted by a majority needs to be enacted and embraced to set a standard for economic development. A universally accepted model by which you are restricted to conduct economic expansion in a way that protects and preserves resources and limits environmentally destructive practices is essential. As long as you follow those basic guidelines you should be free to make as much as can.

As far as how you control the human ego… that will require a proper catalyst. I believe only a universally perceived life-threatening crisis that is clearly accepted and understood by a majority as requiring universal cooperation as having the only chance of success. We are in that life-threatening scenario right now, however too few people have come to that realization. We have seen such a response occur in times of war where there was that perceived "universal threat" so it is in-theory possible. How fast we can convince those who have yet to accept the reality of our current threat will be critical to our level of success in reversing the damage we are currently inflicting to our planet.

Once you conquer the restrictive conditioned responses that limit our abilities to work constructively and collaboratively, you come up against a whole new series of challenges. It will also be necessary to have global buy-in to have global impact. You can't just bail water on one side a sinking ship. You will still sink. You can accomplish global buy-in by opening up opportunities to the masses so they can participate and improve their standard of living, and by providing the means for their training and education. This is the critical starting point from which all other efforts start. We must turn our 7 billion plus consumers into productive stewards of their resources.

Lastly, real economics involves dominant established stakeholders. Any effort must involve those entities directly in any solution in order to avoid the cut-throat competition and restrictive headwinds they can potentially influence. Those counter-productive reactions restricting and opposing innovation and critical response are standard once those large entities such as banks, oil conglomerates, agricultural giants, and so on view those changes as a threat to their stake-hold. It is therefore necessary to come up with solutions that make it worth it for them to participate by not triggering that fear/protection response. In order to establish these new codes of conduct and provide the mechanism for this manageable shift in behavior a common platform for teaching these new rules of engagement will be a key logistical element.

As we said earlier, sustainability means the capacity to endure, endurance being a key requirement of evolution. Right now, we are ending the evolutionary lines of countless species and soon will be in danger of inflicting that same fate on our progeny. If we are to evolve then we must strive to teach, encourage, and empower the virtues of seeking common interest solutions, mutual respect, patience, and ultimately a love for one another and the planet we live on. That is where we start to turn things around. It is a commitment to providing basic levels of societal support through education and individual opportunity to the masses such that the perception and reality of access to a better standard of life and the opportunities for improvement are available to all. These are not the hopes of the innocent, good hearted, or naïve, but the requirements of our species if we are to evolve. Human nature as it now stands will be our greatest challenge.

William Sosinsky

Chapter Ten

The World of 2050

"Humans are distinguished from other species by a massive brain that enables us to imagine a future and influence it by what we do in the present. By using experience, knowledge and insight, our ancestors recognized they could anticipate dangers and opportunities and take steps to exploit advantages and avoid hazards."

~ **David Suzuki**

I think it is important that we try and imagine what our near future is likely to be like. Having covered our most critical challenges so far in this book from a resource/environmental/ human influence perspective, we need to tie all those components together and postulate different potential scenarios of what might or might not occur in the coming years.

We have all grown up on movies that depicted our future from every perspective possible. Almost all conceivable permeations and visions have been covered I believe from post nuclear, zombie ridden desolation, to flying cars and orgasmatrons. As scary, positive, or funny as those projections have been, there is a reality as to what we can anticipate as a likely future that all of us (if we are young enough) and our children will have to contend with. I always like to say that the future will either be Star Trek or Road Warrior. However, the truth is it is likely to be a combination of each of those projected futures depending on where you live and how well you yourself, your community, or your society have prepared.

To try and project any anticipated vision of the future you must factor in all the contributing elements to see how those influences manifest over time. These pieces of the puzzle are difficult to predict as there are so many variables that will ultimately push change in one direction or the other. What new science and technologies will be developed? Will our socio-economic structure be evolving or in a state of decay? Will our population continue to grow or will an epidemic, war, or unprecedented global event reverse that trend? Can we expect that global politics will foster a more collaborative approach or will our bonds disintegrate under an environment of blame, self-interest, and self-preservation? What will happen to our climate and how will those impacts affect different regions and available local resources? To that mix of unknowns, you have to impose the quantifiable trends of how our environment is declining and how we are managing the critical resources and commodities we depend on for our existence and attach time frames, availability, and costs. From that you can start to develop likely scenarios as to how we as a species will adjust and react to a future that will soon be upon us. In many ways this part of our discussion will very much parallel and expand on the ideas put forth in "The Limits to Growth". In this section we will look at the challenges we face in a general sense as well as some of the likely or potential responses which we will expand upon in the following chapters.

As with any theory or prediction about the unknown you have to make assumptions on those key components that you can logically predict will either occur or are likely to continue along their current trajectory. The next step is to look at the variables both likely and unlikely that may develop that can dramatically impact those trajectories. Finally, you must factor in potentially game changing events and scenarios that can intensify our current challenges or greatly accelerate our ability to respond and mitigate our current problems.

So, let's start out with the following general assumptions as we approach the year 2050. These are all predictions based on current environmental and resource availability trends, ongoing efforts from a social/political/technology perspective, and historic human behavioral patterns.

- *The climate will continue to change and intensify as a consequence of increasing CO_2 emissions/concentrations on a nonlinear trajectory for at least the next few decades. This will result from the accelerating release of greenhouse gases into the atmosphere and the decreasing ability of our forests and oceans to absorb and store the CO_2.*

I believe this is a given. The oil/gas/coal industry and global energy policies are not drastically changing direction any time soon. The number of ocean transports and coal burning power plants under construction are increasing every day and will continue expanding for the foreseeable future. These are two of the main contributors to greenhouse gas emissions. Although China (The world's largest CO_2

polluter) recently has made announcements that they will start to close some of their coal fired plants, this will not be enough by itself to offset continuing and increasing damage to the biosphere. Additionally, the accelerating impacts of deforestation and desertification will also be a factor. Droughts will increase and intensify as a consequence along with dramatic/untimely weather events such as hurricanes, floods, and unseasonably hot and cold seasons.

- *Desertification and deforestation will expand at a historic rate as both grasslands and forests continue to dry out and disappear. This will be the combined impact of climate change, continued overuse of those resources, and a natural succession in response to changing seasonal pattern*

New management initiatives will start to take hold, but not quickly enough to stop the increasing forward momentum of these changes. The great northern forests of Asia/Europe and North America will see huge infestations of beetles and other destructive insects, molds, and plant diseases. These impacts will begin to remove species of trees and underbrush that are no longer appropriate for those climatic conditions. This will permanently change the flora composition of those regions. Deforestation in equatorial regions will start to slow as those countries begin to recognize the increased value and profitability that can be derived from those resources but not before regional rain patterns and evapotranspiration patterns are drastically altered.

- *The push for renewable energy and the development of new and more productive energy technologies will continue and make great advances.*

This is one of the more positive things we can look forward to in the years ahead. Inexpensive and plentiful energy is a key enabler when we address all of the other issues created by climate change and resource depletion. Plentiful clean energy impacts food production, water scarcity, and environmental impact. The transformation to a cleaner energy planet will be both welcomed by countries looking to clean up their environments and increase their productivity, and slowed down by the stakeholders who profit from the existing fossil fuel economy. The world will be forced to change, but every step forward will be met with resistance and it will take much longer than necessary to make the transition thus increasing our negative impact on the environment.

Advances in renewable energy are very much expected over the next few years. Big improvements in solar energy in terms of cost and efficiency are right on the horizon. Additionally, the prevalence of installed solar, wind, tidal, and geothermal power plants around the world are increasing dramatically. You can also add smart-grid improvements, advances in building architecture and engineering, and building energy efficiency retrofits as having a substantial impact over the next few decades. Lastly, though it is not renewable energy, advances in new generation nuclear power has the promise of creating large quantities of distributed clean energy starting within the next decade while greatly reducing the potential for accidents.

With our needs squarely focused on developing alternate forms of energy at the moment it is very likely that we will solve our issues relating to developing plentiful, clean, inexpensive energy by mid-century. The fact that solving these challenges will be highly profitable all but insures we will successfully achieve that objective.

- *The population will continue to expand until we run out of supportive resources.*

No population control initiative or reduction/maintenance policy has taken hold or influenced global population growth regardless of the diminishing resource issues we now face. This is particularly evident in the South/Eastern Asia concentration of China, India, Indonesia, and Pakistan where a majority of our global population lives. Under those conditions it is likely we will continue to expand our population towards the 9 billion mark by or around mid-century or until those supportive resources collapse.

- *The lack of potable water access will reach catastrophic levels for populations on every continent before we know it.*

This is a foregone conclusion as it is already happening and there is almost nothing that is being done or can be done in time to offset demand as it relates to supply.

- *We will continue to see a reduction in land that is either available or suitable for agriculture. This will increase pressure on remaining food production operations to step up output in response to increasing demand.*

This is a direct result of a number of factors which include population expansion, loss of farm land to development, soil nutrient depletion, loss of top soils, desertification, and diminishing irrigation water resources to name just a few.

- *Conventional global agricultural production will plummet.*

Remaining farms will have an increased reliance on fertilizer to meet production levels and will ultimately be undermined by a reliance on phosphorous which will dramatically diminish or end their productivity. Additionally, irrigation water availability will start to factor in more and more as once reliable sources start to dry up as will the continued loss of pollinators.

- *Major industrial powers and the richer nations that are suffering resources shortages will look more and more to the developing world to make up needed commodities and will use military intervention if needed to secure those supplies.*

The U.S., Europe, and China are purchasing/leasing huge tracks of land abroad in the developing world specifically for agricultural production. China is building air craft carriers (Following the U.S model for protecting energy supplies) to ensure continuance of the agreements they have signed throughout North Africa for legal access and control of those land

- *Populations in food and water stressed regions will blame their leaders for their suffering and they can be expected to react violently.*

This will be most pronounced throughout Africa, the Middle East/North Africa, Central/Southern Asia where the shortages will hit hardest first and governmental control in certain countries is tenuous at best.

- *The Oceans will be comparatively empty of fish and seafood.*

Whether or not we completely destroy the ocean as a fishery and empty them by mid-century as several studies project, or we finally enact global policies to reduce and manage our ocean fisheries, the oceans are in decline. The coastal wetlands and coral reefs that serve as the nurseries for much of the oceans fish are disappearing or dying. It is also projected that global coral reefs may be gone in or around mid-century. By themselves, reefs account for as much as 25% of all ocean fish nurseries. As PH levels inevitably spike toward higher acidity levels, we are likely to either completely lose our shellfish and crustacean populations or they will at best be scarce. The ocean-based seafood that remains will be spotty, considered a delicacy, and beyond affordable for the majority of our population.

- *Fish farming will expand dramatically in an attempt to make up for declining ocean fish stocks.*

Both large and small local aquaculture operations will sprout up throughout the world as conventional wild sources start to disappear. A spate of new commercialized "imported" species sourced from the developing world will start to become common table fare as industrialized nations replace the former wild species their populations were historically accustomed to and are no longer available on a commercial scale.

- *The Algae industry will expand substantially as a source for soil fertilizer, human and livestock nutritional supplements, food, fuel production, and supplemental feed for aquaculture operations.*

By mid-century algae production facilities both large and small will be common place throughout the world and be one of the single largest and fastest growing industries in the world.

- *Insects and insect protein will increase as a source of food/protein for much of the world replacing meat, poultry, and fish as an affordable nutritional option. Insects will also become a growing source of pelletized livestock and fish feed replacing conventional "garbage fish" and grain sources.*

The relative ease of raising insects, their ability to survive and grow on marginal nutrient sources, and the efficient way they convert nutrients into high quality protein will make insects a key contributor to global nutrition as we move into the 21st century. This pattern is already established in the developing world and is starting to find its markets in the more developed Western cultures.

- *Using advanced recycling methods, waste of all types will become a major source of industrial/commercial source materials, chemicals, and base commodities as conventional resources disappear and relative costs increase.*

We are on the cusp of a revolution in the reuse and recycling of our waste stream. Many components of the waste stream are disappearing in the "natural" world. Both industry and governments will be forced to look to their waste as a way of finding cheaper materials, recapture critical and scarce elements, create energy, and efficiently reduce the costs of their operations and environmental impact. What was formally a problem will start to become an opportunity as waste in harvested and treated as a commodity creating a whole new industry and countless new jobs.

- *Rising sea levels combined with larger and more violent ocean related weather events will make life on islands and low-lying coastal areas tenuous at best.*

Although it is difficult to anticipate just how much sea levels will rise in the coming decades, it is safe to assume that levels will come up at least a few feet throughout this century. That is assuming as we do not slip back into a premature ice age. Combined with the increasing energy available to cyclonic weather systems such as hurricanes, cyclones, and typhoons these new "super" storms will eclipse in voracity and size that which was "normal" for the 20th century. Those extra few feet of available water volume and increased wind intensity will be enough to completely inundate populations and low-lying areas close to the coast. This will include coastal regions much further from the equator that will now become susceptible to catastrophic storms bringing tornado velocity winds and unprecedented storm surges.

- *Massive shifts in population concentrations will occur as a result of available resources, social upheaval, and changing global weather patterns.*

Human populations will be forced to abandon regions where density levels completely overwhelm resource availability, particularly as that relates to water and food scarcity. Additionally, some coastal areas and island nations will not be able to survive. This will be a direct consequence of the more violent nature of their environment, rising sea levels, and the inevitability and regularity of those areas being decimated by catastrophic weather events. In developing nations which lack strong social bonds and secure borders, populations will start to migrate in search of the resources they lack in their home states. This will have serious consequences for neighboring regions which still have remaining resources. The instability that results from a lack of local resources will be the cause of much regional socio-political upheaval. Stressed and angry populations will overthrow their governments, and conflicts will expand beyond borders as nation states desperately try to acquire the basic resources they need to survive. These unstable and dangerous regional conflicts will by themselves be huge factors in the outward migration of affected populations.

- *Nations that have the financial and technical capabilities will look to develop huge infrastructure projects that enable their declining regions to survive by bringing in those critically needed resources.*

This initial effort will be very much centered on water shortages and huge pipeline and desalinization projects bringing in fresh water from far away areas which have surplus resources. We can expect that agriculture and food production in general will undergo a revolutionary transition as regions adjust to the challenging conditions of a changing environment in the 21st century.

- *Individual communities and families will take on an ever-increasing role in providing and managing their own critical basic resources.*

We can expect that onsite energy and food production; water and waste management will increase significantly throughout this century as a higher and higher percentage of these resources are managed locally. In many ways this model will resemble earlier human societies where this was the norm. Although we can anticipate massive improvements in our distributed resource models, our dependency on outside sources for basic survival needs will be reduced as technologies make it possible for people to become more self-reliant. This will be particularly evident in urban societies where buildings will be both constructed and retrofitted to be much more efficient as they relate to both consuming, managing, and producing those essential resources.

Potential Game Changers

Into this equation we have to look at realistic possibilities both good and bad that could rapidly advance or disrupt our efforts to achieve a sustainable balance between our use of resources and the impact we have on the environment. First let's examine some of the positive trends that could start to turn the tide in our favor as we move into the 21st century. These potential developments and "game changers" are:

Clean Abundant Inexpensive Energy-

The anticipated changes that could potentially have major impacts on our energy use are the transition to hydrogen fuel and inexpensive energy storage. Hydrogen energy is a virtually inexhaustible resource and a completely pollutant free fuel that can be derived from ocean water and substituted as an inexpensive replacement for fossil fuels. Affordable energy storage would make the intermittent nature of some renewable energy sources much more practical from a time/usage perspective. We are currently on the cusp of solving both those challenges.

Several more possibilities that are a bit less likely in the near term but could be of equal impact should a major break-through occur are advances in superconductivity, nanotechnologies, thermonuclear fusion, and dark energy

Advancements in these areas would revolutionize the efficiency by which we create, capture, transfer, and distribute power.

Cheap and abundant energy is the key to solving many other major challenges related to sustainable development. For example, it would make desalinization far more affordable which could then eliminate much of our fresh water and irrigation concerns globally. Another issue inexpensive energy would solve is providing the copious amounts of power required for the extensive artificial lighting essential for commercial indoor farms and greenhouses. These "new breed" agricultural operations will be common place by mid-century in response to changing and unreliable outdoor environmental conditions.

The Rapid Market Development of Certain Key Sustainable Industries-

From the production side of the equation it is very possible that much of the projected resource deficits we anticipate could very well be met by new entrepreneurial and commercial development. It is unlikely however that these efforts will make up for all the short-falls we can expect as they relate to energy and food production, and water and waste management. New technologies, protocols, and solutions will only spread quickly once those models prove to be profitable. This will have huge impacts on certain areas of our resource challenges such as waste stream management, energy production and distribution, and food production. As with most of these challenges, both profitability and the relative wealth of the countries wishing to initiate such changes will be the determinative factor as to whether or not they take hold and to what extent. The sad truth is that the only real dependable preemptive measures we can expect to flourish will be based almost entirely on profitability and not need. Such is the conditioned mindset and structure of our global socio/economic model.

The Rapid and Specific Education and Training of our Global Population-

No single contributor to solving our issues on a global scale is, or can be more impactful then providing the knowledge and skills required to transform the way we consume and manage our resources. Production increases are sexy, potentially profitable, and easy to quantify, but they will never solve our problems by themselves. In fact, when we talk about increasing food and energy production it can be argued that you are actually increasing our current challenges. Without modifications to our consumption patterns we will eventually face larger deficits by empowering population growth and thereby increasing the consumption of our diminishing finite resources. If there is any single concept that must be drilled into our global population it is that there are two sides to this equation. We have not as yet begun to truly address the consumption portion of the solution. So it is imperative we change our mindset.

The only realistic and humane avenue available to us to accomplish this end is education. If necessity is the mother of invention, then you must first instill that need for action into your population to promote that response. This is the first step and without it all other efforts are sure to fail. Specific education is the only real initiative we can take on a global scale that has the possibility of encouraging and empowering the changes that have to be made. This effort must not be limited only to those who can afford or those who have access, but must be extended to all who impact the management of global resources where-ever and whoever they may be. With the development of the internet and the ability to disseminate content to every corner of the world now possible, the means for this undertaking are now possible. Successfully done, humankind can quickly mobilize and focus our combined efforts to potentially create dramatic and long-lasting responses to our current downslide.

Some negative impacts that could potentially influence our near future are as follows:

Electromagnetic Surges Wipe out Global Energy Grids-

A real threat to modern societies and our distributed power grids are the electromagnetic surges caused by solar storms. These naturally occurring events can bombard our atmosphere with heavy doses of radiation during times when the sun is actively experiencing powerful coronal mass ejections (CME). Such huge surges of charged particles can create geomagnetic storms in Earth's upper atmosphere frying circuits and overloading capacitors and invertors both in orbiting satellites and electrical systems that are ground based. A large enough event could realistically destroy a nation's power grid and communication networks. It could then take years of rebuilding to get those systems back to their former operational capacity. Essential support systems such as refrigeration, lighting, pumping, industrial/farm equipment, computers/servers and so forth would also be immediately disabled.

It is only recently that these threats have been both generally recognized and plans implemented to address our vulnerabilities. Although improvements and protective measures are underway in many areas of the world, we are still far from having completed those steps and for the moment we remain at risk for such an event.

Premature Climate Shift-

An ominous threat that looms in the background is the concern over premature climate shift. If we should suddenly in the next two decades undergo a massive change in environmental conditions globally (plus or minus 8 degrees Fahrenheit) all bets are off. Even a more moderate shift of 3 degrees or more could have potentially catastrophic impact. It will make no difference as to whether that change leads to a dramatically warmer or cooler climate. Nothing we could do would stem the immediate collapse of our food chain infrastructure. As a direct consequence we would not have had sufficient time to prepare transitional supportive agricultural production. Mass starvation would soon follow on a global scale as conventional food supplies and farm production levels would be disrupted almost immediately.

How realistic this scenario may be is impossible to say? We are certainly headed towards a climate shift, but just when it will happen is beyond anyone's ability to predict accurately. It is however a real possibility and must not be dismissed as we have already surpassed historic levels for CO_2 concentrations which have triggered such events in the past.

Unanticipated Population Reduction-

Zombie apocalypses aside, our global population could theoretically face a number of realistic scenarios that would dramatically impact population density. Some of these possibilities could potentially reduce the demand on our resources considerably and take pressure off of the "consumption" potion of the equation which would have a positive impact. That being said, the unanticipated and premature loss of human life is never a good thing and rapid de-population could also result in a further degrading of our environment and resource availability depending on the way those losses occur.

An unprecedented untreatable viral or disease outbreak is a real possibility considering the current absence of new generation antibiotics and the speed at which contagions can spread throughout our modern world. A new "plague" or "Spanish Flu" with a high mortality rate could have a devastating impact if there were no available drugs or treatments to administer those infected. For your conspiracy theorists out there, such an outbreak could also be a planned desperate last-ditch government-initiated response should they determine no other efforts at stemming resource loss and environmental degradation were working.

Another possibility is the potential for nuclear war. Although an all-out confrontation would seem unlikely in this day and age, the possibility of regional or limited exchanges or bombs being employed by terrorists in isolated attacks is growing with each passing year. This is a direct consequence of the spread of terrorism, the destabilization of government control in countries that possess nuclear capabilities, and the possession and development of these weapons by so called "rouge" nations. Many prominent Think Tanks believe that these types of limited confrontations may be inevitable in the coming years and it is only a matter of time. Radiation as we discussed earlier makes the areas affected too dangerous for habitation or other productive purposes.

Additionally, events such as a "Yellowstone" scale super volcano eruption or an asteroid/comet colliding with Earth present remote possibilities that would have a dramatic impact on our population and the environment. The thing is those occurrences happen so rarely (on a geological time scale) that the likelihood of such an event occurring in this century is extremely doubtful.

Chapter Eleven

Human Capital

(Our most valuable and mismanaged global resource)

"Nobody's going to fix the world for us, but working together, making use of technological innovations and human communities alike, we might just be able to fix it ourselves."

~ Jamais Cascio

Let's face it. We live in a world of unproductive consumers. As our population expands and our expectations for a higher standard of living increase the demands on our global resources are skyrocketing. The need for essential commodities is expanding on an unimagined scale, yet our global resources are ultimately finite. This is the center of the target when looking at the reasons why our efforts to protect the environment have fallen so short. It is human beings that created our current dilemma through mismanaging this delicate balance, and it will be human beings that ultimately confront these challenges successfully or the reason we fail.

The various socio/economic models' mankind has followed throughout the ages that support our daily needs for attaining energy, food, potable water, and disposing of waste, have essentially remained the same since the beginning of recorded history. When we needed more resources, we moved to a new location, fished in a different part of the ocean, dug a new mine, or drilled a new oil well. When we needed to get rid of our waste, we dug a hole, flushed it into a river, dumped it in the ocean, or burned it to ash. The majority of major advances we have made through the ages have all been centered on producing and processing more with little thought towards sustainability. Those days and outdated practices must end immediately if we are to preserve our planet and its resources for our children and future generations. It is therefore essential that the economic growth that is the day to day requirement of a healthy and functioning global society occurs from here-on in a manner that supports environmental stewardship and resource conservation.

Having never had to consider the limits of our global resources and the fragility of the biosphere that supports life on our planet, we now face challenges we were never conditioned to address. Those issues that define our "sustainability" are the combined impacts of individuals and populations throughout the world. To think that we can solve those challenges without their participation is foolish. Human consciousness must now evolve on a global scale.

We now face a historic imperative that will take the combined efforts of those of us who are enlightened to expand that knowledge to those of us who are not. This is not about charity, philanthropy, subsidy, or responsibility. This is about our survival. It is this investment in human capital in which we have to focus our efforts. We must now engage the minds and thoughtful participation of our population if we are to effectively start this process. The challenge then is "How do we manage this essential re-programing of our species?" It all starts with education.

This will require a centralized universal platform to disseminate the knowledge and skills that will allow us to navigate this new age of conservation and efficiency. There needs to be specific goals, methodologies, strategies, and structure in coordinating this unprecedented effort. We must provide the means by which the individuals in our population become more effective producers and more thoughtful consumers.

The undeniable and unavoidable truth is we will all sink or swim together. We are indivisibly dependent on one another if we are to turn things around. If we cannot empower our neighbors to fully participate and work together to protect and preserve the irreplaceable resources, we all must depend on, we all will face a very bleak and austere future. Your individual commitment and support are the keys to this process. No one else will do this for you, and it is up to each of us who realize the necessities of a collaborative global response to actively encourage and work towards getting our neighbors to participate. To ignore this necessary effort is to dismiss the only real hope we have to address and respond to these global threats. If we are to succeed, you and your active communication and actions are the key to that success.

Chapter Twelve

Defining a Methodology for Education and Training

(This is where we start)

"It is in fact a part of the function of education to help us escape, not from our own time -- for we are bound by that -- but from the intellectual and emotional".

~ T.S. Eliot

<u>Overview</u>

How does one reprogram an entire global population? How do you undo the mindsets and pre-disposed views of diverse cultures conditioned by countless generations of reinforced behavior and repetition? What will it take such that people realize the necessity for collaboratively managing their resources and protecting their environment? This is no simple challenge. Much of what we do and how we manage our basic requirements for survival and living is core to our belief systems and a central part of our cultures. This is particularly true in less developed countries where these norms and behavioral patterns are deeply ingrained into lifestyles that have remained virtually unchanged for centuries.

The reality however is that conditions are becoming increasing difficult and expensive in regards to acquiring basic necessities and managing our daily existence throughout the world. These pressures will continue to increase regionally as consumption increases and resources diminish until those impacts reach a critical mass. As situations become desperate and the truth sinks in that the systems, we depend on to manage our resource are changing on an unprecedented scale people will either look for a solution or someone to blame. It is at that point that proper guidance and knowledge empowerment will play a defining role in determining our future.

To accomplish this efficiently and directly there is an absolute need to tie global education and training efforts directly to the specific sustainable infrastructure and regional projects required for our long-term economic development. This involves rebalancing resource management and promoting universal improvements in the standard of living. Additionally, this process must be about empowerment and not exploitation for it to be effective. That is the key to its development to ensure wide spread cultural participation. This approach lays the ground work for the collaborative environment that will be the defining element as to its eventual success.

There is also an extreme need for a common platform through which this education and training takes place. This becomes necessary as to speed up the efficiency and establish the focus that will counter the time element we are collectively up against. Much as the U.S. was able to develop a nuclear weapon in a relatively short period of time with the Manhattan Project in the 1940's, we must now consolidate our efforts to be successful with global resource management. Through standardizing and coordinating our energies we can limit time wasted competing against ourselves when it is imperative, we act together. To ignore this truth is to insure our failure.

When one starts out to design and develop a universal education/training platform that process needs to be driven by specific purpose and goals. This is necessary to define a methodology for implementation and bring clarity to that effort which can be reflected in the design and structure of that platform. It is therefore critical that we must first identify the challenges and essential goals of that mission to define that path. I imagined the following criteria as being the basis for that process.

- The platform must be universally accessible.
- The curriculum needs to be focused on the key aspects of sustainability.
- Remedial and rudimentary courses must be available to help prepare less sophisticated individuals for more advanced courses and concepts.
- The curriculum must be flexibly designed to address specific sustainable management challenges that exist locally.
- Efforts at re-education and training must be directed not just towards students and workers, but to local and regional governments, community leaders, and stakeholders.
- The platform must soon become self-sustaining and financially independent of outside subsidy in order to both continuously operate and expand.

- The teaching methodology must include a strong message of global participation and collaboration.

So, starting with this basic criterion let's look at the challenges that will have to be overcome and the strategies employed to meet these demands.

Universal Accessibility

Simply said, if your solution requires everyone's participation in order to reach its intended goals then that empowerment needs to be universally accessible. This means it must be available locally, offered in a language common to that population, and within the financial means of all who wish to participate. Education on this scale has never been attempted in human history. The reason it is now even somewhat plausible is the recent development of the internet.

The use of the internet as a tool to deliver the education and skills-training required to sustainably manage our resources may ultimately be the single most significant contribution of this evolutionary medium. No other means has proved to be as efficient in providing access to knowledge from a cost/deliverable's basis. This is particularly relevant to poorer/more isolated populations where cost and local availability are the defining factors in acquiring a quality learning experience. That being said the majority of these online education efforts currently available are for-profit and tend to focus on traditional curriculum that is supportive of conventional approaches to economic and social development. What is needed now is specific knowledge and training that directly addresses our need to re-establish a sustainable balance back to our environment.

Curriculum Focus

A core curriculum focused on the universal challenges we all face and the new methods for addressing those issues is central to this process. These courses should be aimed at providing the knowledge and skills that relate to the new technologies, applications, and protocols for managing resources sustainably while increasing production.

These specific areas of focus are:

- Renewable Energy
- Sustainable Agriculture, Farming, and Food Production
- Water Management

- Waste Management
- Economic Growth and Expansion

Programs and courses should be designed to introduce students to the transformational concepts and correct implementation steps required to counter our current non-sustainable trends. Each effort must be tailored to the age and perceptive limitations and education level they are meant to address (i.e.-children first learning to read, primary school students, college level students, existing work force).

There is no shortage of expertise and vision when it comes to addressing what needs to be done for humanity to mount an effective response to our current challenges. What is needed is a structure for that knowledge and those capabilities to reach people who currently lack access to that information and mentoring guidance.

Preparatory Education

Before you can walk you must first crawl. Many areas of the world lack the most basic education opportunities, or options are in such short supply that much of the population does not share in those benefits. This makes potential students and workers incapable of handling more complex concepts or instruction in advanced skills training. Even in nations and regions where there are adequate modern education available students are rarely taught the very basics of sustainable resource management or sustainable economics. So, what we encounter are basically two similar but separate issues that relate to preparing our population for the task at hand. That challenge being you must establish a strong base of general understanding before you introduce a student to more demanding instruction if they are going to be productive contributors.

For the developing world or in poorer regions where quality educational opportunities are sparse at best, you must provide access to basic education. This can be as rudimentary as offering classes and instruction in reading skills, math, and basic science. Thankfully much of that curriculum already exists online and

it is just a matter of adding those courses/capabilities to your platform, translating those materials into local languages, and then developing a content delivery platform.

In more developed societies it is a matter of introducing the student to those concepts and ideas at an earlier stage of their education such that their transition to more complex concepts and materials follows a natural trajectory. For children learning to read, a series of children's books with relatable characters teaching them the basic concepts of recycling, resource preservation, sustainable farming, how renewable energy is made and so forth would be appropriate. The characters in the books would have adventures and overcome challenges that relate to the issues of resource management and environmental stewardship introducing the child to these new ideas.

Primary school children could be taught the basic principles of sustainable growth and economic development through games designed to teach them all the basics of managing our planet as it relates to our large population. This process could be part of an academic competition. These "fun" competitions would introduce the student to new and emerging technologies, methodologies, protocols, and environmental/ infrastructure challenges, while tasking them with building virtual communities that foster expansion and economic growth without diminishing or damaging natural resources.

Regional Environmental, Infrastructure, and Social Compatibility

Although human beings all have the same essential needs, how we provide for those necessary goods and services vary radically depending on several factors. Pre-existing local infrastructure which provides electricity and fuel, delivers water, produces food, and manages sewage and waste can vary greatly from modern state-of-the-art engineering to non-existent depending on where you are. Environmental conditions impact rain and water availability, solar radiance, wind and seasonal weather patterns. Some environments are in the desert, others by the sea. Still others may be located near tropical rainforests while still more may be in the cold barren tundra. There are large sprawling metro-plexus, and remote rural villages. Certain areas are rich with natural wealth while others are barren and struggle with basic supportive resources. As a project developer you may be tasked with modifying that which is already in place, or planning, designing, and building from scratch. Each of these variances has a profound impact on the technologies, applications, and strategies you employ to establish a sustainable balance within that locality.

Any effective education and training platform must be flexible enough to allow for a customizable curriculum in order to adjust to these differences. As I like to say "Solar modules don't produce power in a mine." It is therefore a requirement that the lessons, courses, and materials offered match the needs and respond to the challenges defined by the region and locality.

Regional customs and societal norms can also vary greatly depending on where you are. This can impact every aspect as to how large infrastructure projects evolve. Financing, government involvement, and political influence all impact project viability. Additionally, project structure, oversight, and development issues based on the maturity or limitations of the local supportive infrastructure all come into play. To this you can add the availability and variance of human resources. These can range from a well-educated and prepared workforce to a completely untrained and under-educated populace. Further refinement of the course materials needs to evolve to reflect these challenges and provide appropriate information and guidance. In this way students are then properly prepared for the specific challenges they will face.

Far Reaching Societal Impact

It is not enough to have a well-educated and skilled work force and soon-to-be graduating student population if there is no local or regional public support. Stakeholders within the community need to be educated such that they can actively engage with this process. Business must invest in, and develop the right projects. Governments must enact the correct laws and legal guidelines. Social/religious/ community groups must encourage the necessary changes. The general population needs to support those efforts. Any local or regional attempt to provide education and training must actively engage these stakeholders in the localities where these efforts are taking place in a strategy of continuous, extended out-reach. This is an essential element such that this transformational process is universally understood, the benefits clearly defined, and those efforts fully supported on a societal level.

Education and Training Methodology Linked to Economic Expansion

I have always postulated that economic expansion must be directly linked to mitigating our global resource management challenges if we are ultimately going to re-establish a sustainable balance. The same is true for the education and skills training portion of that process. So, a question I often hear is "How do you plan to pay for this enormous and expensive undertaking without the need for constant subsidy?" My answer is by directly linking the process of empowerment to the rebuilding and modernizing of our global infrastructure. Let me explain.

In order to supplant current non-sustainable systems, we must create new platforms and models that allow for adaptation and expansion of advanced sustainable technologies and protocols. This cannot be accomplished if we continually rely on subsidy to fund those efforts. Failure to create this independent relationship will inevitably lead to a collapse of this change-over as our current global economic model is overtaxed. Financial resources would diminish as a consequence of the increased costs of basic necessities (food, water, energy) thus reducing (relatively) the money available for new projects and education efforts. This re-shifting of expenditures will ultimately undermine any chance we might have to finance the massive infrastructure changes and expanding empowerment efforts required to insure a healthy and vibrant future for our population.

Additionally, rebalancing resource management with consumption is not just a matter of knowing what needs to be done in a general sense. It is necessary to understand the tiered steps that build this process so it can be economically self-sustained and will grow of its own momentum without the need for constant injections of subsidy.

These are extremely complex concepts/equations that must be taught over time providing the correct building blocks in the proper order for this consciousness to become an accepted standard behavior for the general population. Our failure to accomplish this will mean we destroy the biodiversity of our planet, our core food and water support systems, and eventually and ourselves. This is the guaranteed, predictable, and unavoidable result of habitat destruction and resource depletion due to overpopulation, over consumption, and resource mismanagement.

To counter these trends, we would need to establish a new system for providing education and training that reduces the need for public/government subsidized funding. Learning annexes and hands-on training sites would need to be an integral part of every profitable new sustainable infrastructure project you initiate. As the great majority of these core infrastructure projects are initiated, directed, or awarded by local and regional governments to private entities, governments could easily make education and training empowerment a necessary cost of doing business.

This is not a new concept. Corporations have always trained and mentored their workers or provided internships to potential employees. The only difference is this effort would make a wider range of subject materials and training options available on-site at their facilities. Opportunities would not just be limited to workers and employees, but rather extended into the general community. This way, as you re-establish a sustainable balance within a community, town, city, or region through sustainable economic development and specific projects, you are at the same time training and educating that population to be a part of that support effort. This allows them to adjust and understand how they live in balance with their environment and resources, while providing the means by which they acquire the skills they need to man the jobs that will provide these solutions.

The key to corporate participation is that there are huge profits involved in these contracts and projects. In fact, this transition to a "more sustainable" infrastructure will be the largest redistribution and investment of wealth in human history. The days of governments handing out virtually unlimited opportunity and wealth to private corporations without the requirement of reciprocal responsibility must forever come to an end. These "responsibilities" must not be limited to just managing a resource or eliminating an environmental impact, but extended to the overall solution portion of the equation.

Additionally, let's not assume that there is no incentive here for corporations. This process of increasing the skill set, general knowledge, and productivity of their workforce and regional community will greatly increase their profitability. Efficiency, innovation, increased productivity and opportunity are the corner stones of healthy economic development. Smart, well trained people take advantage of opportunity and are more productive. Productive people have more wealth. Wealthy people spend more money.

By its very nature our education and training effort will need to expand to match the increases in our population and require constant reassessment and improvement to keep up with the advances and changes that will be guiding this process. The long-term viability and health of that effort ultimately comes down to a philosophy and methodology as to how you pay for it.

Global Collaboration

All our efforts will fail unless we directly address the human element that inhibits our ability to collaborate. Nothing we teach or instill on a technical level will amount to anything unless we recognize the root causes of our current issues. Any global education effort must instill through persistent reminders and re-education why human frailties and our common competitive and antagonistic history have stood in the way of our ability to work together. This is a critical component for success. It is necessary to bring clarity and understanding to the participant as to why these aspects of human nature can ultimately destroy all our best intentions.

Summation

The key to all these education and training efforts being successful is a guiding methodology, coordination, and focus. It is in everyone's common interest that we rebalance our resource management and become better stewards of our small planet. The quality and vibrancy of our lives, and surely that of our children will depend on our success. It is not enough for there to be effort and good will.

This challenge requires common purpose and a collaborative mindset. We need universal involvement and well trained and skilled partners if we are to be successful.

William Sosinsky

Chapter Thirteen

The Basics of Integrated Sustainable Design (ISD)

"The most general law in nature is equity-the principle of balance and symmetry which guides the growth of forms along the lines of the greatest structural efficiency."

~ **Herbert Read**

Nothing is wasted in nature. In a healthy environment a seamless balance is established between plants and animals as natural selection defines the perfect symbiosis of life, climate, and location. Nature is the ultimate practitioner of efficiency as it is always attempting to rebalance the equilibrium of an environment as changes occur to the key components in any particular bio-system. Integrated Sustainable Design (ISD) seeks to mimic that efficiency by finding that same perfect balance between resource management, productivity, and zero waste. Ultimately ISD becomes the critical conceptual element that can determine our eventual success or failure in building the supportive infrastructure that can help our population adjust to the new demands of the 21st century.

Integrated Sustainable Design is a concept pioneered by Energime. It combines symbiotic technologies and protocols into a common platform that solve a variety of challenges at a common site. Several things are needed to accomplish this. You must have access to a great many diversified technologies. Each locality you deal with has specific challenges that have to be addressed with matching applications designed to solve those challenges efficiently and profitably (i.e. solar panels don't work in caves). You must have a diverse and experienced design and implementation team to provide the technical capabilities to implement these projects. (i.e. creating sewage treatment solutions that provide the nutrient source for algae production used for feed, energy generation, and water purification). You have to have an educated and well-trained work force (the purpose of the education and training protocol) able to deal with the complexity of these integrated systems. Lastly, you must work with investment groups that are both tech and risk savvy that can appreciate the opportunity and understand the steps required to mitigate risks and who have the commitment to participate in that process.

There are certain truths to human behavior that we must be honest about with ourselves if we are to face up to the challenges that lay ahead. People in the most general sense will almost always chose to do what costs less, is easier, takes less thought, or provides more immediate perceived value in the short term regardless of the long-term consequences of those choices. Education, wealth, and conscience may encourage some to be more pro-active in defining their decisions, but for the grand majority of our population this is the absolute truth. So, this preconditioned behavior is ultimately the defining challenge that must shape our development and integration process from an economically adaptive perspective for any change to take hold and have the impact we hope to achieve.

For this very reason ISD is the inevitable, unavoidable, and ultimately logical approach to future projects because it is defined by efficiency. Efficiency as it relates to planning, design, production, process, management, balance, distribution and profitability. This is a central requirement when attempting to create any scalable, vertically integrated system that has as its goal perfect symmetry.

So, getting back to those truths about human behavior; if people will always choose to do what costs less, is easier, takes less thought, or provides more immediate perceived value in the short term, then satisfying those tendencies is your goal. Whatever it is that will solve that challenge while re-establishing a sustainable balance is the target. This has different implications depending on what stage of the flow chart you're focusing on. By that I mean are those people businessmen, investors, engineers, architects, scientists, or ultimately consumers? In terms of this chapter we are going to concentrate on the production side of the ledger.

When you are trying to deliver a basic commodity such as water, food, or energy it is natural that whatever process can dependably deliver that end product at the lowest cost with the highest value/profitability is that which will be successfully adapted. It is a simple supply /demand, cost/production relationship. Investors will back the best solution that provides the highest returns with acceptable risk until they find, or are forced to move in another direction. Coal is cheaper, available, and easier to understand so they build coal burning power plants. When the laws change restricting the burning of coal they move to the next most profitable option.

ISD on the production end is attempting to maximize profitability as it relates to time, space, process, and value. Land is at a premium, particularly in and around major metroplexes where demand is greatest. Transportation is a major cost. Newer technologies are achieving unprecedented efficiencies in terms of speed, levels of production, and economies of scale. Waste removal and disposal is a huge and expensive drain on overhead. In theory if you can maximize production value per square foot, reduce or eliminate transport and waste management costs, and increase process speed by combining state-of-the-art technologies with evolving management protocols you are well on your way to accomplishing the goals of ISD.

In the following chapters we are going to look at the future potential of energy, food production, water and waste management. We'll examine the steps we need to make to ensure the viability of those critical survival impacting components as they relate to long term sustainability. During that discussion I will reference specific strategies and integration options as to how different efforts relate to ISD and how their positive impacts can be amplified by proper coordination and inclusion with other synergistic projects.

Chapter Fourteen

When It Comes to Initiating a Strategy for Re-establishing Regional Sustainability...Be Specific.

"No problem can be solved until it is reduced to some simple form. The changing of a vague difficulty into a specific, concrete form is a very essential element in thinking."

~ J. P. Morgan

There isn't a single regional population on our planet that is not currently faced with resource management issues that are directly impacting their quality of life or their prospects for a sustainable future. As much as we strive for simplicity in our search for a magic solution or single bullet strategy in solving these issues it's never that simple. Each community, region, country, and society have their own special challenges that require a flexible approach. So as much as we might all wish for a simple and all-encompassing path to follow for a more sustainable world, the solutions are in reality quite specific. These particular pre-existing conditions are central to determining a starting point for developing a workable economic strategy to revamp energy, food, water, and waste infrastructure.

This is important to understand as what is most needed in any locality in terms of critical project development is not necessarily what makes the most sense from a short-term economic perspective. The resource that is in greatest demand currently by that population or that will be most needed in the near future may not produce sufficient profitability to attract investment. To disregard this principle ignores the demands of the investment community and insures the continuous need for subsidy when creating projects. Such a course ultimately bankrupts your ability to continuously fund needed expansion. The solution involves building up your capital reserves to offset the costs of those critically needed infrastructure improvements that are either not profitable or have a longer-term return on investment. You accomplish this by investing in other strategic tangent projects that are synergistic to that core mission of rebalancing local resource management which have highly profitable short-term returns.

As an example, a community may need to address their long-term water needs but investing in a desalinization plant or huge pipeline project is prohibitively expensive. This same community may have a waste management issue whereby they are running out of space at their landfills and are exporting much of their waste to neighboring communities at great cost. Additionally, that poorly managed waste source may be polluting lakes and rivers making their waters unsafe sources for human consumption and agricultural use. If that community were able to profitably manage those waste streams such that the investment paid off quickly, they would soon have the financial ability to leverage those profits as a basis for investment into those major water improvements. Those waste management technologies exist today and include recycling, extracting, reformulating, and repurposing applications that transform waste stream components for reuse into a higher purpose. As waste is a pervasive issue in practically every corner of our world, this could be one possible solution to funding that desalinization plant or pipeline project.

Therefore, the challenge from an economic /investment strategy equates to identifying the core resources which are in abundance locally that can be profitably (and sustainably) developed to create those capital reserves. This way, as long as there is project linkage in your strategy, the profit from these more profitable projects can be reinvested and serve as the initial funds to be used in developing efforts in areas of need where resources are sparse and the financial payback less attractive. Also, by grouping projects together, it is possible to average out the return on investment (ROI) on a series of projects to offer an acceptable timeframe for that return on investment in order to make the project attractive to risk capital. This is where Integrated Sustainable Design is crucial.

Determining what assets are plentiful in any particular region comes down to the infrastructure maturity, climate, and ecological/environmental profile of that location. By that I mean how modern and developed is the community, and where is it located in relation to naturally occurring resources? Is there a modern sewer system and water distribution network? What about a centralized electric grid? Is it a warm and arid climate located inland near the equator with lots of sunshine or a more temperate region adjacent to a large river or windy valley? Does it have rich soil and healthy aquifers and water sources? Every detail determines the availability of renewable energy, food production capacity, and water reserves both currently and in the near future. Unless these attributes are clearly identified and understood you cannot establish the critical leverage point that will bring in the continuous cash flow needed to address the balance of the total sustainable build-out.

From a resource/infrastructure perspective this is a much simpler strategy to define when addressing challenges in the developing world. In almost all developing nations there are major voids in production and distribution networks, and in many cases potential resources have not been efficiently tapped or managed. Though food and water issues may be of most immediate concern, waste, and in some cases energy opportunities can be immediately profitable and more easily financed. Waste issues are prevalent practically everywhere in the third world and are an easily tapped resource. New and innovative technologies are being created every day to turn those waste ingredients into valuable feed-stocks for other industrial uses. The major challenges that exist in the developing world almost always relate to existing waste collection networks or the lack thereof. Energy on the other hand is a key enabler providing the essential power for subsequent projects. Additionally, electrical rates are generally more expensive as a commodity in the developing world making it attractive for investors.

When you combine the raw materials derived from the waste stream with the energy needed to run factories it is possible to put in place the key components that fuel industrial growth and an export capacity. An example of this would be the use of rice husks which were formally disposed of in landfills or dumped in local rivers. The rice hulls are now employed as a feeder source for insulation, cement, and even the silicon used in the production of solar cells. What was once a disposal expense for rice producers or an environmental pollutant is now an even larger generator of income than the rice itself in some instances.

In the modern developed world all the systems that serve the day to day needs of that population are already in place. As a result, the process of transforming infrastructure is either a function of retrofitting and replacing obsolete systems, or developing new consumer markets that end up increasing demand that spurs on market growth. Such is the case with consumer demand for organically grown fruits and vegetables creating an opportunity for large indoor farms that can grow those crops more efficiently and at lower per square foot costs.

In both the developed and developing world the single constant is that profitability ends up being the main driving force that initiates the largest portion of these investments in sustainable change. Understanding this tiered approach is at the core of this problem-solving strategy. For this methodology to work it must be profitable in order to attract investment and spur economic expansion. If those profits are systematically reinvested into the far reaching and long-term solutions needed for our future that are less profitable, you would then have the financial means available to offset much of that anticipated need. The strategy for direct linkage between planned economic expansion and essential infrastructure improvements that re-establish and rebalance our use of resources is necessary if we are to preemptively address those future short-falls. The more you are able to devise a strategy that brings economics and sustainability planning needs together the closer you, your community, or your society are to finding that critical balance.

In order to see what those possibilities are and the logic as to how they work or are "linked" together we must have an understanding of the technologies, applications, and protocols that are likely to shape our future. In the following chapters we will examine many of those options.

Chapter Fifteen

Waste is Not Garbage

"Let him who would enjoy a good future waste none of his present."

~ **Robert Babson**

If we are to adequately supply the fundamental material needs of our 21st century population then the concept of "garbage" must soon be obsolete. It is a misnomer. A callous outdated term used by the short-sighted, naïve, lazy, ignorant, and careless masses who do not understand the value of waste. The great majority of our waste stream is composed of that which has been grown, mined, milled, extracted, manufactured, and constructed previously at considerable cost and effort. The reality that the waste is no longer being employed for its originally intended purpose doesn't negate the fact that it still has useful value. Perhaps it would be better for people if they thought of "waste" as the excess, surplus, or remaining left-overs of some other process? By changing the way, we refer to the "left over" materials that result from our consumption perhaps the negative perception we now attach to the term would be transformed into a more positive and productive opinion. In any case, it is imperative we learn to view our waste as a resource and not as garbage.

As defined by the United Nations Statistics Division in the *Glossary of Environment Statistics;* "Wastes are materials that are not prime products (that is products produced for the market) for which the initial user has no further use in terms of his/her own purposes of production, transformation or consumption, and of which he/she wants to dispose. Wastes may be generated during the extraction of raw materials, the processing of raw materials into intermediate and final products, the consumption of final products, and other human activities. Residuals recycled or reused at the place of generation are excluded." [43]

The last line of that definition "Residuals recycled or reused at the place of generation are excluded" is perhaps most important part of that explanation. It is the successful elimination and reuse/repurposing of waste that is one of the core missions of ISD and a critical element in the management of our resources if we are to re-establish our sustainable balance.

Waste comes in many forms some of which are easy to repurpose and some of which can be more challenging. For most people living in modern society the waste that we generate on a daily basis consists of Municipal Solid Waste (MSW), human waste and effluent (Sewage), and atmospheric waste in the form of gases produced through our use of energy in our homes and transportation. Industry and business contribute vast amounts of more complex waste streams some of which are highly dangerous and toxic to humans and to the environment. These can include specialized and dangerous waste streams such as medical, radioactive, heavy medals, and chemical waste.

So, let's examine some of these waste streams to understand their value, evolving protocols and technologies used in their processing, potential ways they can be incorporated into a balanced ISD system, and the importance of eliminating their impacts on our environment.

Municipal Solid Waste

One of the most visible and prevalent sources of waste and what we generally refer to as "garbage" is Municipal Solid Waste or MSW. MSW is composed of a variety of waste that occurs as a result of consumption, construction, demolition, and maintenance of our homes, businesses, and transportation vehicles. On a technical level we divide the mass of the waste into two distinct categories; organic and inorganic waste. Organic waste is composed of items that at one point were made up of materials that were living. Food, yard scraps, the rubber in tires, plastics, coal ash, paints, wood and paper-based products, and many packaging materials such as Styrofoam are some of the subcategories of that particular stream. Metals, cement, glass, and a variety of mineral or stone-based construction materials make up the bulk of the inorganic components.

Many of the items from both the organic and inorganic streams such as varieties of glass, metals, plastics, and paper products are increasing being recycled through pre-sorting at the curbside before pickup. Where there are mature collection systems in place and where there is the public will to do so, percentages of MSW that actually make it to the landfill are being reduced dramatically. That being said this is still the exception and not the rule. In developing nations that percentage of recycled waste in some cases is close to zero and the waste ends up fouling roadsides, landscapes, rivers, and almost every area where people congregate or frequent. There is not a shoreline anywhere on the planet no matter how remote where MSW is not present as it is distributed by ocean currents throughout the world. Additionally, landfills everywhere are filling up and have either reached their maximum capacity or are quickly approaching that threshold making the problem of what to do with that constant flow of waste a real logistical issue.

www.yourarticlelibrary.com   avaxnews.net

The value of MSW is a direct function of how well you can presort, sort onsite, and concentrate all the component stocks such that the distinct waste piles that result are of a single, consistent makeup in terms of chemical/material composition and density. When reusing certain feed stocks for chemical conversion processes material size and a consistent caloric value are additional considerations.

There has been an extraordinary amount of effort these past couple of decades trying to convert the organic materials in MSW for use as sources of energy. Because organic waste is essentially a variety of complex carbon chains it is possible to convert those materials into everything from electricity and diesel fuel, to synthetic gas and jet fuel depending on the before mentioned separation

protocols and the advanced technologies now being developed to process those materials. Some of those methods include gas capture, combustion, pyrolysis, gasification, and plasma arc gasification.

Gas capture for the most part is a process where existing or "mature" landfills that have reached their maximum capacity are "tapped" to recover methane gases. This is accomplished by covering the site in a membrane to concentrate, direct, and thus capture the methane. Those gases are the result of the decomposing organic components buried at the site which produce a steady stream of combustible natural gas. For many municipalities and waste districts this offers a simple way to offset local air pollution issues created by the produced methane while deriving a dependable fuel source and essentially leaving the site undisturbed. This strategy ignores the recycled value of the buried materials and creates the need for more and larger landfills to deal with the continuous stream of incoming waste.

It is also possible to burn (combust) the organic materials at these sites to power turbines and create electricity as is common these days in many parts of the world. This is a simple concept where a perceived problem (waste) is converted to a critical need (electricity) so it is a very popular as it also reduces the need for long term landfill storage. It is my opinion however that this approach is both ignorant and short sighted. As a solution it negates the potential and inherent value of that complex waste stream by turning valuable and in some cases scarce resources into toxic ash. In that regard it is both a wasteful and unsophisticated way to treat such a valuable resource.

Efforts to create synthetic fuels date back almost 180 years. During both the first and the second world wars conversion technologies were improved dramatically as countries attempted to make up for a shortage of petroleum. Germany introduced several innovative processes during that period resulting from intensive research into different methods to convert organic mass into synthetic fuels and gases.

Recently there has been a push by project developers and technology companies for a magic bullet solution whereby entire organic waste streams of combined MSW would be converted to high quality fuels. Almost all, if not all of them have failed miserably. The reason is fairly simple. The carbon chains in plastics vary from one another, which varies from rubber, wood, paper products, and yard waste. Separation and concentration protocols are critical to achieving a consistent result. In each case the controlled conversion process of each of those different materials required precise specific temperatures, pressures, and conversion times in order to achieve a consistent quality end-product. You can draw the analogy of trying to cook a large meal of a roast, potatoes, vegetables, breads, and a desert in the same oven at one temperature for the same amount of time. It is unlikely that all your course components will come out of the oven in the desired shape for your meal.

"Pyrolysis is a thermochemical decomposition of organic material at elevated temperatures in the absence of <u>oxygen</u> (or any halogen). It involves the simultaneous change of chemical composition and physical phase, and is irreversible. The word is coined from the Greek-derived elements *pyro* "fire" and *lysis* "separating". The process is used heavily in the chemical industry, for example, to produce charcoal, activated carbon, methanol, and other chemicals from wood, to convert ethylene dichloride into vinyl chloride to make PVC, to produce coke from coal, to convert biomass into syngas and biochar, to turn waste into safely disposable substances, and for transforming medium-weight hydrocarbons from oil into lighter ones like gasoline." (44)

For regions of the world that lack natural fuel resources and are highly dependent on imports for oil and gas, pyrolysis offers an intriguing option. Waste tires and plastics are particularly rich in high quality carbon chains and as such are the target feedstock for most of these new efforts at producing synthetic fuels. The success however of many pyrolysis projects whose aim has been to produce diesel and gasoline as their main end-product has been hampered greatly by the lack of separation/concentration protocols we referred to earlier. As a result, either those end-products end up as low-grade pyrolysis oil with limited commercial value, or the actual operations close down as the machines break down from the buildup of muck and residual tars that foul their works. Additionally, the burning of low-grade pyrolysis oil is similar to a bunker fuel commonly used in seagoing vessels and as such very "dirty" and a huge contributor to atmospheric pollution.

Gasification processes organic waste into a synthetic gas which can then be combusted to power a turbine to create electricity. The value of gasification is that the "cleaner" gas that it produces combusts much more efficiently at higher temperatures and with less corrosive, toxic, and polluting residues then burning the waste directly. Those "cleaner" gases can be employed directly to run an engine or turbine without damaging the system, or converted to a high-quality liquid fuel using the Fischer–Tropsch process. This approach is being used more and more in industrial applications around the world to create the large quantities of electricity they require for their operations.

Plasma Arc Gasification is also known as "plasma pyrolysis". Using this technology organic waste or feedstock is burned using a plasma arc torch at temperatures between 4,000 to 25,000 degrees Fahrenheit to gasify the materials. This produces "Pure highly calorific synthetic gas consists predominantly of Carbon monoxide (CO), H_2, CH, among other components. The conversion rate of plasma gasification exceeds 99%.[45] Non-flammable inorganic components in the waste stream are not broken down. This includes various metals. A phase change from solid to liquid adds to the volume of slag.

Plasma processing of waste is ecologically clean. The lack of oxygen prevents the formation of many toxic materials. The high temperatures in a reactor also prevent the main components of the gas from forming toxic compounds such as furans, dioxins, nitrogen oxides, or sulfur dioxide. Water filtration removes ash and gaseous pollutants." [46] In addition to creating a relatively clean end-product, plasma arc technology is very useful in disposing of toxic and medical waste as the process renders those elements harmless and keeps them from getting out into the environment.

It is because energy and fuel are essential and such central commodities critical to economic expansion that so much effort at managing MSW is directed towards the production of energy. There are other components however buried in our landfills which are critical to technology and are becoming increasingly scarce that we will soon need to reclaim. Rare Earths are one such material.

Rare earths are comprised of 17 chemical elements that although not as scarce as the name implies, are not found in very many places around the world in any great concentrations. This makes mining and harvesting these important elements in any substantial quantities extremely challenging. Rare earths are critical to many industrial and technical processes including the production of LED and compact florescent lights, liquid crystal displays (LCD's), energy storage, and specialty glass. Rare earths are also key components of high-tech magnets used in hard drives, electric motors and generators, catalytic convertors, loudspeakers, and power tools. Heavy industry uses rare earths as enablers to process crude oil into gasoline and in polishing industrial mirrors used in the production of solar concentrators, telescopes, televisions, and so forth. They are indispensable to these efforts and we will soon be running out of these elements unless we extract and recycle them from our waste stream.

www.fastcoexist.com   graphicillus.jpgphys.org

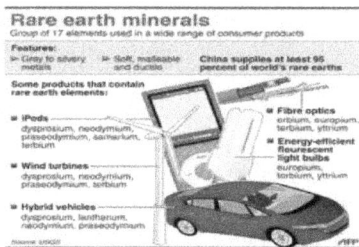

Currently such advanced recycling technology is taking hold in Japan to recover rare earths and is expected to start popping up in other countries that were part of the industrial revolution when most of these elements were landfilled. Additionally, more and more of the modern electronics that are being thrown out are being harvested for these essential elements and we can expect that this is a trend that will increase in the years to come.

A recent trend in managing MSW has to do with efforts directed towards new recycling technologies aimed at repurposing specific waste streams for building and manufacturing. Plastics and rubber waste are being combined with other biomass to create advanced composite materials used in housing, agriculture, storage, and industrial building materials. Lego style prefabricated housing that are a fraction of the cost of conventional materials and have similar or better performance characteristics will soon become the norm in the developing world. Wood and stone is being replaced by plastic and rubber combined with biomass to make sound barriers adjacent to railroads and highways, water resistant docks and decking materials, grain silos, and oil rig mats to name a few.

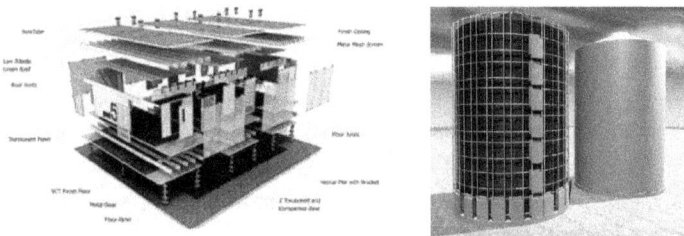

Green Bioproducts/Energime Green Group

These are just some of the many secondary uses possible for consumer waste. With our resources declining rapidly and the environmental impacts at crisis stages in many parts of the world it will be necessary for us to recycle and repurpose MSW with much greater efficiency in the coming years. This is an issue we need to gain control over such that we do not bury ourselves and our children in "garbage". It is an area however that offers tremendous opportunities for job creation and profitability which makes it a prime candidate for initial investment as an enabling starter project in a regional sustainable rebalancing strategy.

Agricultural and "Farm" Waste

In nature, it is the decomposing bio-organic mass of former living organisms or "nature's waste stream" with its key elements and minerals which feed the new generation of organic growth. That same relationship is certainly possible from a strategic sustainable production perspective for the endless volume of bio-organic waste or "biomass" created by human industry, sanitation, and consumer waste. That being said, nowhere is that potential more promising than with farm and agricultural waste streams. Those potential building blocks for our food chain are all present in that residue of livestock, aquaculture, and plant production, yet in many cases we agonize over how to dispose, bury, dump, or burn those stocks which we perceive as a nuisance and not an asset.

That isn't to say that manure is not readily repurposed already as a fertilizer or energy source throughout the world, or that wood pulp, rice hulls, or cow hides don't end up being used in tangent forms of useful production. The issue comes down to how we process much of that unused waste maximizing its potential value while reducing or eliminating the negative impacts our mismanagement has on the environment.

Embedded in most modern farm and agricultural waste is a mixture of natural and human introduced outside elements which include nutrients, pharmaceuticals, fertilizers, pesticides, and assorted toxins that need to be extracted and "sorted" before they are allowed to be reintroduced into a healthy environment. These chemicals and additives are showing up more and more in our water table both affecting the health of the riparian environment and the people who drink from those sources. Additionally, this "modern" mix of agricultural additives are present in the great majority of the meats, poultry, fish, and plant products we produce worldwide contributing to a variety of health and processing concerns affecting our population. Therefore, a strategy as to how we manage those waste streams prioritizing their value and threats becomes critical to our approach when aiming to re-establish a healthy sustainable balance.

Chief among those elements we need to recover and recycle is phosphorus. As we discussed earlier the great majority of the essential phosphorus that we consume in our food is lost through our food waste stream in the form of biomass waste, manure, urine, or "effluent". Phosphorus is of single importance and a critical finite element that is not retained by the consuming individual or animal and is therefore completely recyclable back into our food chain if the waste can be collected and reprocessed. In addition, we lose phosphorus as fertilizer is leached off our farmland through run-off into our streams, rivers, and out into our oceans as a result of poor crop/soil management.

There along with other phosphorous/nitrogen/potassium rich sewage contributes to the condition known as Eutrophication. This in turn pulls the oxygen out of the water as a consequence of runaway algae growth causing large "dead" areas along our coastlines. There are currently more than 400 such areas globally and their number and size are expanding steadily.

"There was a time when humans operated totally self-sufficient farms, tilling the same land for years by managing waste effectively, by simply making sure that everything that came out of the land eventually went back into it. In such a closed-loop scenario, phosphate would have the capacity to be reused approximately 46 times as food, fuel, fertilizer, and food again. [47]In the fertilizing techniques that dominate today, which involve the annual application of phosphate-enriched chemical mixtures on top of nutrient-starved soil, phosphorus is used exactly once, then swept out to sea. This practice is simply unsustainable. Our ancestors learned the importance of conserving nutrients through necessity: if they could not make the soil yield, they would starve; there were no second chances. The world has a chance, now, to learn this lesson again, before it's too late." [48]

Simply put, we need to completely reorganize the way we manage our agricultural models such that we stop wasting phosphates through poor farming methods and overuse, and efficiently recapture the "waste" phosphorous that is part of the production stream. That way it can be put to productive use and reduce its now destructive impact. This is particularly critical in areas such as China, India, and much of the developing world where less than half of the applied fertilizer actually ever makes it into the intended plant. Along with their large populations and tremendous need for food these countries exercise some of the most inefficient management practices as it relates to over-using fertilizers where the excess is allowed to leach into surrounding water systems. For those farmers improved management practices and education as to how much fertilizer is sufficient for the crops, they raise would have a huge positive impact.

In many larger and commercial livestock operations both in the developed and developing world, animal excrement is concentrated in "sewage lagoons". In these large open "cess pools" manure and urine are dumped, drained off, and mixed together. Whereas many of these sites are now using these wastes with the singular aim of capturing the methane produced during decomposition as a "renewable" energy source this is an inefficient and poor waste management strategy as it relates to long term sustainability. Properly separated and processed, a variety of valuable industrial/commercial/agricultural commodities can be derived from those solid and liquid waste streams. In many cases those feed stocks derived from the advanced separation processing of those waste streams are more valuable than the dairy and meat products those animals are primarily raised for.

In the case of phosphates, there are many existing technologies available that work in parallel with these waste streams to extract those elements, some more efficiently and cost effective than others. [49] Currently the price of mined phosphates is relatively less expensive than extraction. This imbalance is anticipated to change by 2030 as natural reserves start to dwindle and countries become much more dependent on agricultural and sewage waste streams to make up short falls. At that point it will come down to available finances to pay for these more advanced technologies as to whether or not they are employed. It is doubtful much of the developing world will be able to afford this infrastructure.

Additionally, this delay in implementation will only worsen our current impact on our inland waterways and oceans as the increasing stream of waste nutrients create more and larger dead zones. Countries such as Sweden and Germany have already made phosphate recovery a major objective in the coming years, but they are in the minority at the moment with most countries lacking any comprehensive strategy as to how to manage this precious resource.

When evaluating the overall component value of both the manure and urine there are all sorts of additional feed sources for commercial production other that phosphates that can be extracted when they are efficiently separated. These end products can include fertilizer and commercial grade urea as well as additives and byproducts that can be used to produce glue, engine cleaner treatments, composite plastics, pigment binders for paints, cement hardeners, and various other applications.

One of the major challenges' processors face is preserving the viability of the feeder source. Some of those potential feed stocks are severely degraded once the solids and liquids are mixed together and ammonia and other highly volatile compounds start to form. Therefore, to maximize the value of those individual waste streams it is essential to devise methods that immediately separate and process those individual streams at their source. Urine contains approximately 80% of the nutrient value of the waste while the solids the bulk of the biomass related components. Advanced livestock recovery systems designed to capture and separate the solid and liquids in the stalls have been developed to accomplish just this end and are just starting to come to market. Similarly, a new generation of consumer toilets are being developed to accomplish this very same goal and are gaining major market share in Europe as those countries seek out new and innovative ways to address separation and recovery methods for their sewage.

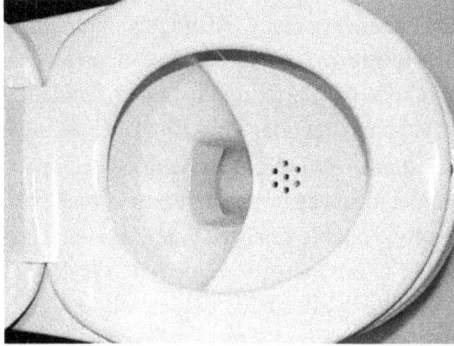

NoMix Toilets

http://inhabitat.com/nomix-toilets-separate-waste-are-super-eco-friendly/

In the developing world much of the agro-waste is now being used to enhance soil health by a producing an end product known as biochar. Biochar is produced by smoldering wood and agricultural waste in a process similar to Pyrolysis whereby carbon is sequestered in the soil in the form of charred biomass. This process increases soil fertility in potential farmlands that lack nutrients or have low PH. It is a form of land regeneration has been in use for centuries by tribes and civilizations in South America before being discovered by European explorers.

Finally, biomass is now being used to create synfuels through a variety of methods we discussed earlier in this book. Along with crops that are raised specifically for fuel such as corn, jatropha, sugar cane, and palm, agricultural waste and non-food crops such as switch grass are now being employed for that same use. How well they perform in terms of an end product however is specific to their caloric/oil content and source separation purity.

Fossil Fuels/CO2

Very few issues are potentially more impactful on our environment than the uncontrolled release of CO_2 into our atmosphere created as a consequence of burning fossil fuels. CO_2 is the main "greenhouse gas" being blamed for climate change and the acid spikes in our oceans PH. Currently less than one third of the

CO2 produced daily, or 25 Million tons of CO2 are sequestered by our oceans. The remaining 50 million tons are vented into the atmosphere. These vented totals are continuing to rise with our increasing population and fossil fuel usage. If we are to reverse this imbalance it is essential, we bring these totals down. Therefore, we are tasked with finding a way to sequester the CO2 in a manner that makes sense and is ultimately economically adaptable.

What most people fail to realize is that CO2 can be an extremely valuable gas when captured, contained, and employed properly. Used effectively it can have a very positive influence on agricultural and aquaculture productivity. Living organisms tend to grow faster and larger when levels of CO2 are increased. During the Jurassic Period when Dinosaurs ruled the earth and grew to enormous sizes, CO2 levels were 5 times what we find today in our modern atmosphere allowing those animals to achieve historically large proportions.

CO2 is an essential building block in the Kreb's cycle and for photosynthesis. When plants are grown in enclosed environments, or farm raised algae are fed with concentrated levels of CO2 their rate of growth and the time it takes them to achieve maturity are reduced significantly. Considering the increased profitability and benefit of larger crops in shorter time frames the value of utilizing CO2 this way becomes clear. Additionally, the carbon in CO2 is transformed into actual carbon as it is consumed by the organism along with other key elements. That carbon can then be sequestered in soils through the distribution of those organisms (algae) where they can serve as a base or natural fertilizer for farmers. This can have a similar impact as creating biochar in terms of fortifying the soil. Thus, a strategy of directing those CO2 waste streams into the living organisms that can sequester and make use of those waste streams would seem to be the best and most logical use of this otherwise potentially destructive gas.

Until now the main focus for CO2 sequestration as far as algae is concerned has been with trying to identify specific strains that develop high oil content that utilize or "eat" those waste streams. For many synthetic and organic fuel pioneers, algae promise to be the holy grail of potential fuel sources. If you consider this for a moment it makes perfect sense. Most of the oil and coal that we use for energy today was at one-point algae before it was converted into fossil fuels as the result of eons of heat and pressure. The major challenge for this type of application is finding the most promising strains of algae, and then dewatering and extracting the oils efficiently to reduce production costs. Thus far it is still comparatively expensive to produce fuel this way as compared to using oil, gas, or coal if you don't take into account the environmental costs.

Depending on the particular variety of algae, certain strains can also have other very desirable qualities that make them ideal for addressing waste gases. First off, algae can reproduce and increase its mass several times in the course of a day growing much faster as compared to land-based plants and animals. This makes it a prime candidate for industrial level production of organic oils. Another attribute of many algal species is the ability to sequester CO_2 equivalent to half their body weight as they grow and expand. One ton of CO_2 can potentially be sequestered in just two tons of algae. Additionally, algae can also absorb other dangerous and undesirable waste gases during the same processing such NO_x as well as a variety of heavy metals and other undesirable pollutants. Finally, certain algal strains have shown the ability to survive in very hot environments such as ocean steam vents and can be employed in directly managing flue gases from power plants and industrial sites in real time. These specific qualities make algae farming an extremely promising candidate in any future planning that addresses the challenges we currently face with CO_2.

Perhaps the largest untapped market and future opportunity for sequestering CO_2 will come in the form of indoor farming. After all, if CO_2 is a greenhouse gas, use it in greenhouses. Advanced designs for growing crops in enclosed environments are looking more and more at creating CO_2 dense environments in order to accelerate plant growth and reduce harvest cycles. Vertical farming uses stacked growing surfaces and feeds plants using aquaponic and aeroponic systems that require constant inputs of nutrients and external resources. Injecting CO_2 waste streams into this environment would make perfect sense. The same is possible for aquaculture operations in the production of algae used for food and nutrients, and in theory, for enhancing fish growth.

When you look at the implications and opportunities for including CO_2 in an ISD model: CO_2 can accelerate plant growth, plants can sequester the CO_2 as they feed on and recycle fish wastes, fish can eat plant and algae nutrients grown with the help of concentrated CO_2. This is a somewhat oversimplified explanation of how that self-contained process would work, but you can get the general idea of the potential as it relates to creating a closed loop system. ISD therefore becomes a major consideration and potential tool as we address the industrial releases of "greenhouse gases" and strategies as to how we reduce and utilize those waste streams.

Chapter Sixteen

Water, Water Everywhere but Not A Drop to Drink

"No water, no life. No blue, no green." ~ **Sylvia Earle**

Nothing is more essential to life, a healthy environment, and personal health than fresh, clean water. The human body requires between 1.8 and 4 liters per day depending on size, age, activity level and location to remain in balance. Yet it is projected that within a 10-year time frame (by 2025)13 of 20 people living on this planet will either lack sufficient potable water for their personal daily requirements or they will be limited to water sources that are too contaminated to be considered safe to drink. A lack of fresh water will most assuredly lead to regional agricultural collapse, mass migration of thirsty populations, abandonment of valuable infrastructure, increases in water related deaths and illnesses, and increased regional tensions for remaining water rights. Viewed from that perspective this is a rather sobering statistic.

Yet as pressing an issue as this is most governments have seemingly addressed this looming catastrophe with the courage of an Ostrich. That is, they have stuck their collective heads in the ground hoping it would just go away. This is wishful thinking at best. The cost to replace the deteriorating water and sanitation infrastructure of industrialized countries may be as high as $200 billion a year. Leakage of untreated and treated water from pipes reduces access to water. Leakage rates of 50% are not uncommon in urban systems. [50] More than ever before in our long history, water management will require higher levels of management and planning if we are to prosper in the 21st century.

Fresh water for the most part has always been a "free" resource. After all, it falls from the sky and if you are lucky enough to live next to a spring, stream, lake, or similar body of water you could always just take what you need when you needed it. That being said only 0.003% of total water available globally is accessible, fresh and unpolluted. [51] With the advent of modern societies, commercial agriculture, pollution, and increasing population density, naturally occurring clean water resources have been stretched beyond their limits. As with all resources it is a matter of how much you need, how much is available, how efficiently you manage and use those resources, and how clever you are in creating new supplies. With catastrophic shortages and droughts becoming common place around the world, solutions to this huge challenge cannot come fast enough.

In terms of availability and cost, clean fresh water may well be the "new oil" of the 21st century. When in need, desperate people will pay almost anything for a drink of water. As discussed earlier, access to sufficient fresh water is on track to become first major issue relating to global sustainability that directly affects regions and their ability to support a local population. Therefore, a strategy to assure long term access and continuity of needed water resources are critical to any sustainability plans and considerations.

From a usage perspective, global agriculture accounts for 92% of freshwater consumption globally. [52] For the greater part of modern history improvements of storage models (dams, levees, cisterns, reservoirs, wells) and irrigation distribution systems has been the singular focus of agrarian societies. Additionally, modern populations are more and more concentrated in cities making resource availability and efficient distribution critical to the viability and maintenance of those urban centers. The design and implementation of current freshwater infrastructure assumed at the time of construction a consistent, dependable, renewable annual supply. With climate change, its impact on changing hydrologic patterns, pollution, and increasing annual demand, these systems in many areas of the world are, or will soon be obsolete.

Let's start out with some basic facts. There is more than enough fresh water on this planet to support hundreds of times our current global population. If one also accounts for ocean water and the potential for desalination, or harvesting atmospheric moisture there is virtually a limitless amount of water available to solve any issues we might have with sufficient supplies. So, this challenge is not about resource availability. The challenge lies in understanding the changing nature of global hydrologic patterns as they relate to climate change, a population's specific proximity to existing supplies, and intelligent management of those available local resources. Let's examine some of the options and strategies we will have to employ in the coming years to address this rapidly evolving issue so critical to our survival and prosperity.

William Sosinsky

Desalination

Our Oceans account for 72% of our global surface area and over 97% of our planetary water by volume. Yet because of its salinity and mineral content ocean water is unfit to drink or for use as an irrigation source for agriculture. By simply removing those solids sea water becomes as potable and useable as the freshest land-based sources. Currently 40% of the world's population lives within 60 miles of an ocean such that desalination offers great potential to offset much of our freshwater demands.

The expenses associated with desalination include facility construction, maintenance, and ongoing production costs. This is generally more costly than other alternatives which include sourcing water from lakes, rivers, aquifers, water recycling, or saved through conservation measures. Those sources however are not always available. With the huge quantities of fresh water most farms and people require to function on a daily basis desalination plants can be enormous, use copious amounts of power, and can be extremely expensive to build. In many cases it is the best last option for certain regions and countries, particularly where sufficient infrastructure funds are available and there is critical need such as the case in the Arab Gulf States and California.

There are basically two main technical applications used in desalination (vacuum distillation and reverse osmosis). Of the two, reverse osmosis is less expensive. One of the challenges with reverse osmosis is it creates "pure" water completely lacking in minerals as it is essentially distilled. This can have a long-term impact on bone and tissue health as the distilled water leeches' minerals from the body once it is ingested. As a consequence, minerals from the body once it is ingested. As a consequence, the water needs to be treated with mineral additives if it is to be used as a person's primary source of drinking water over a long-time frame. Most of the desalination plants currently in operation around the world add those minerals before the water is released for consumption.

With the cost of fresh water rising as a result of need and increasing scarcity desalination is now becoming the popular choice for those governments that can afford to build such facilities. One of the environmental concerns associated with desalination is the residue brine that is left over from the process which is heavy in concentrated salts. Directly reintroduced back into the ocean it can settle to the sea floor and harm aquatic life. Solving the issue of safe brine reuse/disposal and finding energy sources that are clean, renewable, and inexpensive will go a long way towards encouraging additional desalination capacity throughout the world. This would in turn address much of our current global fresh water requirements.

Atmospheric Harvesting

Earth's atmosphere is full of moisture. At any particular moment there are over 3,100 cubic miles of water floating through the air. Sometimes that moisture comes down to the surface as rain, snow, sleet, or dew and sometimes it just stays in the air as suspended gaseous molecules of H2O. A new focus has arisen as of late looking to tap that airborne moisture as a dependable water source. A main advantage to capturing atmospheric water is that it is being constantly regenerated making it the most renewable of resources when it comes to long term sustainability.

Practically everywhere in the world with very few exceptions harvesting "ambient" moisture works as a viable collection strategy. In climates where relative humidity runs as low as 25-30% such as the Australian outback or the American Southwest this can still be a life empowering option. Harvesting atmospheric water is not a new concept. Cultures as old as the Incas used "fog fences" to help condense morning dew which was then stored in cisterns to be used as their fresh water supply. That same simple method is still being employed in many places throughout the developing world as a cheap way of capturing this needed resource.

More recently Atmospheric Water Generators or (AWG's) have been developed to help supply potable water needs in otherwise resource poor environments. With AWG technology water vapor is either condensed by passing it over cooling coils which lowers it below its dew point, or exposing the moisture filled air to desiccants. It is then passed through a purification stage where it is then stored in a holding tank. Systems large enough to supply water for a community or small enough for a single home are being marketed heavily these days but tend to be expensive. This form of water harvesting can also require lots of energy and be somewhat costly to run. That being said prices are coming down with new system improvements and it is becoming a much more affordable option. As with reverse osmosis, atmospheric water is basically distilled and needs to have minerals put back into the solution in order for it to be a long-term source for drinking water.

Water Recycling and Reclamation

Let's face it. All water is basically recycled water. When we talk about recycled or reclaimed water, we are referring to that water which is extracted from a previously used source or in this case wastewater. The definition of reclaimed water, as defined by Levine and Asano, is "The end product of wastewater reclamation that meets water quality requirements for biodegradable materials, suspended matter and pathogens." [53] Simply stated, reclaimed water is water that is used more than one time before it passes back into the natural water cycle. Scientifically-proven advances in water technology allow communities to reuse water for many different purposes, including industrial, irrigation, and drinking. The water is treated differently depending upon the source and use of the water and how it gets delivered. [54]

The practice of recycling or reclaiming water is gaining in popularity around the world in areas desperate for new resources as a consequence of increasing demand and limited reserves that have few better options. Recycling is generally the next step after communities have already instituted local and regional conservation programs and are looking at additional ways to make use of already existing supplies.

Sewage and various industrial operations use huge amounts of water to both transport waste and as part of the production process. Those waste streams contain a variety of components which range from downright unappetizing to extremely toxic and dangerous. Whereas water in this "processed" state is generally not safe to reuse, there are several recovery methods that once employed can extract clean and potable water from those waste streams.

Currently the most common application for recycled water is for reuse in industrial cooling processes or as a source for crop and landscape irrigation. This water is sold to commercial users at a reduced rate to encourage their participation and usage and is often delivered through a piping/distribution system that runs parallel to those carrying non-recycled sources. Because the water used this way is only treated to a preliminary stage, the recycled water generally contains phosphates and nitrogen which bring an added benefit to farmers and landscape end users as they enhance soil nutrients.

More and more however communities are looking towards the recycled/reclaimed option to provide drinking water for their constituents. Recycled water used in this manner requires further filtering and treatment before it is considered safe enough to drink or "potable". Generally, water reused for drinking goes through a reverse osmosis process and ultraviolet disinfection before it re-enters the water supply. In the developing world poorer communities are beginning to recycle questionable water sources by storing that water in clear glass or plastic containers on their rooftops. There the sun's natural ultraviolet radiation kills the organic matter/pathogens present in that water source. Whereas this does not remove any chemicals, heavy metals, or pharmaceuticals that may be present in that water it can certainly make water that is not polluted with those components relatively safe to drink. This ends up being viable option when there are no other alternatives available.

Water Aquifers Beneath the Continental Shelf

One of the very positive by-products of ocean oil exploration off our coastlines has been the discovery of huge reserves of fresh water locked in aquifers below portions of the continental shelves. It seems that about 20,000 years ago during our last ice age when ocean levels were much lower rain and snow melt collected in the sediments below the coastal plains forming huge water deposits. Though the quality varies from pristine to slightly brackish, these water sources are much "cleaner" and considered fresh requiring far less processing and desalination then ocean water to make them potable.

The existence of vast freshwater reserves trapped beneath the ocean floor could sustain future generations as current sources dwindle. Vincent Post, from Australia's Flinders University, said that an estimated 500,000 cubic kilometres (120,000 cubic miles) of low-salinity water had been found buried beneath the seabed on continental shelves off Australia, China, North America and South Africa. "The volume of this water resource is a hundred times greater than the amount we have extracted from the Earth's sub-surface in the past century since 1900" [55]

Massive and expensive drilling operations would be needed to access these caches as well as land-based treatment facilities to filter and improve the water quality. Additionally, as consumption increases those reserves would rapidly start to diminish with no chance of being recharged. In that regard they are not renewable. Whereas these reserves are extensive they are ultimately finite. Perhaps their best use would be as a temporary bridge until we are able to employ better options or for use in times of extreme need or drought. My fear is that our uncontrolled access and ensuing dependency on these reserves will ultimately result in the same overuse and mismanagement we have inflicted on our land-based aquifers.

Advanced Water Distribution Models

Since the beginning of civilization mankind has worked to move fresh water from one place to another. Modern cities have always been located in close proximity to their main water sources or adjacent to neighboring watersheds in order to facilitate the distribution of that critical resource. Farms have evolved over time to follow river systems and inland bodies of water where they could redirect that fresh water into irrigation networks. With the onset of climate change and the shift in hydrologic patterns those models are quickly becoming obsolete in the light of reduced supply and increasing demand. If we are to maintain our population and support some of the massive urban infrastructure, we have built in our recent past then the 21st century is likely to see the most ambitious water distribution projects in human history.

The fact is that the majority of the world's fresh water reserves are encapsulated in ice sheets, glaciers, and jungle rivers in areas that are sparsely populated at best. Imagine if we could just access the Greenland or Antarctic Ice Sheets, draw water from the Amazon River, or tap into Lake Baikal and distribute those resources more thoroughly? We could then put a huge dent in the demand side of the water issues we are now facing. The reality is our major population concentrations tend to be in warmer more temperate regions dependent on river systems that are fed by dependable seasonal hydrologic patterns or snow melt and distant glaciers in far off mountain chains. Once those rain patterns are disrupted, it stops snowing, and the glaciers melt things can get bad quickly. Such is the dilemma we are currently facing.

Water like oil is a liquid that can be transported in larger quantities through pipelines, aqueducts, and by transports such as trains and seagoing tankers. Because daily demand is constant and the quantities needed to satisfy that demand so extreme the logistics of delivering water from one remote location to an area of need can be daunting. Even if there is the will to access far away water resources, the cost and engineering challenges are enormous and require planning, financing, and implementation on a historic scale to implement. Countries that have the resolve, financial and technical ability should be able to manage critical portions of their demand with enough lead time and advance planning in anticipation of shortages. So far that foresight and will has not been apparent and it is my opinion that we will not see these projects come about until we have an example or several examples of major urban centers collapsing around the world due to a lack of water resources such that governments start planning for these largest of public works projects.

Additionally, water tends to be a local resource. Globally there is an uneven distribution of fresh water. While some countries have an abundant supply of fresh water, others do not have as much. For example, Canada has 20% of the world's fresh water supply, while India has only 10% of the world's fresh water supply, even though India's population is more than 30 times larger than that of Canada. [56] Countries and regions in need may have to cross over borders to access those sources. Such needs and issues are the things wars are fought over. An evolved cooperative environment and concept of sharing basic assets will have to win the day

if these challenges are going to be met in the decades ahead.

Localized Purification and Storage

Most local rainwater in developed environments never makes it into water distribution systems or water storage. Those waters generally flow directly into sewer systems or local streams as runoff. Great quantities of water may flow out of downspouts or drain off highway systems for example during a downpour creating an opportunity to collect and manage those resources before they disburse or get seriously polluted.

There are newer technologies currently being tested that can filter in real time runoff from highways allowing them to be collected for storage and reuse. Employing this strategy would be of immense value in developed countries looking for additional ways to increase water availability. Such a concept could be incorporated into future road and highway designs during construction or retrofitted into existing transportation systems where it makes sense. Currently this kind of system is being tested in California where water issues related to drought are increasing yearly.

For individual homes and buildings water could be regularly captured and stored in on-site cisterns or barrels to create a separate supply for landscape and general "grey" water usage. In an age where every drop counts these simple methods of collection may well play an important role in reducing dependence on conventional water reserves.

21st Century Farming

As stated at the beginning of this chapter the single largest draw on water usage is agriculture. It would therefore make sense that if we are attempting to rebalance our sustainable use of water, we should start by creating strategies for farms and livestock operations that make the most efficient use of this finite resource.

The water footprint of a country is related to what its people eat. In 1993, Professor John Allan (2008 Stockholm Water Prize Laureate), strikingly demonstrated this by introducing the "virtual water" concept, [57,58] which measures how water is embedded in the production and trade of food and other products. For example, it is a common thought that the water involved in a cup of coffee is just the water in the cup. [57] There is actually 140 litres of water involved. The 140 litres of water is the amount of water that was used to grow, produce, package, and ship the coffee beans. [57] A hamburger needs an estimated 2,400 litres of water. This hidden water is technically called virtual water. [57] Therefore, eating a lot of meat means a large water footprint. The more food comes from irrigated land, the larger is the water footprint Additionally, an individual's daily diet of fruits, vegetable. Additionally, an individual's daily diet of fruits, vegetables and grains requires more than 1,500 litres (396.3 US gal) of water, as compared to 3,400 litres (898.2 US gal) needed for a daily diet rich in animal protein. [59]

Crops lose a tremendous quantity of water through evapotranspiration. Exposed to the open air, heat, and wind water is drawn from the crops and surrounding ground requiring robust and constant irrigation to maintain their vitality and moisture content. As we will examine in the following chapter indoor farming is going to become a major area of growth in the near future. Aside from increased square foot production and better control of crop growth rates, nutrient content, and exposure to chemicals, a huge reduction in the use of water is a key benefit of this approach.

With an indoor farm that has tight controls over its envelope essentially the only water that leaves the facility is that which is held within the fruit, vegetable, grain, or herb. This can amount to a 95% efficiency savings in the amount of water needed to bring that crop to maturity. Considering the nature of changing hydrologic rain patterns globally and increasing demand a network of these types of facilities can serve as a failsafe protection locally against prolonged droughts and crop collapse as a result of diminishing water resources.

Where such facilities are not employed due to choose or lack of development funds, conventional farmers choosing to grow crops that utilize less water per produced fruit, vegetable or grain is a smart strategy. Corn as an example uses prodigious quantities of water as compared to many varieties of wheat. Additionally, although there is much controversy and resistance to genetically modified crops (GMOs) being introduced globally. The use of drought resistant and water conserving varieties of plants are a valuable contributor to an overall water management strategy. From this perspective perhaps, all GMOs are not necessarily bad.

Finally, meat is being consumed in increasing quantities globally as the population grows and standards of living improve. Getting people to change their tastes and expectations is difficult. The costs of these commodities are bound to increase in price precipitously as those costs for production are reflected more and more in the market place. Finding varieties of protein to replace those more taxing to the environment and to local water supplies are likely to be a constant theme throughout the 21st century. Indoor fish farming is one way to greatly reduce that ratio of water use as it relates to protein production. The fact that fish farming can be seamlessly integrated into a diversified ISD indoor farming production facility makes this potential solution something that has great possibilities in the years ahead.

Water Section Conclusion

Ultimately the critical empowering element to managing water supplies long term may come down to cheap, clean, abundant energy. There is however much that can be done in terms of conservation, efficiency, and usage strategies in the short term that can have a substantial impact. All those options should be instituted by governments as early as is possible to help offset the extreme current imbalance between need and supply that is likely to increase over the next few decades. Once the energy factor is solved desalination and atmospheric condensing becomes a limitless, renewable option. That should eliminate the concern that our population will have adequate potable and fresh water for future generations.

Chapter Seventeen

Remember When Food was Plentiful?

"There are people in the world so hungry, that God cannot appear to them except in the form of bread." ~ **Mahatma Gandhi**

My parents weren't rich but somehow, we never ever worried about having enough to eat. I grew up like many kids in a culture where food was the center of all our social gatherings. Holidays and special occasions were marked by celebrations centered around specially prepared dishes and baked goods. I don't have a memory of my childhood where some exotic food or treat wasn't part of that flash back. This was all part of a history and tradition that had been passed down through generations.

These days I live in New York City. I can't remember a time where there were more options as to what to eat and more places to get whatever it is you crave 24 hours a day. You find restaurants on every corner with twenty different choices on every block. There are supermarkets, delis, bodegas, food courts, street hawkers, vending machines, and specialty trucks. You can drive up in a car and seconds later the food appears at a window. If you don't feel like going out then you can go online or use a smartphone app and whatever you desire shows up at your door as if by magic. The wealthy developed world has gotten use to the good life. From a perspective of selection, accessibility, and instant gratification our relationship with food has never been better. Try telling the average person that all this is about to end forever and they look at you as if you are crazy. How can you blame them?

The fact is we are burning through our food producing potential and resources at an unsustainable rate. Those stocks that we depend on will inevitably collapse in the years ahead if we continue to produce and consume at our current pace employing our standard strategies. For the time being food experts can claim we have enough food to feed everyone on the planet and our only issues are with distribution and unintended waste. Those are the "current" facts. That being said I see no plan to sustainably manage the remaining stocks of ocean fish, no plan that is stemming the loss of our bees, no strategy for maintaining and recapturing our diminishing phosphorous reserves, replenishing our disappearing aquifers and melting glaciers, and no plan for curtailing our exploding population with their ever-increasing appetite… and those are just some of the main issues. It is a perfect storm of converging trend lines the likes of which we have never faced as a species.

Any sane individual can look at the sands running out of an hour glass and predict the eventual outcome. Yet we are doing close to nothing to deal with these critical issues. As a consequence of short-term and short-sighted corporate self-interest supported by paid-off political hand puppets our ignorance, inaction, and lack of courage will be our epitaph. If the 21st century is going to be about food and our inability to manage our finite global resources, our arrogance and faith in those we blindly believe will Sheppard us through these challenges will be its cause.

Our hunger will drive us to decimate and extinct our remaining stocks of endangered higher mammals as we search the wilderness for "bush meat" killing anything and everything for that next meal. Elephants, tigers, lions, and countless other species will be the things you read about in books. If you are fortunate enough you may be able pay the price to see the last remaining specimens in zoos in the few rich and isolated countries that will be able maintain their food production efficacy. Whales, sea lions, dolphins, and countless other sea mammals and larger fish will disappear as they are starved to extinction unable to find the schools of fish and sea animals that they formally fed upon.

Most meat and large wild fish will be considered "luxury" items reserved for special occasions or available only to the rich. McDonalds will no longer be able to sell cheap hamburgers because of their inability to access beef supplies. Fruits, vegetables, and nuts will be unimaginably expensive. The diets of those in the developed world will be austere and limited to whatever proteins, carbs, and produce are available at the market day to day and season and season. Many countries will issue food rationing cards restricting individuals and families as to how much of certain food stocks you are allowed to buy at any one time or for any particular period. Obese societies, all-you-can-eat buffets, and food eating contests will be the stuff of legend.

The news will be filled with stories of countries in Africa and Asia collapsing under the weight of starving populations. Wars and regional conflicts will break out like wild fires as roaming bands of desperate, starving masses leave their borders to search for food in their neighbors' lands. Old scores will be settled and weapons we hoped would never be used will be used. Great walls and fences will be constructed along borders. National armies will be relegated to guarding those walls, patrolling remaining coastal fisheries, and overseeing the remaining food production and distribution centers to ensure supplies are not pilfered. The U.N, Red Cross, and FEMA will not be sending out planes or showing up with trucks filled with bags of food to those in need leaving them to starve.

In the more developed and stable societies it will be common place for people to commit crimes and kill for extra food. Politicians will run for office on food management platforms and people will be suspicious of anyone who is over-weight. Recording artists will be singing songs about feeding our families instead of feeding the world.

As much as I hope this will not be our future, we must prepare ourselves for such eventualities if we fail to act preemptively to avoid these potential consequences. That being said most, if not all of that which I have speculated about in the previous few paragraphs are avoidable if we have the will and foresight to organize and act. Our success will not be measured by the quantity of food we can produce, but rather by the balance we can strike between our consumptive needs and the healthful management of our remaining resources. The fact that this will require not just a technical solution but substantive changes in preconditioned human behavior and understanding to fully implement makes it all the more challenging. In the following sections I will define an outline for us to rebalance our approach to feeding the human race examining the specific challenges and rational behind each step. Ultimately it will be our ability to innovate and a permanent change in human perspective and behavior that will determine the scope of our success.

Nutrition Overview

Critical to the health of any human being is proper nutrition. An insufficient balance of necessary proteins, fats, carbohydrates, vitamins, and minerals will eventually lead to malnutrition. When that imbalance becomes severe enough the result is starvation. Wikipedia defines starvation as a severe deficiency in caloric energy intake! It is the most extreme form of malnutrition. In humans, prolonged starvation can cause permanent organ damage [60] and eventually, death. The term inanition refers to the symptoms and effects of starvation.

According to the World Health Organization, hunger is the single gravest threat to the world's public health. [61] The WHO also states that malnutrition is by far the biggest contributor to child mortality, present in half of all cases. [61] Undernutrition is a contributory factor in the death of 3.1 million children under five every year. [62] Figures on actual starvation are difficult to come by, but according to the Food and Agriculture Organization, the less severe condition of undernourishment currently affects about 842 million people, or about one in eight (12.5%) people in the world population. [63]

A poor diet may have an injurious impact on health, causing deficiency diseases such as blindness, anemia, scurvy, preterm birth, stillbirth and cretinism; [64] health-threatening conditions like obesity[65,66] and metabolic syndrome; [67] and such common chronic systemic diseases as cardiovascular disease, [68,69] diabetes, [70,71] and osteoporosis. [72,73,74]

One of our key goals as we move into the 21st Century must be to eliminate malnutrition and starvation to ensure the lifelong and healthful nutritional needs of every human being wherever they live on this planet. This objective is going to increase in difficulty and scope on an unprecedented scale in the coming decades. It will require innovative and evolutionary concepts and well-orchestrated strategies if we are to respond effectively.

For the past several decades great strides forward have been taken to reduce and eliminate hunger throughout the world producing impressive percentage gains in the reduction of numbers of people suffering. These efforts unfortunately have all too often relied on outside inputs of resources and over-production in order to facilitate those gains and not enough on local empowerment. Ominously the trend towards eliminating global hunger appears to be reversing. Rising food prices, crop failures, and an unprecedented change in global weather patterns have greatly impacted both global production levels and affordability of basic food staples. This has been especially impactful in poorer developing nations.

Additionally, many larger developed nations for the very first time in the modern era have to import that which they used to grow at home and devise strategies that out of necessity must rely heavily on foreign resources for their long-term base nutritional needs. Lands larger in their combined size than France have been leased in Africa alone in just the past few years by the U.S, China, and the European Union specifically for this purpose. It is only a matter of time and ultimately inevitable that we collapse our current system if we stay this course.

William Sosinsky

The Challenges we Must Overcome

As discussed earlier, there is a veritable laundry list of specific challenges we need to address to start turning things around. Some are simpler and more straight forward then others. Some require strength of will, some require innovation, some require we look at ourselves and ask what is important? What do we stand for as a people? Do we truly care about our fellow man and our environment? Are we just savages mesmerized by short term self-interest and are we incapable of making decisions and working together collaboratively for our collective health and well-being?

In that sense the next few decades are going to be the most exciting and impactful period in homo-sapiens evolution. I could not be happier and looking more forward than to be alive to witness this. We will either evolve together and get this right or nature and god will have their way with us as we descend into a new dark age. This is the stuff epic films are made of and this story is all but guaranteed. Hopefully there will be popcorn!

But before the popcorn comes the work. How will we make up for our lost pollinators? How can we protect our crops from the unexpected changes in weather patterns and seasonal regularity they depend on? When will we be able to balance out the water issue? Where will the basic nutrients we (and our food) depend on come from?

Wild organisms are the critical and most often ignored aspect of a healthy and vibrant farm ecosystem. For instance, animal dug provides essential nutrients which are broken down by flies and beetles such that they enrich the dirt. Forests prevent soil erosion, capture and store water, regulate water flow, and increase humidity supporting the local hydrologic rain patterns. Forest canopies are the homes to birds which eat insect pests. Worms, millipedes, and many other small insects, animals, and bacteria are responsible for soil formation. Finally, bees and other insects and mammals are responsible for pollinating plants.

Modern commercial farming destroys this synergistic relationship by removing and clear-cutting neighboring forests reducing local ecosystem biodiversity. This is critical habitat for the health of essential pollinators as it provides a variety of plants to feed on when the food crops are not flowering. Additionally, forest removal reduces local humidity disturbing natural rain patterns while also removing the home for the predatory bird population needed to control pests. The massive tilling and shade removal expose the soils to direct solar radiance raising the soil temperature to a point where it loses its ability to maintain water and kills off the soil forming animals and insects essential for soil health. Pesticides poison the remaining pollinators while herbicides eliminate and remove critical bacteria from the soil finishing the job the increased solar radiance started leaving the soil nutrient deficient.

The result is a system that in the short run may produce higher crop concentrations and yields through the massive use of fertilizers, chemicals, and water resources but is completely reliant on this un-natural and unsustainable support system for its long-term productivity. Today the great majority of our global commercial farming is managed just this way having abandoned conventional logic by treating our lands like factory floors instead of living ecosystems. By eradicating the naturally supportive organisms and eco-structure that make sustainable farming possible modern farming practices essentially undermines themselves. So how do we reverse these practices and re-establish a balanced and sustainable strategy for managing our farm lands?

Lost pollinators; this is a difficult problem to solve. The average person is blissfully ignorant to just how important our bees are. They are the tireless workers of the insect kingdom to which we owe the debt of bringing our crops to maturity. Bees provide the critical pollination step that allows the fruits, vegetables, nuts and grains to grow. It is hard to imagine the volume of effort that would be required to replace their essential and apparently under-appreciated efforts. Although plants can also be pollinated by wind, bats, flies, butterflies, and a variety of other flying insects those species are responsible for but a small fraction of how much bees contribute to this process. Many of those species are in decline as well adding to the problem.

Several years ago, in southwest China the overuse of pesticides led to the complete collapse of their bee population. In order to bring in their Pear and Apple crops workers are forced to collect the pollen in jars and then reapply the pollen to the flowers with a paint brush in order for the trees to pollinate. As Pears and Apples are considered a high value crop in China this makes sense. This approach however would never be practical and would be nearly impossible to repeat on a global basis. There are just not enough people to do the jobs the bees do.

The reality is losing our bees is unthinkable and they would be almost impossible to replace. To help our pollinators prosper we will have to employ common sense planning, labor and innovation in equal quantities. One strategy that may help is to plant rows of wild flowers integrated into crop formations to provide alternate feeding options for the bees while the food crops mature. Another option is to plant a variety of trees (fruit) crops integrated into those fields for the same purpose. This would also help by providing useful shade, increased humidity and water retention, as well as homes for pest removing bird populations. A third option is to leave large tracks of native forests and jungle undisturbed parallel to farming operations and abandon the current "clear cut" mentality that is destroying these regions.

In any case we need to re-evaluate our use of pesticides and consider the long-term damage and impact they are having on the health of these ecosystems and the bees in particular. What most people fail to realize is that the pesticide/herbicide industry grew out of the chemical weapons programs of world war two. When the war was over, they had to find uses for all these advanced, complex, and highly toxic chemicals and so the pesticide/herbicide industry was formed. Since then we have been treating our essential birds, insects, and bacteria (and bees) like concentration camp inmates.

There is also the question of how long-term exposure to these chemicals is impacting the health of the people who eat those crops...which is basically everyone. Residues of these chemicals have shown up throughout our food chain even when our food is raised to be so–called "organic". Commercially used pesticide/herbicides such as DDT, Paraquat, Glyphosate and many others have basically played Russian roulette with our health for decades while having huge impacts on the environment and many animal species. Everything from cancer to increased cases of genetic variations such as autism has been blamed on their use. Considering the volatility and toxicity of these chemicals it is no secret as to why there is ample cause for concern.

If we lose the bees our options will become increasingly limited. Robotic pollinators or hand-held machines that perform the same function as the bees are an option going forward when and if they are invented. Considering what the bees do for free with extreme detail, tenacity and accuracy, it would be tragic if it gets to that point. That being said we would still see a dramatic reduction in crop yields and the related production costs would soar making those foods that much more expensive and out of reach of the poor. It is my opinion that unless we plan on managing all our fruit, vegetable, and nut crops on a factory level where accessibility to those crops are determined by wealth and social position rather than need, we must to do everything within our power to save the bees. Supporting those ongoing efforts immediately with extreme focus and the necessary financial commitment cannot happen soon enough.

Managing our Soil

We are killing our soil. That is to say that we are creating conditions whereby increased solar exposure, overuse and over-tilling, erosion, and a constant diet of pesticides and herbicides are killing the animals, insects, and bacteria that keep the soil productive. Healthy soils are alive with a mixture of living organisms. Those entities are continuously working to manage the conversion of base elements and inorganic soil components into nutrients that support healthy plant growth. Once those organisms are removed the soil becomes an almost sterile medium. That lifeless dirt then requires constant inputs of outside resources in order to provide the basic function of providing an environment where plants can grow…and we are running out of those resources. That pretty much sums up our global commercial agriculture management strategy.

Soil is the mixture of minerals, organic matter, gases, liquids, and countless organisms that together support plant life. Two general classes are topsoil and subsoil. Soil is a natural body that exists as part of the pedosphere and which performs four important functions: it is a medium for plant growth; it is a means of water storage, supply and purification; it is a modifier of the atmosphere of Earth; and it is a habitat for organisms all of which modify the soil.

Soil is considered to be the "skin of the earth" with interfaces between the lithosphere, hydrosphere, atmosphere of Earth, and biosphere. [75] Soil consists of a solid phase (minerals and organic matter) as well as a porous phase that holds gases and water. [76,77,78]

Modern farming has ushered in an age of unimaginably large operations as mechanized production has spread throughout the world. Supported by pesticides and herbicides that were once hailed as miracle solutions productivity has exploded providing the fuel for what is now unsustainable population growth. This in turn has put unprecedented pressure on the soil to produce more and more crops to support those additional numbers. Additionally, as humankind has expanded former productive farmlands have been converted to other uses such as commercial development and living space further reducing available tillable lands.

Humankind has known for centuries that when soil is overused and mismanaged it becomes less and less productive. The stories of poor soil management fill history books and have been the cause of untold suffering. Whether it is a "dust bowl" covering depression era America, or the collapse of a whole civilization such as occurred with the Mayans, poor soil has dramatically impacted societies through the ages. Whereas the Dust Bowl was a matter of poor farming practices it is thought that the Mayans may have led to their demise due to deforestation. In both cases the soils stopped producing and led to a system collapse of their agricultural infrastructure. What we are now seeing on a global scale is capable of doing the same thing to our modern civilizations.

Deforestation is the permanent destruction of a forest and a huge threat to our healthy soils and the health of our planet. When tropical rain forests (i.e.-The Amazon, Indonesia, Madagascar, and Congo) are cleared for their wood, for fuel, for use as farmland or as grazing space for livestock, or for living space or other purposes the soil is gravely damaged. To start with tropical rain forests, have a very thin "productive" layer of soil as the majority of plants live on a thin deposit of nutrient rich dirt. Exposed to high levels of heat from the near equatorial sun organism's native to the soil die. With the loss of trees, plants and their root systems the soil loses its capacity to store water and then becomes vulnerable to erosion. An estimated 18 million acres (7.3 million hectares) of forest, which is roughly the size of the country of Panama, are lost each year, according to the United Nations' Food and Agriculture Organization (FAO). [79]This is turn creates large expanding tropical deserts bleeding soil into formally clear running rivers and streams. Approximately half of our global rain forests have already been permanently lost to deforestation this way and this trend is increasing both in size and speed. Along with Ocean based algae these resources comprise the lungs of our planet producing the very oxygen we need to breathe and we are wiping them out.

Frontpage | Shutterstock   Institute for Humane Education

In more temperate regions and in more developed countries the over-tilling and over-use of soils have had a similar impact. Whereas better farming and soil management practices have taken hold over the decades there is still an unhealthy reliance on fertilizers, pesticides, and herbicides to bring in increasingly larger annual crops. When you combine extreme need and mechanized capabilities with equally poor farming practices as is the case with countries like China, Indonesia, and India for example, the destructive impacts are horrendous.

Additionally, the need for irrigation and a lack of clean water reserves pushes many countries to rely on unsafe and polluted sources such as sewage and industrial runoff for those purposes. As a result, toxins start accumulating in the soil and are transferred to the produce and livestock we consume. Heavy metals, pharmaceuticals, and the aforementioned pesticides and herbicides then start to concentrate in our bodies and over time can have a pronounced impact on our health. This desperate need to produce more and more food has forced many societies to completely disregard and ignore these consequences as they struggle to meet consumption demand.

In order to start reversing our current impact on our soils and to ensure the long-term health and productivity of our farming system globally there are a number of strategies we must start employing immediately. First is rather obvious; we must stop cutting down our irreplaceable and necessary forests and jungles. Their critical and complex role in our planet's health cannot be replaced or overstated.

Once lost, they are gone forever in terms of how that loss relates to our foreseeable future. Governments around the world need to be better educated as to the long-term ramifications of these practices and all efforts must be undertaken as soon as possible to halt these practices once and for all.

Secondly, we must educate farmers and initiate efforts to both protect remaining soils and stop erosion using more intelligent farming practices and erosion control methods. Once you get down to rock and lose those top soils the process of rebuilding and reconditioning the remaining dirt becomes near impossible. It can take centuries to build up a soil base and the value of our remaining soil resources cannot be stated more emphatically. When our food resources start to decline and populations are starving, we will not have centuries to figure out how we are going to feed them.

Next farmers will have to take an active role rebuilding the organic base to the soils they farm by growing and supplementing those components on their farms. This must be a common practice that is undertaken concurrent with producing their main crops to provide the "natural" means for nutrient assimilation. Those organisms and key elements are necessary if they are to feed their crops without the excessive use of fertilizer. "Life" must be brought back to the soil and the practice of using massive amounts of herbicides to control weeds must come to an end. In this particular case advanced GMO crops may have a critical and valuable role to play.

New methods and strategies for phosphate recovery and reuse must be an integral part of every agriculture operation. Application control methods, recycling, and reuse of phosphorus must be core considerations and practiced henceforth. If we do not quickly come to terms with our careless use and disposal of "waste" phosphorous we are headed for disaster. ISD methods of incorporating existing phosphorous rich waste streams into the direct support of our regional agriculture models must be explored, designed and implemented with all due haste.

Lastly, we must replace, diversify, and expand global crop production when and where needed by the implementation of newly developed 21st century farming technologies. These innovations would include such advanced approaches as indoor aeroponic and aquaponic farming, and algae/aquaculture production as core components to conventional agricultural operations. This becomes necessary in order to insure adequate regional nutritional needs while reducing pressure on the currently overtaxed natural environment. By shifting a substantial portion of a farms production to high density indoor farming, it will allow farmers a window of time/opportunity such that they can work on rebuilding the vitality of the soils they until.

The Farm of the Future

In keeping with that last thought, let's look at some of the ways farms and farm production are likely to change as we head into this century.

Humankind is on the verge of a new era when it comes to raising food. We now have the means and knowledge necessary to grow some key crops in much higher densities then conventional farms indoors using tiered growing surfaces. The advantages of indoor farming are several. First, they allow for extremely high densities of produce to be grown in a relatively small space. In this production scenario aeroponic and hydroponic methods of delivering nutrients are supported by specifically tuned LED lights. This way plant development and growth can be controlled with great accuracy and is highly reliable in terms of the timeframes required for the plants to reach maturity. As no soil is required during cultivation water is the medium used for nutrient delivery. This allows for specific quantities of nutrients to be administered with little or no waste. The same is true for water usage if the enclosure has a well-maintained envelope. Only the moisture contained in the plant is removed from the facility upon harvesting. The end result is an optimally nutritious end product raised in the shortest dependable timeframe with little or no need for pesticides or herbicides.

Credit   Urban Organics Newsweek May 2015

Indoor farming however does not come without its challenges. It is by nature energy intensive so the cost of electricity plays an important role in the financial viability of any particular operation. The same can be said for the initial capital investment required to build a facility. Ultimately market demand and pricing play key roles in determining the viability of creating such a production structure and the kinds of crops to be raised. Additionally, not all crops can be harvested indoors using these techniques. Species that require pollination offer a special challenge that would require innovation in order for them to be raised in an enclosed facility. The possibility of keeping bee populations captive within these structures or developing the means by which robotic pollination is possible could provide answers to this particular challenge

In addition to farmers having to take on the added responsibility of providing the base nutrients and organic additives to rebuild and maintain healthy soil onsite, similar production will offer them a diversified option in creating other profitable crops. Algae production will become much more of a staple and core farming crop for conventional agricultural operations in the years ahead. The ability of algae to grow and increase in mass in short time frames producing useful and valuable end products in unrivaled in the plant and animal kingdom.

Another crop which some people may find a bit surprising which will blossom in the coming years will be insects and insect protein. Currently insects make up a sizable proportion of the protein intake in several Asian and African countries. Insects such as locusts, grasshoppers, grubs, and spiders have many of the same characteristics as algae in their ability to grow quickly and produce high quality protein and nutrients with limited effort and resource consumption. In the West, more and more people are trying insects for the first time whether that first taste is with chocolate covered ants or sautéed insect larvae and finding the experience surprisingly agreeable. Pelletized insect protein will find an ever-increasing role in providing livestock nutrition and should before long find their way in the regular diet of western countries.

Additionally, fish farming, particularly with species that can survive on various algae bio-flocks, plant, and insect matter will increase regionally. These operations will flourish in order to supplement the loss of wild species and the protein they provide as well as provide "affordable" protein to those populations. A critical defining attribute of the species raised for this purpose will be their ability to covert raw protein into edible fish "weight". That ratio and the efficiency of conversion will greatly impact production costs, and the species that achieve mature weight at lower costs will be highly sought after as potential "crop" fish. In this regard many warm water species such as Tilapia, Catfish, and assorted fresh water species may have an advantage in replacing diminishing wild ocean stocks. River systems such as the Amazon may be able to provide new and exciting species that can be cultivated in an aquiculture setting that will start to establish new markets in the years ahead. One potential drawback of these species however is their inability to concentrate needed Omega 3 making them somewhat less desirable from a nutritional standpoint then the high "oil species" we now consume and use for fish feed. Perhaps a change in the algae diet they historically consume can help in addressing that particular challenge.

ISD is a Necessity

Efficiency, production costs, and increased profitability will be the driving force to these changes in the years ahead. Future livestock facilities will be designed to make as much use of the animal waste products as the dairy and meat those animals now provide. Farms will raise a much wider diversity of synergistic crops integrated into a structured eco-system in order to rebalance their impact on local resources and the environment. Properly planned and managed these changes offer unlimited promise in reversing our current imbalances.

One of the critical potential drivers that can further enhance agricultural efficiencies will be a rethinking of 21st century industrial and commercial operations and how those waste streams can be directly tied into farming operations. Currently zoning laws, an absence of fundamental knowledge, and a lack of coordinated planning and will are standing in the way of these types of projects. Much in the same way we think of economics and the environment as being mutually exclusive concepts, the idea of combining industrial production with food production is something the average person (Or civic leader) dismisses without further consideration. The thing is many of the component elements, gases, energy, and heat that are a waste product of industry and civil infrastructure could be put to direct use in food production with appropriate processing and integration. All that is needed is for people to start to see those tangents and areas of intersection. It should be a goal of all societies that the clever reuse of those waste resources is maximized for highest profitability and minimal environmental impact; CO_2 from power facilities emissions as a growth accelerant, phosphates and organic components from sewage as fertilizer and so forth.

Ultimately the future of food production will be defined by our ability to maintain the local vibrancy of supportive eco-systems along with our seamlessly integrating new production technologies and the totality of our waste production into highest use recycling. Right now, we are in the beginning stages of understanding the need for such symbiotic and synergistic relationships.

Government efforts and a refocusing of our financial community's support will be critical in building this effort. The ability to create these systems maximizing profitability relative to existing models will spur on needed investment and ultimately be determinative as to its initial adaptability and acceptance.

William Sosinsky

Chapter Eighteen

The Future of Energy (It is the Power that Enables Change)

"I have no doubt we will be successful at harnessing the sun's energy. If sunbeams were weapons of war, we would have had solar energy centuries ago."

~ Sir George Porter

If climate change has captured our primary focus in terms of the environmental threats, we now face then energy and the issues surrounding its production, control, value, and impact are certainly at the core of our sustainability efforts. Energy, when all is said and done, plays the central role as both our biggest challenge and key enabler when it comes to change. It has always been a complex double-edged sword. On one hand without abundant energy you do not have economic growth, transportation, production capacity, refrigeration, storage, etc... There is little to no technology advancements in which energy is not a key driving force and consideration. On the other hand, it has been our misuse, mishandling, and errors in judgement with energy that has caused our most pressing and globally impactful environmental issues which we now need to address.

Energy is singularly the most valued and easily centralized and controlled necessity that our modern society relies upon for our prosperity. That attribute has been the stuff wars are fought over and which governments, business interests, and economies plan their futures around. In this way energy is more of a political issue and the driver of recent global change then any of the other key areas which affect long term sustainability. Such are the issues surrounding energy and why it requires the most thoughtful and measured approach in the ways we go about solving the challenges connected to its use, development, and control.

Very often the 20th century is referred to as the "American" century, however it may well be remembered in future texts historically as the century of oil. No other single commodity or resource has had more of a direct impact on the environment, economic growth, wealth creation, standards of living, politics, global conflict, and overall societal impact then humankind's dependence on petroleum. The financial and human resources that have been expended to explore, extract, obtain, defend, and control those reserves are unprecedented and have shaped our recent history.

A chronology of oil in the 20th century reads like the pages of a history book. Standard oil and John D Rockefeller developed the oil industry that powered America's early growth into an industrial superpower and with that he became the richest man in history. Japan fought a war of imperialistic expansion to obtain more resources for their people with oil reserves being a main goal. The American oil embargo of Japan in 1941 in response to those aggressions preceded the Japanese attack on Pearl Harbor and provided the impetus as to why Japan declared war on the U.S. America's bombing campaign in WW2 on Germany and Japan had a primary objective to diminish axis fuel/oil reserves and was a key to eventually winning the war. Germany invaded the Crimea in order to capture needed oil resources to support their war effort.

After WW2 America cultivated relationships throughout the Middle East to support its industrial growth by backing sometimes unpopular leaders who would work with them to insure those supplies. The Arab oil embargo following the 1973 Yom Kippur war between the Arab States and Israel ushered in an American Strategy of keeping a regular Naval presence in the area and putting military bases throughout the region to guarantee no further interruptions in supply. OPEC was then formed to nationalize production creating unimagined wealth for the upper classes/leaders of the oil rich Gulf States and for a number of leaders and businessmen in Africa and Asia in countries with substantial oil reserves. That change shifted global wealth and created major changes in international banking and investment decision making. The Gulf wars of 1990 and 2003 were fought to protect the flow of those supplies.

I suppose the point I am trying to make is that global politics and political power has in one form or another been incredibly influenced by oil. National policies, international agreements, regional tensions, and global economic and social influences have been dictated by its need and control. Fossil fuels are the current top producer and creator of wealth on our planet and the ability to control petroleum reserves and markets has been hard fought. With many Trillions of dollars in untapped resources yet to pull out of the ground and sell, those countries, corporations, and leaders who control those reserves and the banks, politicians, and armies that back their wishes make them a very formidable force to reckon with.

They will go to untold lengths when defending their vested interests. Just an elite few control the single largest financial and political power stake hold in the world and they will not relinquish that position without a fight. That is unless someone can come up with an alternative that allows them to maintain their position and wealth such that they can change. That solution to that quandary or lack thereof may be the determining reason as to whether or not we can save our environment and turn things around before it is too late.

When it comes to responding to the need for more energy that does not impact our biosphere with the same virulence as fossil fuels, science and technology developers have been hard at work trying to find those answers. When you look around you, energy and the potential to capture energy is virtually everywhere. It shines down on us, blows by us, and is encapsulated in the materials we throw out and use every day. Energy bubbles up from the ground, flows by in rivers, pulses with the tides, heats up our streets and roof tops, and ultimately exists on a sub-atomic level in the invisible universe that surrounds us to which we are hardly aware of. In the following sections we will take a look at several possibilities and how each may potentially be part of an eventual solution.

Solar

When we categorize an energy source as "solar" energy it can be a bit confusing. In reality, very many of the sources of energy we now use in one form or another come from, or are created by the sun. Fossil fuels for example are energy sources that stored solar energy as living organisms to be later released through combustion. Wind energy is caused by temperature and pressure variations in our atmosphere directly influenced by solar irradiation. For this section the types of solar capturing technologies and methods we will discuss are those that directly convert the sun's spectrum into useable energy sources we can tap.

The Earth receives 174,000 terawatts (TW) of incoming solar radiation (insolation) at the upper atmosphere. [80] Approximately 30% is reflected back to space while the rest is absorbed by clouds, oceans and land masses. The spectrum of solar light at the Earth's surface is mostly spread across the visible and near-infrared ranges with a small part in the near-ultraviolet. [81] Most people around the world live in areas with insolation levels of 150 to 300 watt per square meter or 3.5 to 7.0 kWh/m^2 per day. The total solar energy absorbed by Earth's atmosphere, oceans and land masses is approximately 3,850,000 exajoules (EJ) per year. [82] In 2002, this was more energy in one hour than the world used in one year. [83,84,85] Along with hydrogen, solar energy offers one of the two potential inexhaustible "conventional" renewable energy sources we have available to develop.

Solar energy falls into two basic categories, active solar and passive solar depending on how the energy is captured and distributed. Some active solar methods to harness the sun's power include photovoltaics, solar concentrators/collectors, solar thermal, ambient solar thermal, and solar water heating technologies. Passive solar examples deal more with the way buildings and structures are designed and oriented to use the sun's energy, assist in air circulation, disperse light, and function as thermal mass storage. To increase the use and integration of active solar energy production and passive design techniques many countries, states and regions have actively encouraged investment in such systems. Policies and programs aimed at assisting in this transition come in the form of grants, rebates, incentives, and feed-in tariffs.

When we look at solar power as it relates to how we use energy it is important to differentiate as to what type of energy you are trying to supplement or replace. This understanding defines what methods are most efficient with delivering that need. With that I mean to say is that British Thermal Units (BTU's) or Calories are the measurement equivalents we associate with heating/cooling purposes while Watts are a function of electrical usage. Both BTUs and Wattage can be harnessed directly from different portions of the solar spectrum depending on the active or passive technologies and applications you use to capture them.

There are literally dozens of "solar" technologies and applications in use today with more being developed daily as new and inventive ways are discovered to capture the limitless power of the sun. To detail all of those technologies and fully explain their application would require another book so I will keep this section as general as possible. That being said the power of the sun can be used to enormous advantage when designing structures and buildings for both residential and commercial space. As those possibilities are incorporated into advanced architectural and engineering designs and concepts by our "solar visionaries" our reliance on other forms of energy will be reduced significantly.

The most common "active" solar technology in use today is photovoltaics. Those are the modules or "panels" that are popping up seemingly everywhere there are roof tops, light poles, or open fields bathed by the sun. The main attraction people have to solar modules is their ability to directly convert portions of the solar spectrum directly into electricity. This attribute makes it a simple and efficient way to bring electricity into an off-grid setting, or to supplement electrical needs where there is available sun and space to mount or site modules at relatively low cost.

Source-Solar Energy Wikipedia

Photovoltaics have been around for decades. It is only in the past 15 years or so that there has been a large increase in research and development to improve their efficiency. A booming global market place has encouraged developers and scientists to improve this technology making it more accessible to consumers as a common energy option. As a result of global production competition and an ever-increasing demand, module prices have come down substantially. They are now on par in terms of "electrical" costs with fossil fuels in many markets.

Most operating systems in use today are now operating at well below 15% efficiency in converting the solar spectrum to electricity. Proximity to the equator, cloud cover, air pollution, and shading issues are all big technical considerations when considering where to site a system as they can greatly impact production. Current conversion efficiencies for photovoltaics top out at close to 20%, however some lab applications in development are promising future efficiencies nearing 40%.

A good percentage of commercial and home energy use requires BTUs as opposed to electricity and in these applications solar thermal technologies can be the better choice. BTUs are generally produced by combusting/burning fossil fuels such as oil, gas, or coal to create heat. In those cases, "active" solar water heaters and solar concentrators, or "passive" thermal mass or ambient solar collection systems are far more efficient than photovoltaics. Another advantage is heat capturing systems and technologies generally deliver BTUs at a much lower cost than converting the Sun's light spectrum into electricity. These technologies, systems, and designs capture the much larger thermal portion of the solar spectrum with conversion rates approaching 60% in some cases. A majority of these technologies are made from much simpler and inexpensive materials and the production processes tend to be less involved making them cheaper to produce. Ultimately, they are far more economical and better suited for heating/cooling related uses.

Source-Solatronics Energy-Solar Water Heater   Source-Energime Water Solar Concentrator

In the urban environment and in industrial settings very often BTU usage is the much larger portion of on-site energy consumption. These systems can be employed for heating, water heating, and air conditioning (with the addition of an absorption chiller) which can all be huge consumers of BTUs.

A main component and consideration of energy efficient building and LEED design is the inclusion of passive solar elements to reduce the need for lighting, heating, cooling, and air flow technologies. Referring to a component as "passive" indicates that steps have been taken in its design and implementation that either reduce or increase the impact of the solar spectrum simply by the way it reacts to the structure or system. Strategic shading, baffles, and thermal window film/e-glass reduce interior thermal gain from the sun keeping it cooler indoors and limiting the need for air conditioning. Painting building roofs and exterior surfaces white will reflect sunlight contributing to that same end.

Open floor plans and strategically oriented placement of the structure on the building site can provide increased natural light, reducing the need for extensive daytime lighting.

Examples of Passive Solar Buildings

SIEEB Solar Energy-Efficient Building in Beijing   Passive solar building design - Wikipedia

The following are key design elements for residential and commercial buildings in temperate climates.

- Placement of room-types, internal doors and walls, and equipment in the building.
- Orienting the building to face the equator (or a few degrees to the East to capture the morning sun) [86]
- Extending the building dimension along the east/west axis
- Adequately sizing windows to face the midday sun in the winter, and be shaded in the summer. [132]
- Minimizing windows on other sides, especially western windows[87]
- Erecting correctly sized, latitude-specific roof overhangs, [88] or shading elements (shrubbery, trees, trellises, fences, shutters, etc.) [89]
- Using the appropriate amount and type of insulation including radiant barriers and bulk insulation to minimize seasonal excessive heat gain or loss[133]
- Using thermal mass to store excess solar energy during the winter day (which is then re-radiated during the night) [90,91]

For larger commercial buildings there are many passive systems now available which can be employed directly to help preheat makeup air for an HVAC system. Installations such as "solar walls" or "solar roofs" bring preheated air from a baffled collector plate on the exterior sun-facing surface or roof of a building using heat transfer to accomplish that purpose. Transpired solar collectors greatly reduce the need for other energy sources to produce required BTUs. This process is similar to how some pools preheat their water by circulating otherwise cold water through black rubber membranes or pipes exposed to the sun.

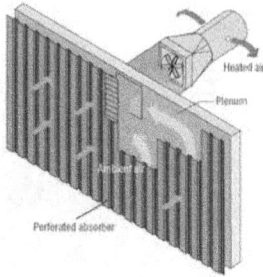

Source Wikipedia Solar Thermal Energy   Source Solar Wall by Conserval Engineering Inc.

Heat in a solar thermal system is guided by five basic principles: heat gain; heat transfer; heat storage; heat transport; and heat insulation. [92] When you consider the amount of energy naturally collected and stored in building surfaces and structural mass, heat transfer is a natural way to provide much needed "free" energy to reduce our dependence on alternate sources.

When we look at commercial or utility sized solar installations to generate electricity it is much more common these days to see solar collectors or "concentrators" being used then photovoltaics. With this method "Fresnel" mirrors or focused lenses are combined with a tracking system to concentrate large amounts of sunlight into a very small area creating extremely high temperatures. Collection dishes or troughs project the sun's rays/heat onto a fluid source which can be anything from water to oil. The super-heated liquid is then directed to a steam turbine that converts that heat into electricity. One of the main advantages to using a thermal based system is the ability to easily store the heat produced in order to generate energy at times when the sun is not directly feeding the system. Another advantage is increased conversion efficiencies which can top out at better than 30%.

There are literally dozens of creative designs and methods being built to capture solar energy in this way. These systems can be either made up of small individual units working together in unison or a single enormous collector depending on the particular method/application. Concentrator applications as a result of their active design are much more complex and maintenance intensive then photovoltaic modules. Increased production and higher conversion efficiencies however generally make concentrated solar a much better choice for utility sized projects.

Source Wikipedia Solar Thermal Energy   Source Wikipedia Solar Thermal Energy

The last technology I want to touch on in regards to solar energy is "Ambient solar thermal" technology. This is the newest and most advanced solar application soon to be in operation around the world. This technology operates on the principle that there is always energy present in any environment where the temperature is not absolute zero. At zero degrees Kelvin, or $-273.15°$ Celsius, there is an absence of all non-kinetic energy. In all other instances above absolute zero there is available ambient energy that can potentially be collected. The higher the ambient temperature the more energy there is available. Direct sun light and warmer surroundings are ideal, but these systems can still collect energy at the South Pole in the dead of winter. Large dishes are used in this application to produce energy and can convert as much as 98% of the solar spectrum. These are much higher efficiencies than either solar concentrators or photovoltaics will ever likely be capable of.

Source Red Sun Technology Earth Power Inc.

To sum up; Solar energy is singularly the most abundant and easily captured renewable power source we currently have available to us. With all the technologies and applications that are now on the market, there are very few regions and structures in the world that cannot make use of some form of solar technology to their advantage. Additionally, we are on the brink of many great advances, production improvements, and cost reductions in the field of solar energy. That should finally make this plentiful energy source easily adaptable and a staple of every new and retrofitted construction project where power is a need. If current trends continue solar energy is anticipated to be the leading source of global electricity by mid-century.

Wind

One of the fastest growing segments in the renewable energy market is wind power. Whether those installations are located on the open plains, off our coastlines, or lining the rooftops and edges of our urban landscapes, wind turbines it seems are turning up everywhere these days. When wind is dependably available with high enough velocities capturing those flows can be one of the most productive and cost-effective methods of creating renewable electrical power.

The use of wind as an energy source is not a new concept. The wind wheel first appeared in ancient Greece in the first century AD and soon after that in China and Tibet as a way to pump water for irrigation and for mechanical power. By the ninth century it is believed that windmills were being employed to grind grain and lift /pump water in Persia. For centuries the world was explored and settled by seagoing adventurers traveling on ships powered by wind filled sails. It was only at the end of the nineteenth century that the first wind turbines built to convert wind into electricity would be introduced.

Wind turbines come in two basic varieties those being horizontal and vertical axis configurations. Horizontal axis turbines are generally of the pin wheel design and come in a variety of sizes. Some land and ocean-based turbines can reach incredible dimensions with heights and widths rivaling those of large skyscrapers. These are the design type more associated with large wind farms. Those farms can consist of hundreds of individual units connected to one another through a central grid. Larger wind farms are generally situated on open plains, mountain ridges, river valleys, and along coastal areas where they can take advantage of strong, consistent wind patterns.

William Sosinsky

Vertical axis turbines are a newer concept now finding their way into urban and residential settings. These designs have spurred a developing industry which is in its early stages as these fascinating kinetic structures are architecturally integrated and retrofitted into the built environment.

Source Oklahoma City Medical Research Tower

The science of siting vertical axis wind turbines is far more complex relative to their specific positioning compared with their larger horizontal cousins. Modern cities with their patchwork streets and high rises create a whole new set of challenges. Artificial canyons and variations in the solar absorption rates of different surface materials can create powerful concentrated flow patterns and thermal up-drafts. This interaction of wind with man-made structures also tends to create added turbulence which is undesirable as it has a negative impact on consistent flow rates and turbine energy production.

There has been much debate as of late as to the practicality and success of building integrated wind turbine projects as some have performed rather poorly. This is more the result of insufficient planning and improper placement rather than any deficiencies with the systems and should not be considered a condemnation of the concept. Vertical wind turbines integrated into the urban landscape are potentially a very valuable tool in producing clean urban energy. Ultimately wind only blows when and where it blows. Setting up a turbine in the wrong location in the hope it will produce energy will most likely result in an occasionally revolving piece of kinetic sculpture.

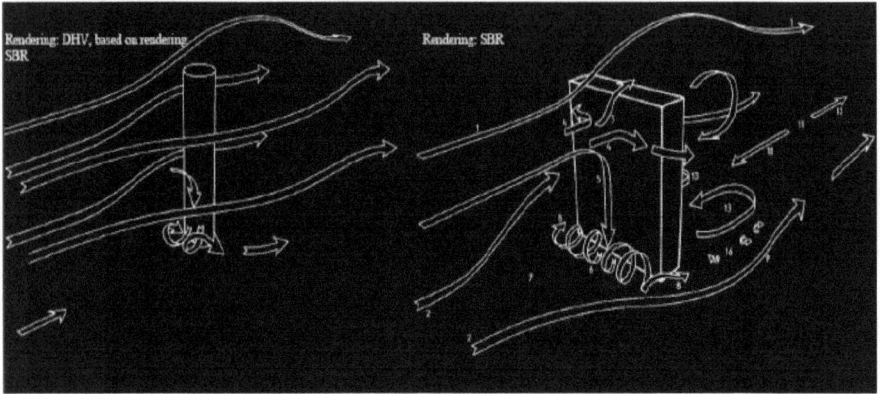

Source Synergy International

In order to avoid such missteps engineers and designers are now understanding that they need to spend a considerable amount of time analyzing wind patterns in advance of siting the turbines in order to determine optimal positioning. Baffles and conduits may be employed to direct and even out those air flow patterns. Additionally, these constructs can draw in or "suck" the air and substantially speed up the flow rate so as to add to the production potential of the turbine.

Several other factors play key roles in determining where to position wind turbines. The "Wind Rose" is the seasonal air flow pattern as it relates to a particular site and must be clearly understood in advance of construction. The optimal height as to where you position a turbine can also vary greatly and needs to be defined. In general, wind patterns tend to be stronger and more consistent the higher up you go. The Nation Renewable Energy Laboratory (NREL) has created detailed and extensive maps of the U.S. and abroad in an attempt to clearly illustrate the potential for wind harvesting and to help wind farm developers assess the viability of any particular site or region. In urban setting however, there is no substitute for specific site information where setting a turbine back a few feet or up a few feet can be the difference between a productive project and a waste of time and money.

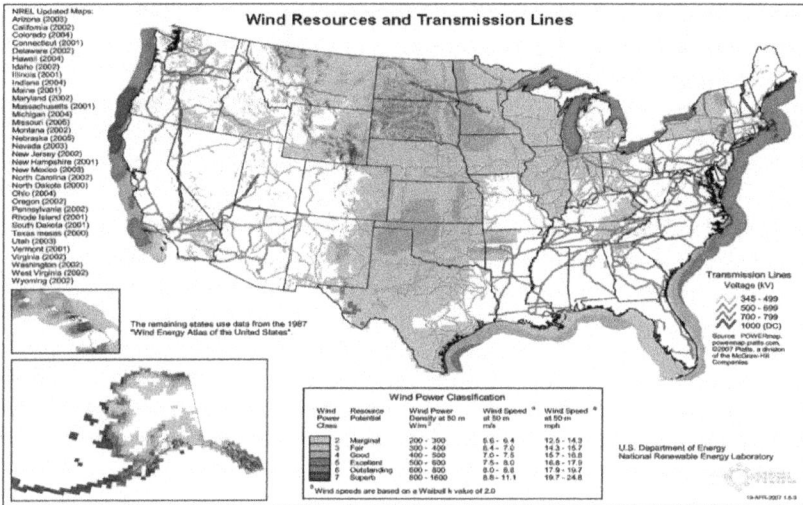

Source National Renewable Energy Laboratory

Another challenge with wind power is the intermittent nature of seasonal air flow patterns that make wind production an unreliable source as a stand-alone contributor to grid based energy. Although seasonal totals are very reliable from year to year, there is no guarantee that the wind will be blowing on any particular day or at any specific time. As energy generally needs to be used the spilt second it is generated before it dissipates, expensive storage capacity is required to make the singular use of wind power a viable alternative for supplying a consistent source of dependable energy.

In the absence of energy storage tangent projects that consume excess energy are good strategies such that the overage does not go to waste. This can occur late at night when energy is not needed, when there is excessive production from high winds, or when other adequate feed-in sources are supplying the local grid. Using that untimely production to produce hydrogen-based fuels or power industrial processes that can run intermittently at off-hours for example are productive ways to manage this challenge and can present money saving opportunities to end users.

Geothermal (and Ground Geothermal)

Earth is a huge thermal mass storage vessel. Under the crust of our planet burn the fires that created our universe along with an ongoing process of radioactive decay. The active molten outer core formed of liquid iron and nickel fourteen hundred miles thick lies below our mantle and outside the Earths solid inner core. The heat created by these natural processes is continuously trying to work its way up and out as a function of thermal conduction. At points in the planet crust where the outer mantle gets a bit thin or just to the rears of where tectonic plates meet, magma from that outer core is pushed upwards in the form of volcanoes and steam vents. Such areas present a great opportunity for tapping into what is essentially an unlimited source of thermal energy.

Much like solar thermal collectors, how that energy is used and harvested is defined by the need. Thermal energy can be used to drive a turbine to create electricity or used directly as a heat source providing BTUs for heating and cooling purposes. Geothermal power is cost effective, reliable, sustainable, and environmentally friendly, [93] but has historically been limited to areas near tectonic plate boundaries. Recent technological advances have dramatically expanded the range and size of viable resources, especially for applications such as home heating, opening the potential for widespread exploitation. The Earth's geothermal resources are theoretically more than adequate to supply humanity's energy needs, but only a very small fraction may be profitably exploited. Drilling and exploration for deep resources is very expensive. [94]

Up until the twentieth century geothermal sources were used exclusively for heating purposes. As far back as the third century BC hot springs in China were employed as baths with the first geothermal heating districts popping up in France by the fourteen hundred. It is only since the dawn of the industrial revolution that scientists have endeavored to drive turbines with geothermal power in an attempt to create electricity. In areas where vents and magma sources are close to the surface such as the country of Iceland this is an option that really makes economic sense.

Another form of harvesting geothermal energy that is far more useful on a global economic scale is "ground" geothermal energy. This method uses heat pumps to exchange the moderating temperatures of the ground or other thermal masses such as bodies of water to provide make-up heating and cooling BTUs for homes and other actively used structures. Ground temperatures and those of large thermal mass storage sites tend to change very slowly and maintain a constancy of temperature which is much more stable than those of changing outdoor conditions. As a result, geothermal heat exchange is an ideal source and inexpensive method for supplementing other types of energy needed to provide BTUs.

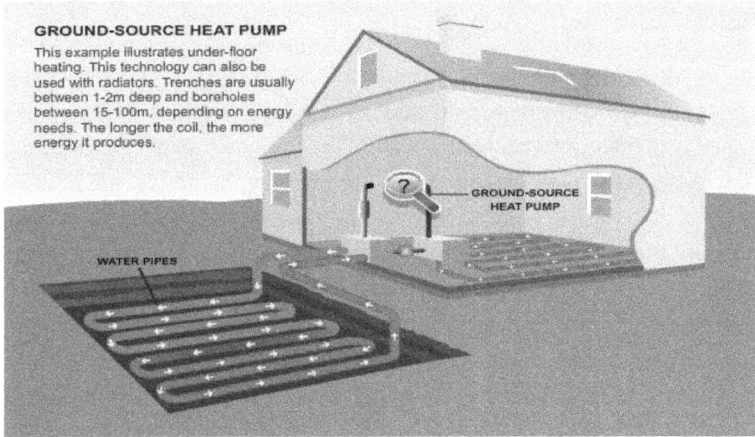

GROUND-SOURCE HEAT PUMP

This example illustrates under-floor heating. This technology can also be used with radiators. Trenches are usually between 1-2m deep and boreholes between 15-100m, depending on energy needs. The longer the coil, the more energy it produces.

GROUND-SOURCE HEAT PUMP

WATER PIPES

Source OurLifeHus

This approach is nothing new to building design and is evident in its use in structures dating back centuries. In North Africa for instance, different cultures for centuries have dug their huts into the soil below grade with a hole at the apex of their roof such that the interior remains cool even in the warmest of climates. This simple design was taken from observing termite mounds which can maintain internal temperatures in the 60-70-degree Fahrenheit range using this simple heat exchange method when it is 120 degrees or more outside. Ground temperatures outside most arctic environments generally range from the low fifty-degree Fahrenheit range into the low seventies.

The viability of determining whether or not ground geothermal applications makes sense at any particular site generally involves an evaluation of what are referred to as "degree days". This method defines the variations in outdoor temperatures from what is considered an indoor "comfort" range. The total numbers of degrees needed to be artificially added or subtracted from the interior in order to get into that comfort range during the course of a year defines the total number of degree days for that site. The higher the number of degree days the better chances that site is a candidate for such an application. Climates with very warm summers and cold winters tend to work best. Considering the percentage of our energy use that goes directly to heating and cooling purposes this is a technology that makes a great deal of sense.

Hydro-electric

Moving water has more than 800 times the kinetic energy as air flowing at the same velocity. It is this simple attribute and humankind's ability to harness this power that has fueled the development and spread of humanity to many regions of the world that were formally rural and untamed. Additionally, hydro-electric power throughout our recent past has been the considered the cleanest and most sustainable energy source for producing electricity. Projects designed to capture those potential kilowatts include some of the largest and most ambitious construction efforts in human history. Dams such as the Aswan, Hoover, Grand Coulee, and Three Gorges have changed the economic and development course of regions just as assuredly as they have impacted their local environments. It is no wonder that large dam projects are now commonplace around the world and one of the first areas governments look to when they aspire to increase local power supplies.

Unfortunately, climate change and evolving hydrologic distribution patterns world-wide may impact many of these dams. As such they are in jeopardy of having their water supplies diminish to the point where their production is adversely impacted. Should these changes continue and increase, many of these constructs will no longer be able to function as designed and cease to generate the resources they formally provided.

In an effort to circumvent the need for such formations a new form of hydro-electric harvesting is starting to take hold. In-line moveable turbine technology captures kinetic river flows and shows considerable promise in a way that does not require huge capital investments into stationary structures.

Source Tidal-Turbine.Tumblr.com.

Source Alstom   Source Offshorewind.biz

As a result of this promise there has been considerable investments made into technologies that can capture this energy flow. More predictable and dependable than either solar or wind, tidal energy can be captured using a number of strategies. Turbines can be situated directly in coastal currents or positioned at the mouths of rivers, bays and inlets where they can extract energy from surges as tides flow in and out. One of the more promising methods is to contain the inflows in large storage ponds, then to process the retreating water through turbines as they drain back into the sea. Considering the huge percentage of our global population that live within 100 miles of the ocean shore, this particular technology can be very impactful in solving our long-term energy consumption challenges.

Wave Power which is more a derivative of wind power and not tidal energy may at some point play significant role in providing options for energy generation. Thus far however it is still in its beginning stages and has yet to be demonstrated on a large enough scale to be considered a significant long-term contributor. Additionally, its interference with seas going vessels, ocean commerce and potential fishing grounds makes it problematic as far as wide spread adaptability is concerned.

Nuclear

Most people are very cautious when tying our future hopes for electric power to nuclear energy and with good reason. Recent experience with Fukushima and Chernobyl were historic reminders of the dangers involved with using fissionable materials to create power. Add to that the less spoken about issues with illegal nuclear dump sites, mishaps managing nuclear waste, and our current potential destruction and environmental impacts on the North Pacific and those consequences are frightening. We won't even address the potential nightmare of terrorism. That being said, perhaps a more even and less hysteric perspective would be helpful when considering the use and further development of nuclear energy as a power source.

Traveling Wave Reactors (or TRWs) are the next generation in nuclear reactor technology. Backed by such notables as Bill Gates, Siemens, and the DOE Terra-Power has designed a reactor that runs on depleted uranium and is rumored to operate much more safely than current reactors. Using depleted uranium eliminates the need for reprocessing and greatly simplifies the process of fuel preparation. It may also conceivably reduce nuclear waste. TerraPower says there are 700 000 metric tons of spent fuel in the U.S. alone, and 8 metric tons could power 2.5 million homes for a year. [95] Some reports claim that the high fuel efficiency of TWRs, combined with the ability to use uranium recovered from river or sea water, means enough fuel is available to generate electricity for 10 billion people at U.S. per capita levels for million-year time-scales. [96] The development group expects to have a prototype up and running by 2020 with the first commercial facility operational by the end of that decade.

The holy grail of nuclear technology is the commercial development of a fusion reactor. Fusion energy is the type of power produced by the sun and can generate virtually limitless clean energy using hydrogen as its main fuel source. There would be no pollutants or toxins resulting from this technology making it perhaps the ultimate environmentally safe technology concept. Scientists have been struggling for decades attempting to develop such a reactor as its creation could single handedly solve any future challenges, we might encounter with energy supplies. Commercial development of fusion applications however, and the use of energy created through fusion are not expected before 2050 at the earliest.

Nuclear energy more than any other current technology has the potential to provide a realistic long-term answer to our global grid-based energy needs. Used intelligently and carefully managed it can be the ultimate solution as to why we are able to reduce our use of fossil fuels and CO2 impact on the biosphere. Additionally, most if not all of the issues we have had with the safe use of nuclear fuel have been a result of ignorance, short sighted greed, a lack of experience, sophistication, and out-right stupidity. To assume that humans will all of a sudden become wise stewards of this potentially catastrophe causing technology, or not use the radioactive materials that are part of those systems for violent or destructive purpose is way beyond my range of reasonable skepticism. Unless and until nuclear energy is managed with the discipline of a Samurai and every conceivable safety precaution imaginable incorporated into each plants design, our potential dependency on nuclear fuel for our power will keep me up at night.

Hydrogen

The most abundant element in the universe is hydrogen. It is the fusion of that element that feeds the sun and stars and allows them to burn for billions of years. Although hydrogen is not commonly found on earth in its pure form, it is a major component of water. Water is composed of two hydrogen atoms and one oxygen atom. NOAA's National Geophysical Data Center estimates that there are 321,003,271 cubic miles of water in the ocean.[97]

As most of us learned in our first chemistry class water molecules are fairly simple to separate into hydrogen and oxygen with the help of a little electricity. Hydrogen is also a clean burning fuel with no harmful emissions. When burned it recombines with oxygen molecules to form water. Knowing these basic facts, it is easy to see why being able to harvest and manage the hydrogen here on Earth as a fuel and power source could very quickly put an end to our energy needs once and for all.

There are also some very clear issues with hydrogen that make using it as a fuel source more of a challenge. First, the amount of electricity it takes to separate out the hydrogen from the oxygen atom is more than the energy potential gained. This net loss makes it an inefficient and inequitable exchange of energy. Secondly, although hydrogen is an extraordinary fuel it is also one of the most volatile gases imaginable. The frequent accidents that occurred in the early days of the dirigibles/zeppelins from accidental combustion were the reason they eventually gave up on hydrogen in exchange for non-combustible helium. It is these two factors which have so far limited the use of hydrogen as a solution provider for our energy needs. As such scientists have struggled for years to find efficient ways to separate hydrogen from water molecules and safe ways to utilize this abundant energy carrier.

As a direct fuel source hydrogen is perceived to be unsafe. This is in fact somewhat of a misnomer. The truth is that hydrogen may in fact be a much safer liquid for transportation use than gas. It burns cooler and because of its light weight disperses up into the atmosphere almost instantaneously when combusted or otherwise released to the open air. So, what about the zeppelins people are apt to argue? The real facts relating to those accidents are that the cloth membranes of the dirigibles were covered with highly flammable acetates to repel water and aluminum power similar to that of rocket fuel to reflect sunlight. When those chemicals ignited such as was the case (and cause) with the Hindenburg, the flames burned upwards leaving the travelers below practically unaffected. Thirty five of the thirty-six fatalities came from people jumping off the dirigible and crashing to the ground. All those that stayed on onboard survived the catastrophe.

Additionally, the history of hydrogen fuel use in the U.S for example has been one marked by safe performance and minimal issues in regards to unintended explosions or spontaneous combustion compared to petrochemicals and fossil gases.

It needs to be recognized and understood however that hydrogen does burn with extreme force and ignites much easier than fossil fuels. To incorporate hydrogen as a fuel source for automobiles is more of an issue of creating storage or "tanks" which are much better able to handle the impacts common with on road accidents and the need to improve system flows that virtually eliminate leakage. Both are complex issues requiring technical advances over what has previously existed in automobiles. Without these improvements and innovations cars would be rolling time bombs. Composite materials seem to offer more promise than steel. Tanks made of polyethylene are lightweight, can be shaped to fit a car and are designed to powder -- absorb the energy of an impact, reducing the tank to dust and ostensibly releasing the hydrogen safely into the atmosphere. [98]

In terms of producing hydrogen, one solution we touched on earlier was using the excess electricity generated at off hours by wind turbines or other "renewable" sources to separate the hydrogen atoms from the water molecule. The hydrogen could then be transferred or stored for later use. Although you would still have the disparity in energy conversion efficiencies the hydrogen would serve as a de-facto storage source for the energy generated by other renewable sources.

Other attempts to harvest and use hydrogen in real time have included high temperature "separation" methods. Nuclear fusion is one potential method which was discussed in the previous section. Another possible means of harvesting hydrogen with the use of high temperatures has to do with the application of incendiary chemicals to cause a controlled burn of the hydrogen. Chemicals such as thermite, which is itself fuel can be used to create those optimal temperatures. These are the same chemicals used in wartime to firebomb targets and which contain various elements such as aluminum, magnesium, zinc, silicon, boron, and titanium. Once the thermite ignites it creates such high temperatures that water spontaneously combusts releasing the energy contained in both the hydrogen and oxygen atoms. Feasibility of such systems would be a function of containment and the cost of the incendiary elements as they relate to electrical production values.

Hydrogen fuel cells are another area where there has been great interest and focused development as of late. Forward thinking companies such as Google, Apple, and Walmart have employed these systems to provide site energy for their corporate headquarters. They are currently looking to incorporate these systems in their operations and product designs. A fuel cell is a device that converts the chemical energy from a fuel into electricity through a chemical reaction of positively charged hydrogen ions with oxygen or another oxidizing agent. [99] Fuel cells are different from batteries in that they require a continuous source of fuel and oxygen or air to sustain the chemical reaction, whereas in a battery the chemicals present in the battery react with each other to generate an electromotive force (emf). Fuel cells can produce electricity continuously for as long as these inputs are supplied. [100]

The average efficiency of fuel cells used for transportation can range from the mid-thirty to mid-forty percent range. Honda has demonstrated a cell powered electric car that uses a stacked system which has reached sixty percent efficiency. Compared to combustion engines which average about twenty five percent efficiencies these are huge improvements. Because fuel cells have no moving parts and do not involve combustion, in ideal conditions they can achieve up to 99.9999% reliability. [101] This equates to less than one minute of downtime in a six-year period. [101]

Fuel cells built specifically for generating energy for building and factory applications are achieving even higher average efficiencies than transportation versions. As the cost of purchasing fuel cell technologies comes down their efficiencies in generating energy, system reliability, and cost savings will make them a much more compelling option for the average business or consumer.

Heat Exchange

Heat transfer and capture has been a staple of industrial production for decades. Excess heat produced by one process is directly recycled to assist in the energy demands of a neighboring effort. The waste heat from a commercial oven as an example might be directed to an incoming water source to help heat that inflow to temperatures appropriate for sanitary cleaning. Those same basic sensibilities are now finding their way into innovative designs that are starting to show up in our built environment.

Anyone living in an urban center is well aware of that horribly uncomfortable feeling you get during the hot summer months as the blazing midday sun beats down on your back baking the asphalt and cement that surrounds you. The feeling is akin to be cooked slowly in a fry pan. In fact, if you crack an egg onto the asphalt, cement, or a metal surface being bathed by the sun's rays that egg will start to cook right in front of your eyes. That takes quite a bit of heat!

Architects, civil engineers, and city planners are only now beginning to realize the potential for capturing that abundant source of untapped energy that blankets the buildings and streets of our urban environment during the day. Heat exchange has the potential to be a huge game changer when we look at providing energy not only in city environments, but anywhere the sun shines briskly. As with ground geothermal technologies which extract/exchange moderating temperatures from the ground, solar rays contain free BTU's. Those BTUs transferred to urban surfaces during the day can be used for heating, cooling using an absorption chiller, or moving directed air flows through turbines to create electrical power. All you need to do is design structures and structural systems that can capture, move, or store that energy so it can be used directly, or employed at a later time of your choosing.

Streets, buildings, and civil constructs are by default large thermal mass collectors. Technologies that can store that heat and slowly release the energy when the sun goes down can greatly reduce dependence on fossil fuels to heat interior space or for hot water. Whether that collection system is under the pavement, designed into the outer skin of a building, or incorporated into the framework of a bridge, there is potential for that structure to be an energy collector.

The same way a forest or field of flowers wake up and come alive at the sun's first light, so do we have the potential to build into these structures integrated collection systems to tap those very same energy patterns. Imagine a network of hot air collectors built into city streets. Those systems could direct those rising morning hot air currents into tubes running up the sides of office buildings filled with inline wind turbines to create daytime electricity. Building skins could be made of clear water filled glass panels transferring those heated streams to showers and faucets, or warming the floors beneath our feet on a cold day. The idea is simple. In the years ahead, we can expect that the look and function of new construction will evolve with our increasing need for clean energy. How that happens and what those innovations will be are only limited by the imagination of the people who design and build those structures.

Dark Energy

You know Luke Skywalker and Obi-Wan Kenobi may have been on to something with the idea of "The Force". I would feel remiss if I didn't at least include a small section on dark energy as it is the future of energy for mankind should we evolve past our current challenges. Dark energy is in fact "The Force". To paraphrase my Jedi brothers it is around us, it flows through us. It makes up the very fabric of time and space. Whereas that may sound a bit fanciful and cosmically confusing to most of us, let me try and bring this concept back down to earth.

The universe is made up of matter. Much of that material is visible to the naked eye. Stars, comets, meteors, asteroids, planets, moons, and galaxies are just some of the cosmic mass we can look up into the sky on a clear night and perhaps gaze upon. What most people fail to realize is that which we see, or that which is potentially visible with the use of a high-powered telescope is only a small fraction of what is floating around in the vastness of space. In between all those points of light and surrounding every visible object in the universe is the invisible matter and energy contained within that invisible mass. Whether you want to refer to those objects or material as star dust, black holes, singularities, electromagnetic waves, radiation, auras, or cosmic debris, that is in fact the stuff of what dark matter is made of. Scientifically speaking, all matter contains components of energy. All the energy from that dark matter and the invisible matter we cannot visibly see or account for is dark energy.

Dark energy is not an insignificant portion of total cosmic content. In fact, it is the stuff that the universe is made of. According to the Planck mission team, and based on the standard model of cosmology, on a mass–energy equivalence basis, the observable universe contains 26.8% dark matter, 68.3% dark energy (for a total of 95.1%) and 4.9% ordinary matter. [102,103,104,105]

How humankind relates to dark energy and its possible future use has everything to do with local energy fields and how those energy fields are structured. For example, the earth has a large molten outer core as discussed earlier. It is the magnetic fields generated through convective currents by those molten metals in the outer core that create the protective electro-magnetic shield which surrounds and protects our atmosphere from the ravages of solar storms and winds. Every school kid from an early age knows all about the north and south magnetic poles. Very few of us however understand, or ever learn the significance of how the structure of that magnetic field relates to the science of potentially harvesting it as an energy source.

The magnetic energy that circles around the Earth flows in a pattern known as a *toroidal* energy field. This same identical pattern of energy flow is repeated and surrounds every object in the universe from flowers and people to stars and galaxies. When viewed through a spectrometer a toroidal energy field appears to flow in an almost doughnut like shape with the waves of energy wrapping around the center equator and connecting inward at each of the opposite poles.

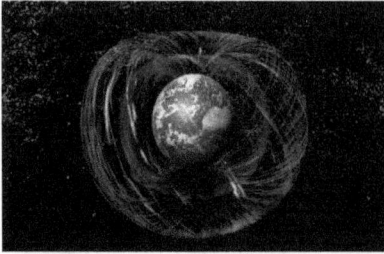

Source imgbuddy.com   Source Renderstuff

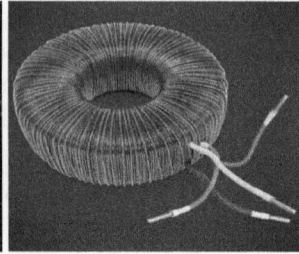

The ability to capture or tap into those energy waves with the use of sophisticated electro-magnetic coils or generators is thought to be a real possibility to our eventual mastery of this poorly understood energy source. Such an application would be able to provide virtually limitless amount of clean, renewable energy. Nicola Tesla the Serbian born American physicist and electrical engineer seemed to have solved this challenge at the beginning of the twentieth century. It is only now that Tesla's extraordinary genius is being widely recognized by the scientific community as they strive to understand, re-create, and complete the work he started so many years ago. Many inventors have claimed to have solved these challenges. There have been claims and accusations made that their inventions and discoveries are being kept off the market by those who feel threatened by the concept of unlimited free electricity. As I have heard these stories more than a few times from highly reputable and knowledgeable sources it gives me pause.

Energy Storage and The Smart Grid

To tie up this section on energy I thought I would just touch on some other key areas that will be critical in the future if we are ever to master energy as a resource.

Energy storage is a very big deal. Most electrical energy must be used the instant it is generated unless it is stored in a battery or via thermal storage for later use. That inability to store energy inexpensively makes all the current renewable energies such as solar, wind, tidal and so forth impossible to rely upon as dependable grid sources. It is their intermittent nature of capturing energy only when it is available that creates unacceptable lapses in production and makes them problematic for grid distribution requirements.

Lithium based batteries have been hailed as a potential solution to this challenge. Batteries made with lithium have been used extensively in automobiles and consumer product applications with great success to date. The issue with lithium is its cost and limited supplies. There is simply not enough lithium considering estimated global reserves to handle more than a small portion of transportation needs globally. In terms of grid-based storage which is far more significant to any battery-based solution it is a complete non-factor.

Cheap storage however is coming in the form of sophisticated thermal applications. By transferring energy into a thermal or molten state, that energy can be released slowly powering electric generators well after that energy was initially produced. Whether that medium for storage is thermal mass or molten metals and salts those newer applications hold the promise of drastically reducing associated storage costs. Though it is highly unlikely you will see these applications showing up in cell phones or automobiles, they will eventually have a dramatic impact on grid-based energy systems and make renewable energy that much more appealing.

The smart grid is all about transmission and balancing the supply/demand equation. Our global use of electricity is currently defined by waste and inefficient system management. An intelligent management system attempts to address those shortfalls in several ways by having the end-user system directly communicate with the supplier/utility. This way the utility can match precise energy production to demand without wasteful over-production. At times of peak demand, instead of increasing production the smart grid can tell those systems that have the option to run at other times to shut off lessening that critical demand. Also, energy tends to dissipate as it travels long distances over power lines. By limiting peak demand surges, utilities do not have to draw power from far away facilities tapping into inefficient sources to make up for their power supply needs. The final result is the need to produce less energy using fewer facilities and a reduction in waste.

Section Conclusion

In the coming years it is essential that design and planning for energy production and use change drastically if we are to thrive. Thoughtful integration of new and evolving energy capture and storage technologies should be an essential base concern and ingredient to any construction project or enterprise. This includes any endeavor geared towards human habitation and survival, transportation, food production, industry, or service that requires energy to operate. That means everything everywhere. It is unlikely we solve these challenges with one magic bullet solution. Using the proper application for the specific circumstances and available resources are critical to this process. Without this approach we will fail to accomplish the reduction of dangerous greenhouse gases by supplanting them with appropriate renewable applications. Combining thoughtful energy management practices with other sustainable efforts managing food, water, and waste through the discipline of ISD we can reduce capital costs and create long term savings. This in turn makes those enterprises more adaptable and in some cases much more profitable.

When we look at energy consumption and potential adaptability, logic tells us that those decisions will ultimately be determined by a simple equation. Whatever energy source can deliver kilowatts, calories, or BTUs at the lowest local price with the highest efficiency and minimal impact to the environment will be the logical choice that is most likely to be adapted. We are therefore tasked with finding the best long term sustainable and clean solutions to our energy needs that meet these criteria.

Logic however I am afraid will have little to do with that process. The sad reality is that everyone backs their own horse no matter what the consequences to the environment. Right now, that lead horse is fossil fuels. The leaders and business entities behind energy production on this planet are the most powerful and influential group in the world. They are an immovable, omnipresent, empowering and directive force that cannot be supplanted without our entire global structure collapsing. With tens of trillions of dollars in untapped fossil fuel resources still in the ground and within their grasp that change will not come easily. Unless we can influence those current stakeholders to stop restricting and inhibiting this transitional process by including them directly in these solutions and offering them an equally compelling financial and strategic path to change, we will eventually run out of time before irreversible damage to our environment occurs. If we should fail to understand this unavoidable truth surviving generations will forever pay a terrible price for our stubborn ignorance.

Chapter Nineteen

Is Algae the Key to our Future Survival?

"No matter how politely one says it, we owe our existence to the farts of blue-green algae." ~ ***Diane Ackerman***

The emergence of algae as a life form on Earth 1.6-1.7 billion years ago was the basis for all life that was to come after. We owe our breathable atmosphere, food chain, and fossil fuels to the existence of these seemingly simple, yet highly diversified and complex mix of water borne animals and plants. The Algal Collection of the US National Herbarium (located in the National Museum of Natural History) consists of approximately 320,500 dried specimens, which, although not exhaustive (no exhaustive collection exists), gives an idea of the order of magnitude of the number of algal species (that number remains unknown.) [106] Current estimates suggest there are more than 70,000 algae species alive today. Various strains are as different from one another as elephants are to pineapples. Like the bees, they are comprised of some of the most productive and critically important species in the world and the attributes of those strains may well determine the future of human beings on Earth.

If we are to "rebuild" our environment's health and vitality, we need to start with the best tools that god and nature have given us. Algae's roll as a managed resource cannot be overstated. Understanding our current global challenges with diminishing soil nutrient content, increasing malnutrition, resource depletion, and reliance on fossil fuels, algae may be our last best hope.

Algaculture

Algae can be cultivated for a variety of commercial and industrial applications. The many different species lend themselves to producing end products which include food ingredients and additives such as omega-3 fatty acids, food dyes, and strains of seaweed which are food staples in various cultures. Additional uses include the production of fertilizer, bioplastics, nutraceuticals, pharmaceuticals, industrial feedstock additives, biofuels, and as a means of processing and controlling a range of pollutants. This versatility and the speed at which algae can multiply and double in mass makes algae a prime candidate for inclusion with many ISD projects.

Algae farms and algae-culture operations come in all sorts of shapes and sizes. In general, single species or monoculture operations are the standard as they target the specific attributes of an individual strain for cultivation. The great majority of operations grow phytoplankton or microalgae species. In the developing world and in less technology intensive operations algae are generally grown in ponds, lakes, or open raceways. Although this method is much less expensive then technology intensive operations, this leaves the targeted algae open to bacterial contamination and the potential growth of other less desirable algal strains. As the Algaculture market matures we are seeing all sorts of innovations and process improvements from photo-bioreactors to covered raceways and operations that occur completely indoors. These operations have much higher production rates and extremely efficient but can be very capital intensive to build and maintain.

Source OccuWorld   Source Climatetechwiki

Photo-bioreactors are at the core of the current technology movement to grow algae. These systems are destined to have a big future as operations become more integrated into urban environments and conventional farm operations. Production space is currently at a premium and the potential nutrient feed stocks necessary for supporting algae growth are generally local in nature. As a result, future algaculture farming efforts will need to fit into flexible, limited and defined spaces. Operations that can "stack" production vertically should become a common sight in the coming decades.

Growing algae requires some very basic ingredients those being water, light energy, and CO_2. There is also the possibility of growing algae in dark environments by simply substituting basic sugars in replacement of CO_2, however this is a slower and less productive method. Specific species are sensitive to temperature and need to be grown in solutions that generally range between 25 and 35 degrees Celsius. Whether the algae are grown indoors or outdoors light plays an important role in increasing algae growth rates and production levels.

In a typical algal-cultivation system, such as an open pond, light only penetrates the top 3 to 4 inches (76–102 mm) of the water, though this depends on the algae density. As the algae grow and multiply, the culture becomes so dense that it blocks light from reaching deeper into the water. Direct sunlight is too strong for most algae, which can use only about $1/10$ the amount of light they receive from direct sunlight; however, exposing an algae culture to direct sunlight (rather than shading it) is often the best course for strong growth, as the algae underneath the surface get more light. [107]

To use deeper ponds, growers agitate the water, circulating the algae so that it does not remain on the surface. Paddle wheels can stir the water and compressed air coming from the bottom lifts algae from the lower regions. Agitation also helps prevent over-exposure to the sun. [108]

Another means of supplying light is to place the light in the system. Glow plates made from sheets of plastic or glass and placed within the tank offer precise control over light intensity, and distribute it more evenly. They are seldom used, however, due to high cost. [109] In expensive energy therefore will have a tremendous impact on bringing down the costs related to harvesting algae particularly in confined/indoor environments.

Another major challenge with algae production has to do with dewatering and extraction of the key target element within the algae cell. Extraction technology is an area of intense focus as the costs related to these processes are often high. Methods for extracting include crushing/pressing, ultrasound, shock waves, chemical solvents, and the use of enzymes.

Nutrition

Phytoplankton are essentially the lungs of our planet producing as much as an estimated 50-85% our oxygen although exact levels are impossible to determine. [131] Another critical role, algae can play for current and future generations may well be as a core nutritional supplement.

Naturally growing seaweeds are an important source of food, especially in Asia. They provide many vitamins including: A, B_1, B_2, B_6, niacin and C, and are rich in iodine, potassium, iron, magnesium and calcium. [110] In addition, commercially cultivated microalgae, including both algae and cyanobacteria, are marketed as nutritional supplements, such as Spirulina, [111] Chlorella and the Vitamin-C supplement, Dunaliella, high in beta-carotene.

Spirulina (A blue-green algae) is of particular interest when it comes to nutrition and as a possible farmed crop. In 1974, the World Health Organization described Spirulina as "an interesting food for multiple reasons, rich in iron and protein, and is able to be administered to children without any risk," considering it "a very suitable food." [110] The United Nations established the Intergovernmental Institution for the use of Micro-algae Spirulina Against Malnutrition in 2003. [111] In the late 1980s and early 90s, both NASA (CELSS) [112] and the European Space Agency (MELISSA) [113] proposed Spirulina as one of the primary foods to be cultivated during long-term space missions. Spirulina is commonly administered by first responders to people dying of starvation. In general recovery times are shorter and the percentages of people who are actually saved using Spirulina as the main nutrient source are higher than any other food option.

Scores of different algal species are consumed globally and are a regular menu item in the diets of cultures from the Far East to the North Atlantic and South Pacific. Many algal species are able to concentrate high levels of omega 3 and a variety of other unsaturated essential fatty acids efficiently which are highly sought after as nutrients that support heart and circulatory health. Fish that consume these varieties of micro-algae are themselves high in omega 3 and very much prized for their nutritional attributes as they further concentrate that essential fatty acid. It is however possible to bypass the fish completely in terms of harvesting this critical health supporting ingredient by cultivating suitable strains of micro-algae in farm-like settings. The challenge with this process is that omega 3 only makes up a small portion of the oils that can be extracted form omega 3 rich algal sources. Therefore, further refinement and separation is required to achieve a pure end-product.

One of the more critical roles algae are likely to play in the coming years is as a feed source for livestock and aquaculture. The inclusion of certain strains of protein/omega-3 rich algae has been finding their way into livestock operations around the world. Dairy products such as milk and eggs harvested from animals on an algae supplement diet concentrate omega-3 offering an added health benefit to those food groups. In addition, recent studies show that pigs, chicken, and lamb fed a high algae diet are growing faster and healthier. This has presented an option to many farmers who formally had to rely on soy shipped from great distances as their primary feed source.

As ocean fish stocks continue to decline, more and more of our "seafood" will come from aquaculture. Algal bio-flocks are a combination of various algae species living in a common environment. To make up for the disappearing "feeder fish" which formally comprised much of the aquaculture diet, inclusion of formulated algae groups will be essential. Every cultured species has particular dietary needs and live in specific temperature/PH/salinity environments. Those conditions impact the choice of the algal strains which must be matched to those exact parameters. Algae bio-flocks will provide many of the base nutrients those farmed species require for healthy growth. Additionally, there are many cases the algae are there to provide the top of the food chain feeding other small animals that are then eaten by the fish. Such is the case when microalgae are used to cultivate brine shrimp as an example. The cultured shrimp produce dormant eggs which can then be hatched when needed to feed various crustaceans, fish larvae, and mature fish.

Algae bio-flock development promises to be a critically important and growing science if we are to have viable aquaculture production and raise healthy and nutritious farmed seafood in the coming years. Much research and development is necessary to determine those precise mixes. Along with raising insects for protein and livestock feed, this field is in the early stages of becoming a huge industry.

Fertilizer and Farm Waste Control

The days of farmers depending on endless supplies of factory delivered fertilizer will soon to come to an end. This is a little bit more than a threatening possibility if you have a farm or are one of the many people who like to eat fruits, vegetables, or grains. Most soil used for farming around the world is now almost completely dependent on inputs of critical nutrients in order to support crop growth. Without regular soil enhancement with fertilizer farmers would have no crops to harvest. The solution to this challenge may be as simple as incorporating algae production into the conventional farm structure.

As a result of being water borne organisms algae have the wonderful ability of being able to feed on and concentrate nutrients in solution. Chief among these nutrients are the phosphates, nitrogen, and carbon found in the fertilizer used to enhance crop growth, and common to the effluent streams of livestock and sewage. Because of this attribute algae are an ideal choice for treating waste-water and the liquid effluent streams created during the cultivation of plants and animals.

One of the big issues facing farmers when addressing agricultural waste is the uncontrolled runoff of irrigation water leeching undesirable elements and chemicals into neighboring water systems. As detailed in earlier chapters this can cause widespread damage as excess phosphates and nitrogen components in that runoff create algae blooms in neighboring water ways. By consuming those waste nutrients, the algae grow uncontrollably. As they die off and decompose that process uses up all the oxygen in the water creating what are known as hypoxic events or "dead zones". This has decimated many coastal waters and lakes throughout the world.In a controlled or "captive" setting however, this same ability has extreme value to the farmer or rancher. Cultured algae fed a regular diet of farm runoff grow quickly and can then be spread onto the soil in place of other fertilizers. It will be necessary in the future to redesign farms irrigation systems such that water runoff is re-directed to onsite ponds and treatment raceways such that these valuable and potentially harmful elements remain on the farm and not in our waterways.

Source Flickr   B Source Homeland Security News Wire

Livestock operations create massive amounts of solid and liquid waste. Much of that waste is already recycled to enhance soil productivity around the world. In more advanced and modern operations very often that waste ends up in sewage lagoons. Still a considerable quantity still seems to find its way into adjacent water ways and aquifers. Whether the waste comes from cows, pigs, chickens, goats, or any of the many other animals raised for their meat and dairy products, it is considered a major nuisance. Disposing of those wastes can also be very involved depending on local laws and restrictions. Additionally, there may be considerable costs involved.

Processing this waste through algae ponds gives the farmer the ability to both eliminate these concerns while developing the capacity to recycle valuable nutrients. This would appear to be a perfect solution to this challenge

"Agricultural Research Service scientists found that 60–90% of nitrogen runoff and 70–100% of phosphorus runoff can be captured from manure effluents using a horizontal algae scrubber, also called an algal turf scrubber (ATS). Scientists developed the ATS, which are shallow, 100-foot raceways of nylon netting where algae colonies can form, and studied its efficacy for three years. They found that algae can readily be used to reduce the nutrient runoff from agricultural fields and increase the quality of water flowing into rivers, streams, and oceans. The enriched algae itself also can be used as a fertilizer. Researchers collected and dried the nutrient-rich algae from the ATS and studied its potential as an organic fertilizer. They found that cucumber and corn seedlings grew just as well using ATS organic fertilizer as they did with commercial fertilizers. [114] Algae scrubbers, using bubbling up flow or vertical waterfall versions, are now also being used to filter aquariums and ponds." [115]

Algae can also be used by many livestock operations as a feed source. In this way many of the nutrients pulled from the waste streams can essentially be recycled time and again having a dramatic positive impact to the farmer's operational expenses. Various forms of algae can be cultured in clear tanks, or pumped through ponds and raceways to be directly harvested for this purpose.

Of course, to accomplish this and create a much more sustainable farming operation will require careful thought in designing and building modern farm infrastructure. Many new technologies exist to help in these efforts however the money needed to bring these improvements about is often unavailable. This is particularly true in the developing world and with smaller farming operations.

Additionally, there is also the perception that these changes are purely to help the environment and not cost effective such that farmers resist taking these critical steps. This couldn't be further from the truth as the payback from such planned operations can be a major boast to the operation's bottom line. In many cases such improvements can be the reason a farm is able to remain viable and profitable and thus "sustainable". In the case of livestock, the waste created can be potentially as valuable as the dairy and meat products they provide when they are processed properly.

Pollution Control

Growing massive amounts of "industrial" algae may ultimately be one of the best strategies when it comes to actively reducing CO2 in the biosphere. Like all plants algae digests CO2 as part of their growth cycle. Algae grow rapidly doubling in size over very short periods of time which make them an excellent storage source for excess and unwanted CO2. Whether that CO2 is already in the atmosphere and oceans, or being produced as a waste stream of industrial production, there is much value in managing those potential feed sources.

There are two different strategies that could potentially be employed to reduce CO2 over an extended time frame. The first involves raising algae in enormous engineered open holding ponds, inland lakes, and raceways. Although this makes the algae susceptible to contamination it would maximize production while greatly minimizing costs. There are vast areas of coastal and inland "bad" lands which could be developed with large infrastructure projects that would be perfect for this type of concept. The Australian outback is a perfect example. By pumping huge quantities of sea water into these large engineered inland seas it would be possible to start redefining the supply chain for a number of critical markets. The algae could eventually replace declining feed and commodity resources while greatly increasing global CO2 absorption capacity. This could also provide an ancillary benefit to regions struggling with sewage/wastewater treatment strategies. We are talking about development projects on a fantastic scale with capital expenditures that would be historic. That being said an entire new industry would be formed providing countless jobs and limitless profitability.

This process will only have the desired impacts on CO2 levels however if we simultaneously stop some of our current destructive practices. That includes ongoing deforestation, the non-regulation of pollution standards for sea-going transports and container ships, and increasing power plant and factory emissions... which brings us to the second portion of the solution.

Algae farms need to be designed and built in conjunction and parallel with the power plants and industries that create much of the emissions we are currently pumping into our atmosphere. Right now, there many such demonstration projects underway that are attempting to prove out the viability of such models. Various species of microalgae are being cultivated using the emissions of power stations for a variety of algae-based end products which we have covered in this chapter.

One of the issues that will have to be addressed if there is to be wide spread adoption of the ISD concept is land use restrictions. Zoning regulations in many developed nations understandably divide land used for farming from land used for industry due to health concerns. Technology now exists to filter those emissions and redirect "sanitary" CO_2 such that it can be used for algae and plant development. By building facilities that can emit those gases adjacent to the site you can greatly increase production levels of the crops while recycling the CO_2 back into living organisms. This would have a huge impact in countries that rely heavily on burning coal for their electricity such as China. It would also be necessary to use additional technologies to deal with other toxic and waste gases in the emission stream, but given the commitment and focus this is achievable.

Algae are also very useful in treating sewage and industrial waste. The use of algae as a filtering "processing" agent can eliminate the need for harmful chemicals that might otherwise be used in that process. Additionally, certain strains of algae have shown the ability to turn otherwise toxic chemicals into less harmful elements. This is an incredibly useful attribute considering the difficulty involved with disposing of some of these more dangerous compounds.

Fuel

The ultimate goal for many of the companies and investors now focusing on algae development is the production of biofuel. More focus and money have been spent on this potential market than all other areas of algae production combined. It has garnered the interest of mostly all of the major oil companies. Those companies such as Exxon have then created partnerships with the largest algae development companies in an attempt to develop this market.

In the U.S much of this effort has been spurred on by the Navy announcing a goal of having a 50% biofuel fleet by 2020. Similar initiatives have been announced by the airlines, and several European Nations are now pushing for this change-over within the next decade. The U.S Navy and naval air force are the single largest consumers of fuel on our planet. To prove out the viability of such a policy shift a demonstration of the potential use of biofuels is deemed necessary. "Rather than one group of ships the Navy plans for biofuels to comprise up to 50% of the fuel used by deploying ships and aircraft throughout the fleet in calendar year 2016. Procurement has already begun for advanced drop-in biofuels." [116] This conversion effort has been led by Chris Tindal, director for operational energy under the direction of Secretary of the Navy Admiral Ray Mabus. It calls for advanced biofuel production stipulating that the sources of the fuel be non-food based. This has eliminated fuels derived from corn, sugar, palm and many other crops from their consideration. As a result, the interest in producing fuel from lipid rich strains of algae has skyrocketed.

Source Sapphire Energy

Thus far it has been a huge challenge to produce algae fuel at a cost that is competitive with standard fossil fuels. It is first necessary to find the proper lipid rich strains from the vast numbers of algal species. Then the algae must be "broken" apart to remove the oil and dewatered as part of the production process. With existing technologies this can be a labor intensive and expensive process. Much of the development effort has had to be subsidized to try and reach these production goals. To supply fleets with adequate quantities for demonstration operations the navy has had to pay upwards of $30 a gallon for "drop-in" biofuel. Trial biofuels delivered into the Afghanistan theatre have cost the Army over $430 per gallon. If algae fuel is to replace conventional oil and gas as a viable fuel source these price points will have to be on par or lower than comparable fossil fuels to attract consumers. Industry experts admit that algae development for fuel is not yet profitable and as such have been supplementing development costs with strains sold for other purposes such as nutraceuticals and high-end chemical additives.

 Current projections of anticipated improvements and technical breakthroughs have algae fuel development reaching that critical fuel price point by around 2025.

Section Conclusion

Humankind has inflicted a great deal of damage to our global environment. That destruction is ongoing and threatening the very core systems that provide the means by which we will survive and thrive in the near future. It only makes logical sense to employ the same bio-organisms that created our atmosphere, cleaned up the pre-existing toxicity of our primeval environment, and provided the base of our food chain to play a key role in reversing and rebalancing that equation. The potential of algae to treat waste streams while creating a huge number of critically needed resources and commodities that are in great demand and diminishing supply cannot be overstated.

If we are to be successful in this effort then the inclusion of algae in a great variety of applications that apply to production, housing, site management, and waste treatment will have to be the norm. It is the very versatility and integrative capacity that makes algae the ideal partner for almost any ISD project which includes organic waste streams. We need our inventors and developers looking not just at large commercial projects, but rather the creation of smaller onsite applications suitable for homes, businesses, and rural villages. Those that can process waste or create critically needed fertilizer, animal feed, nutrients and supplemental food sources are of particular importance. Such applications will help to offset the anticipated short falls in future global food output. Additionally, algae can play a major role in reducing the damaging impacts of uncontrolled releases of nitrogen and phosphorous that ravage our riparian environments.

Algae will also have a key role to play in replacing current fossil fuels and reducing global CO_2 concentrations. The fact that algae consumes CO_2 as it produces those specific fuel lipids will help offset the CO_2 released by its use. Issues related to extraction, dewatering, and processing will have to be resolved. Many local governments will be tasked with re-evaluating zoning methodology in order for commercial operations to operate in close proximity to industry/agriculture.

The 21st century will have to be a time where humankind finally recognizes the value and necessity of these organisms that we have up to now taken for granted.

It was because of algae that humankind has evolved to this point. If we are to evolve any further it may well owe our future to the thoughtful use of these same miraculous organisms.

Chapter Twenty

Protecting Our Priceless Biodiversity

"Don't it always seem to go that you don't know what you've got till it's gone?"

~ Joni Mitchell

It is only because of the arrogance and infinite ignorance of human beings that we believe we can exist on Earth without the very organisms that have been critical to our accentuation as a species. Bio-diversity is essential to our ongoing survival. It is our treatment of the various life forms with which we share this planet that brand humankind as interstellar barbarians and ecological ingrates. We think of ourselves as civilized when our legacy has been nothing short of mindless destruction and unrestrained killing. It's not bad enough that we treat our forgotten family that way by mindlessly competing and waring against one another. The tragedy is that we have extended that mindset to the environment by destroying the very balance of the natural order. We have accomplished this thoughtless and despicable end as we foolishly compete and fight each other for the rights to consume the riches of this world oblivious to the damage we inflict on those resources. Humankind is a plague.

Harsh sentiments for sure, but that is a pretty accurate assessment of recent human activity on planet Earth. "The Holocene extinction, sometimes called the Sixth Extinction, is a name proposed to describe the currently ongoing extinction event of species during the present Holocene epoch (since around 10,000 BCE) mainly due to human activity. The large number of extinctions span numerous families of plants and animals including mammals, birds, amphibians, reptiles and arthropods. Although 875 extinctions occurring between 1500 and 2009 have been documented by the International Union for Conservation of Nature and Natural Resources, [117] the vast majority are undocumented. According to the species-area theory and based on upper-bound estimating, the present rate of extinction may be up to 140,000 species per year." [118,119]

"Rapid environmental changes typically cause mass extinctions. [120,121,122] More than 99 percent of all species, amounting to over five billion species, [123] that ever lived on Earth are estimated to be extinct. [124,125] Estimates on the number of Earth's current species range from 10 million to 14 million, [126] of which about 1.2 million have been documented and over 86 percent have not yet been described." [127,128]

As discussed earlier in this book bio-diversity is of incalculable value and perhaps the single most important and priceless asset we are earthly stewards over. If we are to emerge from this century with a world that is remotely similar to what I have experienced during my lifetime we need to come to grips with this threat. Humankind must recognize the consequences of our actions and find ourselves equal to the challenge of altering our resource management behaviors. This will require a coordinated and cooperative global strategy unprecedented in our human experience. Without such a plan the future will assuredly and predictably resemble one of those many sci-fi movies I have watched during my lifetime that depict desperate future civilizations surviving off what's left of our barren world. How can we be so ignorant and unfeeling such that we are condemning our children and grandchildren to this fate?

What I am proposing is a plan to avoid this eventuality. We can counter this trend by linking the efforts of all the great global institutions of learning, zoos, aquariums, government agencies, and environmental organizations to the experts within the science community doing work on genomics. This would include all the entities that focus their efforts on preserving, managing, and protecting the creatures and plants in our earthly environment. All efforts would then be directed at identifying specific species and varied at-risk ecosystems in a coordinated strategy of collection, storing and preservation of genetic materials.

Science is on the brink of great advancements when it comes to cloning and our abilities to regenerate species for which they have full and complete genomic samples. What is required is a globally coordinated effort to collect and store genetic samples of every at-risk species both animal and plant on land or in water. Those samples of genetic materials need to be indexed and safely stored before those declining species disappear permanently. A complete library must be established in every varied ecosystem on our planet such that those plants and animals native to those environments may be reintroduced at a later date when their survival can be better managed and unthreatened.

This should be a major goal we start immediately proceeding with all due haste as time is a factor. It is an effort that will only become more necessary as changes to the environment and destruction of ecosystems continue with the increasing momentum of climate and chemical changes in our biosphere. As far as our immediate future we should prepare for the worst and take all prudent steps to make possible the regeneration of our planet in future years. This is essential if we one day hope to re-establish the rich biodiversity we now enjoy today.

Similar programs which store and protect the seeds of historic grains have been in operation around the world for decades. The Svalbard Global Seed Vault located in Norway has a mission to provide a safety net against accidental loss of diversity in traditional gene banks. While the popular press has emphasized its possible utility in the event of a major regional or global catastrophe, it will be more frequently accessed when gene banks lose samples due to mismanagement, accident, equipment failures, funding cuts, and natural disasters. These events occur with some regularity. War and civil strife have a history of destroying some gene banks. The national seed bank of the Philippines was damaged by flooding and later destroyed by a fire; the seed banks of Afghanistan and Iraq have been lost completely. [129] According to The Economist, "the Svalbard vault is a backup for the world's 1,750 seed banks, storehouses of 1." [130]

There are enormous amounts of money currently being spent on habitat protection and species preservation. Despite our best efforts at insuring long term survival of these species and ecosystems, we may fail in our individual efforts. It would be prudent to establish safeguards for those irreplaceable species and habitats in such worst-case scenarios. Though it may take centuries to re-establish certain species and ecosystems it is conceivably within our technical capacity to do so given enough time and focused efforts.

Humankind in this short, specific period in our current history has overwhelmed the natural order. Regardless of what we now do, we will only have a limited impact on stopping the continuing damage that is occurring to the environment. It is past time we recognize this truth of our current dilemma. We need to make all necessary plans taking all immediate steps to plan for the remediation and re-establishment process that will have to take place as things settle out by the end of this century. At that point we can access the damage and make long term plans to correct that which we can and start to regenerate and reintroduce that which was lost. To accept this responsibility and take on this challenge will require great foresight, understanding, and active participation of our global leaders. They need to be concerned and they must act now. Those concerns start and end with our biodiversity.

Chapter Twenty-One

The Energime Model and Mission.

A Tiered Approach to Sustainable Development

"If Gandhi were ever to be reincarnated as a company, corporation, or economic entity, his soul and his very dreams for humanity would be expressed as Energime."

~ **William Sosinsky**

The idea for Energime came to me when I was a very young man of seventeen. At that point it was just a passing thought. I believed humankind would soon address all our impending issues with the environment and resource management well before such an entity would ever be necessary. Certainly, we could see the writing on the wall such that we would eventually find a way to work together to stave off unthinkable disaster. Certainly, we would not be that foolish. I was wrong.

The truth is homo-sapiens have certain traits and weaknesses as a species which are so deeply ingrained as to make it almost impossible for us to work together in common purpose. It is the un-anticipated and unfortunate consequence of varying traditional approaches and differences in cultural conditioning that will destroy us. Our passions overwhelm our logic as sure as our short-term self-interests undermine our long-term security. Every culture I have had the honor and joy to learn from and spend time in during my years of travel have traits both positive and limiting. These perspectives work in their favor while at the same time conspiring against their best hopes for the future. When differences in opinion and approach are apparent between co-existing cultures conflict always seems to be the response. Whether those disagreements manifest themselves in the violence of war or tactical economic aggression it seems we know no other way to respond. The same is unfortunately true for individuals whose personal interests and egos undermine their ability to cooperate effectively on mutually beneficial strategies. So the question is "How do you get people who are not capable of working together collaboratively to collaborate if working in common purpose is essential for their mutual survival and prosperity?" The answer I came up with was what eventually became known as Energime.

When people ask me what Energime is and I attempt to describe it in its most simple and eloquent terms, I say to them "Energime is a socio-economic evolutionary entity disguised as a corporation". Most times they just cross their eyes and shake their heads not having the slightest concept of what I am talking about. Other times they nod approval in what ends up being nothing more than patronizing good manners. I have tried in vain thousands of times to describe in detail the core mission of Energime and the steps we have undertaken to accomplish these goals. It is because of my failure to clearly define and impart that vision to a critical mass of people such that they initiate determinative action that I have taken the time to write this book. It is because of that mission that I work without rest to make sure our children will have a future free of fear and suffering. An entity such as Energime is essential if we are going to make it past this century.

First of all, Energime is not a monolithic corporation. Energime is a movement, a coordinating force, a collaborative network, and a symbol of hope. Energime is the world's first truly humanitarian corporation. We are an entity that is trying to bring structural order such that our response to our current challenges of resource management and environmental stewardship are as comprehensive, coordinated, efficient, and impactful as possible.

Although Energime University is a 501 (3C) non-for-profit charitable effort, the main structure of Energime is a for-profit corporation. This was done with purpose. As the world is ultimately ruled by financial interests, a vehicle was needed to directly compete, partner, and influence those entities in order to alter their focus and operations. This effort would be far less effective as a charitable or humanities-based organization as that entity would have limited funds and reduced capacity to direct resources and make sweeping financial decisions with the speed and agility required for a timely and sufficient response.

The structural strategy for Energime expansion is fairly simple. Let's take the latter part of the twentieth century and the first part of the twenty-first century as a starting point. The internet for the first time in history has made it possible for an entity to reach a global audience with utmost efficiency and clarity. Microsoft introduced DOS software in 1981 which led a revolution in the way large quantities of information could be disseminated between different sites over great distances. Companies led by Cisco systems cultivated the lines of transmission and communication allowing that information to flow quickly and efficiently throughout the world. Google and other search engines made it possible to selectively access almost any subject you wished to investigate opening up unprecedented access to information. Energime is the natural forth step. Energime is attempting to use the incredible coordinating and communication potential of the internet to disseminate the required knowledge, skills, methodologies and strategies to empower people around the world as to how to correctly manage their sustainable existence. In that sense Energime is attempting to build and develop all the synaptic connections that can facilitate positive human change and forward evolution with the highest efficiency, speed, and impact. After all, as I have stated over and over, time is not on our side. This way the internet could serve what ultimately could be its single and most important potential function.

Reversing our current course is a global challenge that necessitates a global response. It is a relatively simple concept in theory, however the devil is in the details. In order to affectively accomplish this end requires the participation and capabilities of a great many players all of whom view the world differently. You must manage a responsive force/team, all of whom have similar aims but different expectations, stake holds, interests, skills, capabilities, and ideas as how to best solve any particular challenge. Once engaged with one another we have seen time and time again the inhibitors of fear, self-interest, and ego derail any truly positive forward movement. Therefore, I saw the need for a system of change that could operate as an independent entity to address all the issues that our global societies seemed unable or unwilling to address effectively amongst themselves.

Energime was set up as a collaborative model that owes its allegiance to humankind. In that sense it belongs to no one country and yet belongs to anyone and everyone willing to participate in contributing to an overall solution. Energime does not judge, discriminate, nor withhold effort or assistance when it comes to religion, ethnicity, country, political ideology, or creed. All Energime wishes to do is help. We do not judge. As a fair and balanced servant of humanity we stay out of politics, and we do not take sides other than making every effort to help those who are in need of food, water, and basic necessities.

The way I imagined Energime operating was to employ several approaches based on the maturity, culture, and relative wealth of the country or society we were looking to partner with. In the developing world the idea would be to set up a "parallel" economy. Investments would be made into Energime projects that supported waste management, food production, energy, and water management. Those profits would then be reinvested to fund an independent but coordinated ongoing infrastructure improvement strategy within that country. In this way governments who lack sufficient financial resources to do these kinds of projects would be relieved of substantial responsibilities as to its cost and implementation. Energime would seek out in-country partnership with both private and public groups to develop step by step strategies in building out sustainable infrastructure and consumer integration models. By necessity these methodologies stress profitability, job creation, economic development, and increases in the general standard of living. Without such an approach the model would not be adapted as it would be unattractive to investors and government leadership, or would quickly collapse as a consequence of competing market pressures.

In the developed world it is much more about changing industrial production, property management, consumer purchasing and consumption patterns. This is accomplished by replacing standard market development models with those practices, goods and services that support sustainable management of resources. Lower prices, better quality, higher efficiency, and superior convenience are the keys to encouraging this change-over. In this way you would improve "sustainable" working conditions and one's quality of life through a familiar and natural market progression. This makes the emphasis as simple as providing a better product or solution at a lower price with greater convenience.

Regardless of what projects Energime may become involved with, education and empowerment are the critical elements that go hand and hand with the economics of that particular platform, project, or model. Re-educating the human element that is served by that consumption cycle is critical to establishing true sustainability. Without the added element of improved individual management knowledge all efforts of providing more food, water, or energy to rebalance supply/demand are doomed to eventually fail. The result will only lead to increased consumption. Energime insists that a teaching and training protocol accompany all infrastructure projects. We plan to accomplish that mission with the inclusion of Energime University annexes being simultaneously introduced and accompanying all of our regional efforts and project build outs. Additionally, we plan to include informative and education materials, advertising, and promotional efforts with all our consumer initiatives. In this way a constant stream of re-conditioning sustainable knowledge and skills will slowly but surely be disseminated throughout our global population.

Energime has the goal to be one of the larger corporations in operation anywhere. We intend to vest branches and establish partnerships with collaborative companies and groups throughout the world. As part of that effort Energime is asking for great leeway and consideration from local governments and groups with which we work in terms of allowing us access to their markets. We are also hoping to provide guidance/consultancy over the implementation of regional resource management planning strategies. That has the potential to create conflicts of interest.

We understand that the potential for profitability in the production and management areas we are looking to develop with these relationships could create a great amount of wealth. It is therefore essential that the company and movement exercise the very highest degree of transparency and honorable intention such that it is crystal clear our mission is of a humanitarian/environmental nature and not just aimed at wealth creation for the few and privileged. To use these confidences to maximize the participation of concerned groups to generate profits for the primary sake of individual interests would be nothing short of evil and potentially quite destructive to the collaborative environment we are attempting to establish. As such the Energime profit structure must be well defined so that the bulk of the profits we directly receive in those partnerships are reinvested into tangent efforts in the host countries.

I do not have the ability to make everyone in Energime or with whom we work or partner with be anything other than what they are. Some people will work with us strictly for the money while others will be inclined to participate because of their concerns and commitment to the causes we promote. As the head and CEO of this company with the power of final decisions I can only say that I will never, under any circumstance, or for any price or enticement fail to withhold the guiding principles of Energime. As such I have taken a public pledge to forgo my own earning potential by solemnly pledging to never take out any Energime shares nor live extravagantly as a result of my work and contributions to the growth and success of the company for the duration of my lifetime. What others in my company decide to do and what our partners do I cannot control and I have no expectations for how they live their lives and spend their earnings. I can only speak for myself such that any group that wishes to partner with us understands it is not about personal wealth for me. All decisions will be made in the best interests of the people we serve and to provide the best solutions for the challenges we are addressing. Money and financial leverage are a tool which Energime needs to help save our world and I am completely dedicated to that singular principle. For that reason, I shall never live my life in a manner that is in any way different in terms of life style than the modest existence my family and I now enjoy.

A word of caution is needed. People should be very aware and suspect of companies and entities claiming to have the same mission or claiming ties to Energime when they are in fact using those claims for less honorable purposes. There are those that will say whatever they can to create a deceptive public perception or create a favorable "green" image to get your "concerned" or "targeted" money. Energime, our name, and our message are constantly being pirated by groups who have no intention to follow through or support the unified effort we are working so diligently to establish. Additionally, many corporations, politicians, public interest groups, and financial groups do whatever they can to promote those images when in fact they do very little and have no intention to work in a focused and collaborative manner to contribute to the solutions Energime aspires to address. I would advise anyone committing funds, spending their money on products and services, or lending their support to entities that claim to have these goals to please be sure to do your research carefully. Divisive competition and insincere and unproductive entities merely trying to gain resources or public favor will strip this effort of the critical capital and passionate participation required for an efficient and effective global response. These efforts are extremely dangerous as they undermine our collective response to these issues as surely as they diminish trust and good will. These entities confuse, distract, and redirect support and funds from those who are genuinely concerned with methodically and collaboratively providing the appropriate and correct solutions.

For Energime to work we must all be a part of this effort. Whether that is expressed by changing your personal consumption habits or initiating great change in the workplace or with the entities you align yourself with, participation and thoughtful collaborative steps are essential to us turning things around.

Energime are the subatomic particles that make up the mass and constitute the very essence of matter. In this analogy we are all Energime when it comes to the health and vibrancy of our planet and our environment. You who are reading this book are inexorably tied to me. We are all of that same family that separated so long ago on the primeval plains of Africa. We share that same beginning and unless we remember that essential truth, we will we surely share the same end. Humanly love, concern, and responsibility for one another must be the defining step we take as we evolve from the barbarian commonly known as Homo Sapiens to the advanced beings we one day had hoped to become. Please find the faith and courage to take that step. After all, you are my family and we are all Energime.

Chapter Twenty Two

The World We Leave Our Children

"True love, concern, and honor is not singularly defined by intent, but rather an expression of impassioned will."

~ **William Sosinsky**

I often wonder how we will be remembered by future generations. Will we be cursed for our ignorance, or remembered for our courage? Will we still live separated by tribal customs founded in fear or mistrust, or will we finally bond together in mutual respect and recognize our common lineage? Will we limit our concern to only those we accept as our kin, or will we extend that love, support, and responsibility to those with customs we do not share and whose beliefs differ from our own? Will we evolve or will we perish?

My life has been blessed in so many ways. When I think of what matters, what has impacted me in my time on this earth, and what I will remember as I pass from this life it always comes back to the people I love. I will remember my family, my friends, my mentors and the moments we shared when my time comes. All I am or will ever be is a tapestry and expression of that which was gifted to me. I can be nothing other than grateful.

It is my only wish that I can pass on those same gifts to my children. I want that their lives should be filled with the promise, support, and happiness that I been so fortunate to experience during my short time here. I want them to know how deeply their father cherished them and that I was willing to sacrifice anything and everything of my own existence to make sure their futures were as bright.

I know that deep down in everyone's heart that we all wish those same fortunes for the ones we hold dear. It is time for us all to focus on that goal and the responsibilities that come with it and consider the future we are about to leave to our children. Will they remember us with affection and gratitude for our concern and wisdom, or will they perish because of our ignorance? Could anything be more important?

With all the love, passion, and respect in my heart... please find the courage to engage and take up this fight with me. You are my family. If we stand together, we can save the future for our children. If not...

Our success depends on you.

The End

REFERENCES

(1) Pg. 16, The Guardian 2/2/2015- 14 of the 15 hottest years on record have occurred since 2000, UN says

(2) Pg. 18, Millero, Frank J. (1995). "Thermodynamics of the carbon dioxide system in the oceans". *Geochimica et Cosmochimica Acta* 59 (4): 661–677. Bibcode:1995GeCoA..59..661M. doi:10.1016/0016-7037(94)00354-O

(3) Pg. 18, Feely, R. A. et al. (July 2004). "Impact of Anthropogenic CO2 on the CaCO3 System in the Oceans". *Science* 305 (5682): 362–366. Bibcode:2004Sci...305..362F. doi:10.1126/science.1097329. PMID 15256664

(4) Pg. 18, Jacobson, M. Z. (2005). "Studying ocean acidification with conservative, stable numerical schemes for nonequilibrium air-ocean exchange and ocean equilibrium chemistry". Journal of Geophysical Research – *Atmospheres* 110: D07302. Bibcode:2005JGRD..11007302J. doi:10.1029/2004JD005220

(5) Pg. 19, How Acidification Threatens Oceans from the Inside Out Fiona Harvey, environment correspondent (2013-08-25).

(6) Pg. 19, Huffington Post, 9 July 2012, "Ocean Acidification Is Climate Change's 'Equally Evil Twin,' NOAA Chief Says,"

(7) Pg. 19, "Rising levels of acids in seas may endanger marine life, says study | Environment" The Guardian. Retrieved 2013-08-29

(8) Pg. 19, Climate Progress-Nature Stunner: "Global warming blamed for 40% decline in the ocean's phytoplankton" by Joe Romm Jul 29, 2010

(9) Pg. 19, Spalding, M.D., C. Ravilious, and E.P. Green. 2001. United Nations Environment Programme, World Conservation Monitoring Centre. World Atlas of Coral Reefs. University of California Press: Berkeley. 416 pp.

(10) Pg. 20, McInherney, F.A.; Wing, S. (2011). "A perturbation of carbon cycle, climate, and biosphere with implications for the future". *Annual Reviews of Earth Science* 39: 489–516. Bibcode:2000Geo....28..927R. doi:10.1130/0091-7613(2000)28<927:NCFTLP>2.0.CO;2 Zachos, J.C.; Dickens, G.R.; Zeebe, R.E. (2008). "An early Cenozoic perspective on greenhouse warming and carbon-cycle dynamics"(PDF). Nature (journal) **451** (7176): 279–83. Bibcode:2008Natur.451..279Z. doi:10.1038/nature06588. PMID 18202643

(11) Pg. 20, "The Geological Record of Ocean Acidification". JournalistsResource.org, retrieved 14 March 2012 -Hönisch, Bärbel; Ridgwell, Andy; Schmidt, Daniela N.; Thomas, E.; Gibbs, S. J.; Sluijs, A.; Zeebe, R.; Kump, L.; Martindale, R. C.; Greene, S. E.; Kiessling, W.; Ries, J.; Zachos, J. C.; Royer, D. L.; Barker, S.; Marchitto, T. M.; Moyer, R.; Pelejero, C.; Ziveri, P.; Foster, G. L.; Williams, B. (2012). "The Geological Record of Ocean Acidification". Science 335 (6072): 1058–1063. Bibcode:2012Sci...335.1058H. doi:10.1126/science.1208277. PMID 22383840

(134) Pg. 21, NASA (8 December 2011). "Paleoclimate Record Points Toward Potential Rapid Climate Changes"

(12) Pg. 22, "Is sea level rising?". NOAA National Ocean Service. 2014-06-19.

(13) Pg. 22, SEA LEVEL VARIATIONS OVER GEOLOGIC TIME M. A. Kominz , Western Michigan University,Kalamazoo, MI, USACopyright 2001 Academic Press

(14) Pg. 22, Anisimov et al., Section 11.2.1.2: Models of thermal expansion (Sea Levels), Table 1.3, in IPCC TAR WG1 2001.

(15) Pg. 22, Geologic Contral on Fast Ice Flow – West Antarctic Ice Sheet

(16) Pg. 23, Green Peace-Sea level rise- 4 July, 2012

(17) Pg. 24, Atmospheric intensity Emanuel, K. 2005. Increasing destructiveness of tropical cyclones over the past 30 years. Nature 436:686-688.

(18) Pg. 24, Atmospheric intensity Emanuel, K. 2005. Emanuel Replies. Nature 438:E13.

(19) Pg. 24, Atmospheric intensity Webster, P.J., G.J. Holland, J.A. Curry, and H-R. Chang. 2005. Changes in tropical cyclone number, duration, and intensity in a warming environment. Science 309:1844-1846.

(20) Pg. 24, Atmospheric intensity Brenda Ekwurzel (Union of Concerned Scientists) prepared this summary with helpful reviews by Kevin Trenberth (National Center for Atmospheric Research) and Kerry Emanuel (Massachusetts Institute of Technology). ©2006 Union of Concerned Scientists.

(21) Pg. 24, Desertification Google Dictionary (2012)

(22) Pg. 25, Desertification –Didyouknow.Org Deserts and desertification (2010)

(23) Pg. 25, Desertification. LOWDERMILK, W C. "CONQUEST OF THE LAND THROUGH SEVEN THOUSAND YEARS". *Soil Conservation Service*. United States Department of Agriculture. Retrieved 9 April 2014.

(24) Pg. 25, Desertification Dregne, H.E. "Desertification of Arid Lands". Columbia University. Retrieved 3 December 2013.

(134) Pg. 26, "Desertification map" by USDA employee - http://www.nrcs.usda.gov/wps/portal/nrcs/detail/national/nedc/training/soil/?cid=nrc s142p2_054003. Licensed under Public Domain via Wikimedia Commons http://commons.wikimedia.org/wiki/File:Desertification_map.png#mediaviewer/File :Desertification_map.png

(25) Pg. 28, Fabricant DS, Farnsworth NR (March 2001). "The value of plants used in traditional medicine for drug discovery". *Environ. Health Perspect*. 109 Suppl 1 (Suppl 1): 69–75. doi:10.1289/ehp.01109s169. PMC 1240543. PMID 11250806

(26) Pg. 29, Water Scarcity | International Decade for Action 'Water for Life' 2005-2015". 20 October 2013.

(27) Pg. 30, The Water Project http://thewaterproject.org/water_scarcity_2/Blue Planet Facts http://www.blueplanet.nsw.edu.au/water-facts/.aspx

28) Pg. 34, Great Pacific garbage patch - Marks, Kathy (5 February 2008). "The world's rubbish dump". *The Independent* (London). Retrieved 4 May 2010.

(29) Pg. 36, Air Pollution /Article byPaul Evans *April 23, 2009*

(30) Pg. 37, EDGAR: Trends in global CO2 emissions: 2014 report

(31) Pg. 38, NRDC (Nuclear Program Staff Publication) nuc_01009302a_112b.pdf

(32) Pg. 38, BBC News "Mafia Sank Ships of Toxic Waste" 9/16/2009

(33) Pg. 38, The Moscow Times- Sunken Soviet Submarines Threaten Nuclear Catastrophe in Russia's Arctic By **Matthew Bodner** Nov. 13 2014

(34) Pg. 46, Reuters Sep 19, 2014 Top rice exporter India importing over 100,000 T on temporary supply squeeze NEW DELHI | By Mayank Bhardwaj

The World We Leave Our Children

(135) Pg. 39, (Dzerzhinsk Makes It to the Top Ten Most Ecologically Adverse Cities of the Russian Federation)

(35) Wed Dec 24, 2014 2:04pm EST Russia's grain exports stop: farm lobby MOSCOW/ABU DHABI | By Polina Devitt and Maha El Dahan

(36) China Looks Abroad for Greener Pastures-Los Angeles Times By Barbara Demick 3/29/2014

(37) Pg. 49, "Colony Collapse Disorder Progress Report" United States Department of Agriculture. June 2010. Retrieved 2012-05-24.

(38) Pg. 49, "US sets up honey bee loss task force" BBC News. 20 Jun 2014. Retrieved 21 Jun 2014.

(39) Pg. 52, Grafton, Q. R., & Hussey, K. (2011). Water Resources Planning and Management. New York: Cambridge University Press.

(40) Pg. 52, UN Water - Coping with Water Scarcity 2007

(41) Pg. 54, One World One Ocean http://www.oneworldoneocean.com/pages/our-goals

(136) Pg. 54, http://qz.com/164029/tropical-race-4-global-banana-industry-is-killing-the-worlds-favorite-fruit/

(42) Pg. 74, World With 11 Billion People? New Population Projections Shatter Earlier Estimates Dueling projections of population growth present different visions of the world's future. By Robert Kunzig, National Geographic PUBLISHED September 19, 2014

(43) Waste Pg. 111, "Glossary of Environment Statistics." 1997. UNSD. 1997. unstats.un.org (100) MSW p115, Wikipedia -Pyrolysis.

(44) MSW p117, Wikipedia -Pyrolysis.

(45) Pg. 118, "Plasma Gasification" United States Department of Energy. Retrieved 2010-08-07.

(46) MSW Pg. 118, Wikipedia -Plasma Arc Gasification.

- 196 -

(47). Farm Waste Pg. 121, Bundy, L., & Good , L. (2006, January). Development and validation of the wisconsin phosphorus index. Retrieved from http://www.soils.wisc.edu/extension/materials/PI_Validation.pdf

(48) Farm Waste Pg. 121, Fighting Peak Phosphorus, http://web.mit.edu/12.000/www/m2016/finalwebsite/solutions/phosphorus.html The Future of Strategic Natural Resources

(49) Farm Waste Pg. 121, Lead market potential for phosphorus recycling technologies in Germany Christian Sartorius Fraunhofer Institute for Systems and Innovation Research ISI, Karlsruhe, Germany http://www.isi.fraunhofer.de/isi-wAssets/docs/n/en/publikationen/Sartorius-2012_Lead-market_P-recycling_DE-1.pdf

(50) Pg. 127, United Nations. World Water Assessment Programme (2009). "Water in a Changing World: Facts and Figures." World Water Development Report 3. p.58 Accessed 2012-06-13.

(51) Pg. 127, Nitti, Gianfranco (May 2011). "Water is not an infinite resource and the world is thirsty". *The Italian Insider* (Rome).

(52) Pg. 128, Agriculture Consumes 92% of Freshwater Used Globally - US Leads Per Capita Consumption   http://www.treehugger.com/sustainable-agriculture/agriculture-consumes-92-all-freshwater-used-globally-and-us-leads-capita-consumption.html

(53) Pg. 131, Levine, Audrey D.; Takashi Asano (1 June 2004). "Peer Reviewed: Recovering Sustainable Water from Wastewater". *Environmental Science & Technology* 45: 203A. doi:10.1021/es040504n. Retrieved 20 March 2012.

(54) Pg. 131, Reclaimed water-Wikipedia-http://en.wikipedia.org/wiki/Reclaimed_water

(55) Pg. 132, Offshore fresh groundwater reserves as a global phenomenon. Vincent E.A. Post, Jacobus Groen, Henk Kooi, Mark Person, Shemin Ge & W. Mike Edmunds

(56) Pg. 134, Wikipedia Fresh Water- http://en.wikipedia.org/wiki/Fresh_water

(59) Pg. 135, Nitti, Gianfranco (May 2011). "Water Is Not an Infinite Resource and the World is Thirsty". *The Italian Insider* (Rome). p. 8.

(57) Pg. 135, "Waterfootprint.org: Water footprint and virtual water". The Water Footprint Network. Retrieved 9 April 2014.

(58) Pg. 135, Allan, Tony (2011). *Virtual water : tackling the threat to our planet's most precious resource.* London: I.B. Tauris. ISBN 978-1845119836.

(59) Pg. 135, Morelli, Angela (2012). "Virtual Water - Discover how much WATER we EAT everyday". Retrieved 9 April 2014.

(60) Pg. 140, Disease-Related Malnutrition: An Evidence-Based Approach to Treatment"When [food] intake is poor or absent for a long time (weeks), weight loss is associated with organ failure and death."

(61) Pg. 140, Malnutrition The Starvelings

(62) Pg. 140, "Hunger Stats"*World Food Programme.*

(63) Pg. 140, FAO The State of Food Insecurity in the World

(64) Pg. 140, Whitney, Ellie and Rolfes, Sharon Rady (2013). *Understanding Nutrition* (13 ed.). Wadsworth, Cengage Learning. pp. 667, 670. ISBN 978-1133587521.

(65) Pg. 141, Obesity, Weight Linked to Prostate Cancer Deaths – National Cancer Institute. Cancer.gov. Retrieved on 2011-10-17.

(66) Pg. 141, Obesity and Overweight for Professionals: Causes | DNPAO | CDC . Cdc.gov (2011-05-16). Retrieved on 2011-10-17.

(67) Pg. 141, Metabolic syndrome – PubMed Health. Ncbi.nlm.nih.gov. Retrieved on 2011-10-17.

(68) Pg. 141, Omega 3 Fatty Acid Deficiency – 11 Signs of Omega 3 Fatty Acid Deficiency. Bodybuildingforyou.com. Retrieved on 2011-10-17.

(69) Pg. 141, Omega-3 fatty acids. Umm.edu (2011-10-05). Retrieved on 2011-10-17.

(70) Pg. 141, What I need to know about Eating and Diabetes – National Diabetes Information Clearinghouse. Diabetes.niddk.nih.gov. Retrieved on 2011-10-17.

(71) Pg. 141, Diabetes Diet and Food Tips: Eating to Prevent and Control Diabetes. Helpguide.org. Retrieved on 2011-10-17.

(72) Pg. 141, Osteoporosis & Vitamin D: Deficiency, How Much, Benefits, and More. Webmd.com (2005-07-07). Retrieved on 2011-10-17.

(73) Pg. 141, Dietary Supplement Fact Sheet: Vitamin D. Ods.od.nih.gov. Retrieved on 2011-10-17.

(74) Pg. 141, Brody, Jane E. (March 19, 1998). "Osteoporosis Linked to Vitamin D Deficiency" . *The New York Times*. Archived from the original on 2008-03-09.

(75) Pg. 145, Chesworth, Ward, ed. (2008). *Encyclopedia of soil science*. Dordrecht, Netherlands: Springer. xxiv. ISBN 1-4020-3994-8.

(76) Pg. 145, Voroney, R. P. (2006). "The Soil Habitat". In Paul, Eldor A. *Soil Microbiology, Ecology and Biochemistry*. ISBN 0-12-546807-5.

(77) Pg. 145, Danoff-Burg, James A. "The Terrestrial Influence: Geology and Soils". Earth Institute Center for Environmental Sustainability. Columbia University. Retrieved 27 July 2014.

(78) Pg. 145, Taylor, S. A.; Ashcroft, G. L. (1972). *Physical Edaphology*.

(79) Pg. 146, Live Science - Deforestation: Facts, Causes & Effects by Alina Bradford, http://www.livescience.com/27692-deforestation.html

(80) Pg. 154, Smil (1991), p. 240

(81) Pg. 154, "Natural Forcing of the Climate System"

(82) Pg. 154, Smil (2006), p. 12

(83) Pg. 154, http://www.nature.com/nature/journal/v443/n7107/full/443019a.html

(84) Pg. 154, "Powering the Planet: Chemical challenges in solar energy utilization"

(PDF). Retrieved 7 August 2008.

(85) Pg. 153, Intergovernmental Panel on Climate Change. Retrieved 2007-09-29.

(86) Pg. 158, Your Home - Orientation
http://www.yourhome.gov.au/technical/fs43.html

(87) Pg. 158, "Glazing". Archived from the original on December 15, 2007. Retrieved 2011-11-03.

(88) Pg. 158, Springer, John L. (December 1954). "The 'Big Piece' Way to Build". *Popular Science* 165 (6): 157.

(89) Pg. 158, Your Home - Insulation
http://www.yourhome.gov.au/technical/fs43.html

(90) Pg. 156, "BERC - Airtightness". Ornl.gov. 2004-05-26. Retrieved 2010-03-16.

(91) Pg. 158, Passive solar building design-Wikipedia

(92) Pg. 159, Five Solar Thermal Principles Canivan, John, JC Solarhomes, 26 May 2008

(93) Pg. 165, Glassley, William E. (2010). *Geothermal Energy: Renewable Energy and the Environment*, CRC Press, ISBN 9781420075700

(94) Pg. 165, Wikipedia-Geothermal Energy

(95) Pg. 170, "Depleted Uranium as Fuel Cuts Path to Less Waste" Intellectual Ventures Management, LLC. Retrieved 19 August 2012.

(96) Pg. 170, Ellis, T.; R. Petroski (2010). "Traveling-wave reactors: A truly sustainable and full-scale resource for global energy needs" *American Nuclear Society* 42 (44): 546–558. Retrieved 19 August 2012.

(97) Pg. 171, NOAA's National Geophysical Data Center

(98) Pg. 172, "Fuel storage." Princton University. -Is hydrogen fuel dangerous? Josh Clark http://www.princeton.edu/~chm333/2002/spring/FuelCells/H_storage.shtml

(99) Pg. 173, Khurmi, R. S. Material Science

(100) Pg. 173, Wikipedia- Fuel Cell

(101) Pg. 173, "Fuel Cell Basics: Benefits" Fuel Cells 2000. Retrieved 2007-05-27.

(102) Pg. 176, Ade, P. A. R.; Aghanim, N.; Armitage-Caplan, C.; et al. (Planck Collaboration), C.; Arnaud, M.; Ashdown, M.; Atrio-Barandela, F.; Aumont, J.; Aussel, H.; Baccigalupi, C.; Banday, A. J.; Barreiro, R. B.; Barrena, R.; Bartelmann, M.; Bartlett, J. G.; Bartolo, N.; Basak, S.; Battaner, E.; Battye, R.; Benabed, K.; Benoît, A.; Benoit-Lévy, A.; Bernard, J.-P.; Bersanelli, M.; Bertincourt, B.; Bethermin, M.; Bielewicz, P.; Bikmaev, I.; Blanchard, A. et al. (22 March 2013). "Planck 2013 results. I. Overview of products and scientific results – Table 9".

Astronomy and Astrophysics 571: A1. arXiv:1303.5062.
Bibcode:2014A&A...571A...1P. doi:10.1051/0004-6361/201321529

(103), Pg. 176, Ade, P. A. R.; Aghanim, N.; Armitage-Caplan, C.; et al. (Planck Collaboration), C.; Arnaud, M.; Ashdown, M.; Atrio-Barandela, F.; Aumont, J.; Aussel, H.; Baccigalupi, C.; Banday, A. J.; Barreiro, R. B.; Barrena, R.; Bartelmann, M.; Bartlett, J. G.; Bartolo, N.; Basak, S.; Battaner, E.; Battye, R.; Benabed, K.; Benoît, A.; Benoit-Lévy, A.; Bernard, J.-P.; Bersanelli, M.; Bertincourt, B.; Bethermin, M.; Bielewicz, P.; Bikmaev, I.; Blanchard, A. et al. (31 March 2013). "Planck 2013 Results Papers" . Astronomy and Astrophysics 571: A1. arXiv:1303.5062. Bibcode:2014A&A...571A...1P. doi:10.1051/0004-6361/201321529

(104) Pg. 176, "First Planck results: the Universe is still weird and interesting"

(105) Pg. 176, Sean Carroll, Ph.D., Cal Tech, 2007, The Teaching Company, *Dark Matter, Dark Energy: The Dark Side of the Universe*, Guidebook Part 2 page 46. Retrieved Oct. 7, 2013, "...dark energy: A smooth, persistent component of invisible energy, thought to make up about 70 percent of the current energy density of the universe. Dark energy is known to be smooth because it doesn't accumulate preferentially in galaxies and clusters..."

(106) Pg. 180, "Algae Herbarium". National Museum of Natural History, Department of Botany. 2008.

(107) Pg. 182, Simoons, Frederick J (1991). "6, Seaweeds and Other Algae". *Food in China: A Cultural and Historical Inquiry*. CRC Press. pp. 179–190. ISBN 978-0-936923-29-1. Wikipedia

(108) Pg. 182, Morton, Steve L. "Modern Uses of Cultivated Algae". *Ethnobotanical Leaflets*. Southern Illinois University Carbondale. Archived from the original on 23 December 2008. Wikipedia

(109) Pg. 182, Algaculture Wikipedia

(110) Pg. 183, "What the United Nations says about Spirulina" (PDF). *Spirulina and the Millennium Development Goals*. Intergovernmental Institution for the use of Micro-algae Spirulina Against Malnutrition. December 2010. Retrieved 2 July 2014. Wikipedia

(111) Pg. 183, "Charter" (PDF). Intergovernmental Institution for the use of Micro-algae Spirulina Against Malnutrition. 5 March 2003. Retrieved 2 July 2014. Wikipedia

(112) Pg. 183, Characterization of Spirulina biomass for CELSS diet potential. Normal, Al.: Alabama A&M University, 1988. Wikipedia

(113) Pg. 183, Cornet J.F., Dubertret G. "The cyanobacterium Spirulina in the photosynthetic compartment of the MELISSA artificial ecosystem." Workshop on artificial ecological systems, DARA-CNES, Marseille, France, October 24–26, 1990 Wikipedia

(114) Pg. 186, "Algae: A Mean, Green Cleaning Machine" . USDA Agricultural Research Service. 7 May 2010.

(115) Pg. 186, Wikipedia-Algae

(116) Pg. 189, Navy Looks to Biofuels to Sail the Great Green Fleet in 2016 Story Number: NNS140703-14 Release Date: 7/3/2014 10:34:00 PM By Mark Matsunaga, U.S. Pacific Fleet Public Affairs

(117) Pg. 192, "Extinction continues apace". International Union for Conservation of Nature. 3 November 2009. Retrieved 18 October 2012.

(118) Pg. 192, S.L. Pimm, G.J. Russell, J.L. Gittleman and T.M. Brooks, *The Future of Biodiversity*, Science 269: 347–350 (1995)

(119) Pg. 192, Wikipedia Holocene Extinction

(120) Pg. 192, Cockell, Charles (2006). *Biological processes associated with impact events ESF IMPACT* (1. ed.). Berlin: Springer. pp. 197–219. ISBN 978-3-540-25735-6.

(121) Pg. 192, Algeo, T. J.; Scheckler, S. E. (29 January 1998). "Terrestrial-marine teleconnections in the Devonian: links between the evolution of land plants, weathering processes, and marine anoxic events". *Philosophical Transactions of the Royal Society B: Biological Sciences* **353** (1365): 113–130. doi:10.1098/rstb.1998.0195

(122) Pg. 192, Bond, David P.G.; Wignall, Paul B. (1 June 2008). "The role of sea-level change and marine anoxia in the Frasnian–Famennian (Late Devonian) mass

extinction". *Palaeogeography, Palaeoclimatology, Palaeoecology* 263 (3–4): 107–118. doi:10.1016/j.palaeo.2008.02.015

(123) Pg. 192, Kunin, W.E.; Gaston, Kevin, eds. (31 December 1996). The Biology of Rarity: Causes and consequences of rare—common differences. ISBN 978-0412633805. Retrieved 26 May 2015.

(124) Pg. 192, Stearns, Beverly Peterson; Stearns, S. C.; Stearns, Stephen C. (2000). Watching, from the Edge of Extinction. Yale University Press. p. 1921. ISBN 978-0-300-08469-6. Retrieved 2014-12-27.

(125) Pg. 192, Novacek, Michael J. (8 November 2014). "Prehistory's Brilliant Future". New York Times. Retrieved 2014-12-25.

(126) Pg. 192, G. Miller; Scott Spoolman (2012). Environmental Science - Biodiversity Is a Crucial Part of the Earth's Natural Capital. Cengage Learning. p. 62. ISBN 1-133-70787-4. Retrieved 2014-12-27.

(127) Pg. 192, Mora, C.; Tittensor, D.P.; Adl, S.; Simpson, A.G.; Worm, B. (23 August 2011). "How many species are there on Earth and in the ocean?". PLOS Biology. doi:10.1371/journal.pbio.1001127

(128) Pg. 192, Wikipedia-Biodiversity

(129) Pg. 193, "Banking against Doomsday". The Economist. 10 March 2012. Retrieved 7 May 2014.

(130) Pg. 193, Svalbard Global Seed Vault-Wikipedia

(132) Pg. 158, Your Home - Passive Cooling
http://www.yourhome.gov.au/technical/fs43.html

(133) Pg. 158, "EERE Radiant Barriers". Eere.energy.gov. 2009-05-28. Retrieved 2010-03-16.

Periodicals, Resources, Studies, and Suggested Reading

"The Limits to Growth"
by Dennis Meadows, Donella Meadows, Jørgen Randers, and William W. Behrens III

"Six Degrees," by Mark Lynas

"This Changes Everything," by Naomi Klein

"Climate Wars," by Gwynne Dyer

"The Age of Sustainable Development," by Jeffrey D. Sachs

"Comfortably Unaware," by Richard A. Oppenlander

"The Sixth Extinction," by Elizabeth Kolbert

"Merchants of Doubt," by Naomi Oreskes and Erik M. Conway

What is Ocean Acidification?
http://www.pmel.noaa.gov/co2/story/What+is+Ocean+Acidification%3F
NOAA PMEL Carbon Program

"The End of the Long Summer," by Dianne Dumanoski

"Ocean Acidification" by The Ocean Portal Team; Reviewed by Jennifer Bennett
(NOAA)

"Offshore fresh groundwater reserves as a global phenomenon" Vincent E.A. Post,
Jacobus Groen, Henk Kooi, Mark Person, Shemin Ge & W. Mike Edmunds

"NASA Finds Oceans Slowed Global Temperature Rise"
http://www.jpl.nasa.gov/news/news.php?feature=4655 http://www.nasa.gov/earth

"How Soil is Destroyed"
http://www.fao.org/docrep/t0389e/T0389E02.htm#Erosion%20destroyed%20civiliza
tions

"Water Scarcity and Humanitarian Action: Key Emerging Trends and Challenges
https://docs.unocha.org/sites/dms/Documents/OCHA%20OPB%20Water%20%2011
Nov10%20fnl.pdf

"Sea Level" http://climate.nasa.gov/vital-signs/sea-level/

NASA: "Rising Sea Levels More Dangerous Than Thought"
by Tia Ghose http://www.livescience.com/51990-sea-level-rise-unknowns.html

"How is sea level rise related to climate change?"
http://oceanservice.noaa.gov/facts/sealevelclimate.html

"Desertification: a visual synthesis - UNCCD"
http://www.unccd.int/Lists/SiteDocumentLibrary/Publications/Desertification-
EN.pdf

"Biodiversity"
http://www.who.int/globalchange/ecosystems/biodiversity/en/

"Study on understanding the causes of biodiversity loss and the policy assessment
framework"
http://www.fondazionesvilupposostenibile.org/f/sharing/Causes+of+biodiversity+los
s+and+the+policy+assessment+framework+_EU+comm.pdf

"World Water Day" http://www.unwater.org/water-cooperation-2013/water-
cooperation/facts-and-figures/en/"The World's Water Supply Could Dip Sharply in
15 Years" **http://time.com/3753332/world-water-day-un-warning/**

"Freshwater Crisis"
**http://environment.nationalgeographic.com/environment/freshwater/freshwater
-crisis/**

"Marine Pollution" **http://ocean.nationalgeographic.com/ocean/explore/pristine-
seas/critical-issues-marine-pollution/**

"What is the biggest source of pollution in the ocean?"
http://oceanservice.noaa.gov/facts/pollution.html

"Sea of Trash" By DONOVAN HOHN
http://www.nytimes.com/2008/06/22/magazine/22Plastics-t.html?pagewanted=all

"Fukushima and the Dumping of Radioactive Materials into the Ocean. Enormity
and Scale of this

Unspoken Global Crisis" **http://www.globalresearch.ca/fukushima-and-the-
dumping-of-radioactive-materials-into-the-ocean-enormity-and-scale-of-this-
unspoken-global-crisis/5486732**

"Nuclear Waste Sits on Ocean Floor" By John R. Emshwiller and Dionne Searcey
http://www.wsj.com/articles/SB10001424052702304773104579268563658319 19

"Air Pollution" http://environment.nationalgeographic.com/environment/global-warming/pollution-overview/

"Atmospheric Pollution" http://www.learner.org/courses/envsci/unit/pdfs/unit11.pdf

"Solutions for Industrial Pollution"
http://web.mit.edu/12.000/www/m2015/2015/solutions_for_industrial_pollution.htm l

"Industrial Society and Chemical Pollution" - Baltic University
www.balticuniv.uu.se/.../750-chapter-13

"The Sources and Solutions: Agriculture"
http://www2.epa.gov/nutrientpollution/sources-and-solutions-agriculture

"Municipal Solid Waste" http://www3.epa.gov/epawaste/nonhaz/municipal/

"World production of Municipal Solid Waste (MSW), 2012*–2025"
http://www.proparco.fr/webdav/site/proparco/shared/PORTAILS/Secteur_pri ve_developpement/PDF/SPD15/SPD15_key_data_uk.pdf

"World population trends | UNFPA - United Nations
"www.unfpa.org/world-population-trends

"State of World Population 2014" Author: UNFPA

"Population and sustainable development in the Post-2015 agenda"
http://www.unfpa.org/publications/population-and-sustainable-development-post-2015-agenda#sthash.Fi8jHzkB.dpuf

"Climate Change -Agriculture and Food Supply"
http://www3.epa.gov/climatechange/impacts/agriculture.html

"ARS : Honey Bee Health and Colony Collapse Disorder"
www.ars.usda.gov/CCD

"Colony Collapse Disorder" http://www2.epa.gov/pollinator-protection/colony-collapse-disorder

"Disappearing Farmland - The Globalist" **www.theglobalist.com/disappearing-farmland/**

"What If the World's Soil Runs Out?" *world.time.com/2012/12/14/what-if-the-worlds-soil-runs-out/*

"Does Peak Phosphorus Loom?" *www.americanscientist.org*

"Phosphorus: Essential to Life—Are We Running Out?" by **Renee Cho**
http://blogs.ei.columbia.edu/2013/04/01/phosphorus-essential-to-life-are-we-running-out/"New NASA data show how the world is running out of water."
https://www.washingtonpost.com/news/wonk/wp/2015/06/16/new-nasastudies-show-how-the-world-is-   running-out-of-water/

"IMPACTS ON BIODIVERSITY AND ECOSYSTEMS FROM CONVENTIONAL EXPANSION OF FOOD PRODUCTION"
http://www.grida.no/publications/rr/food-crisis/page/3569.aspx

"Biological Meltdown: The Loss of Agricultural Biodiversity"
http://reimaginerpe.org/node/921Implications of Fossil Fuel Dependence for the Food System" **http://www.resilience.org/stories/2006-06-11/implications-fossil-fuel-dependence-food-system**

"Energy-smart" agriculture needed to escape fossil fuel trap"
http://www.fao.org/news/story/en/item/95161/icode/

"How the world's oceans could be running out of fish"
www.bbc.com/future/story/20120920

"Overfishing -- Pristine Seas"
http://ocean.nationalgeographic.com/ocean/explore/pristine-seas/critical-issues-overfishing/

"Politics and the Environment: From Theory to Practice"
by James Connelly (Author), Graham Smith (Author), David Benson (Author), Clare Saunders (Author)

"Environmental Principles and Policies: An Interdisciplinary Introduction Paperback" by **Sharon Beder** (Author)

"Cloak of Green: The Links between Key Environmental Groups, Government and Big Business" by **Elaine Dewar**

"The Deliberate Corruption of Climate Science " by **Tim Ball**

"The 11th Hour" By Leonardo DiCaprio

"What DNA Says About Human Ancestry—and Bigotry" Village Voice Mark Schoofs http://web.mit.edu/racescience/in_media/what_dna_says_about_human/

" A Socratic Perspective on the Nature of Human Evil" by Max Maxwell
http://www.socraticmethod.net/socratic_essay_nature_of_human_evil.htm

"Carbon Dioxide and Climate" By **Gilbert N. Plass**

National Renewable Energy Laboratory (NREL) Home Page www.nrel.gov/

William Sosinsky

Renewable Energy http://www.energy.gov/science-innovation/energy-sources/renewable-energy

"World is facing a natural resources crisis worse than financial crunch" http://www.theguardian.com/environment/2008/oct/29/climatechange-endangeredhabitats

"The Race for What's Left: The Global Scramble for the World's Last Resources" by **Michael Klare**

"**Seafood May Be Gone by 2048, Study Says**" by John Roach http://news.nationalgeographic.com/news/2006/11/061102-seafood-threat.html

"**Algae: The Future of Just About Everything We Need**" www.outerplaces.com

"**U.N. Urges Eating Insects; 8 Popular Bugs to Try**" news.nationalgeographic.com/

"**Insects for food and feed**" www.fao.org/

"**Recycling - Natural Resources Defense Council**" www.nrdc.org/recycling/

"**Climate Change and Sea Level Rise**" - **The Climate Institute www.climate.org/topics/sea-level/**

"**International Migration**" - **United Nations Population Division ...** www.un.org/en/development/.../international-migration/

"Assessing the Impact of Climate Change on Migration and Conflict" by Clionadh Raleigh, Lisa Jordan and Idean Salehyan http://siteresources.worldbank.org/EXTSOCIALDEVELOPMENT/Resources/SDC CWorkingPaper_MigrationandConflict.pdf

"Hydrogen and Fuel Cells - Hydrogen Power"
http://www.altenergy.org/renewables/hydrogen_power.html

"The dangers of solar storms: That which gives power can also take it away"
http://www.earthmagazine.org/article/dangers-solar-storms-which-gives-power-can-also-take-it-away

"Rapid Climate Change" https://www.aip.org/history/climate/rapid.htm

"Rare Earth Metals: Will We Have Enough?" - State of the Planet
blogs.ei.columbia.edu/

"The World's Water" **http://water.usgs.gov/edu/earthwherewater.html**

"The Coming Famine", Julian Cribb www.amazon.com

"Solar Energy Engineering, Second Edition: Processes and Systems 2nd Edition" by **Soteris A. Kalogirou**

"Dark Energy, Dark Matter" **http://science.nasa.gov/astrophysics/focus-areas/what-is-dark-energy/**

"The future of agriculture is an indoor vertical farm half the size of a Wal-Mart" **Chris Well**

William Sosinsky

ACKNOWLEDGMENTS

Special Thanks to Dr. Richard Sapienza, Dr. Joseph Ravet, Jay Dubinsky, David Gershuny, Norma Burnson, David Weaver, Ali Ashu, Allison Cassels, Robert McQueen, Gerald Newsom, Mike Kalet, and the rest of my extended Energime family in their support of this book and their continued efforts.

ABOUT THE AUTHOR
William Sosinsky

William Sosinsky is the Founder, Co-Owner, and CEO of The Energime Family of Companies including Energime Sustainable Technologies, Energime Power, Energime Energy Efficiency and is the Chairman of the Board for The Energime Foundation. Bill is also the Founder and Director of Energime University.

He served as the opinion editor for EcoSeed writing articles on Integrated Sustainable Design, Green Investment, Sustainable Economics, Advanced Food Production, Global Agricultural Trends, and Advanced Waste Management. A sitting board member on the Lifeboat Foundation Sustainability Board, African Sustainable Development Council, Member of the United Nations Academic Impact, as well as many other environmental and humanitarian groups and organizations.

Bill has a strong background and extensive practical experience in economics, economic theory, marketing, business development, renewable energy, agriculture, aquaculture, waste management technologies, integrated sustainable design, environmental sciences, building energy efficiency and water conservation, project management, education, and communications.

For more information about Bill's work visit www.energimeuniversity.org